city-lit

LONDON

D1076533

Oxygen Books

30130 164389396

Published by Oxygen Books 2009

This selection and commentary copyright © Heather Reyes

A CIP catalogue record for this book is available from the British Library.

ISBN 978–0–9559700–5–4

Typeset in Sabon by Bookcraft Limited, Stroud, Gloucestershire

Printed and bound in India by Imago

**Essex County
Council Libraries**

Praise for *city-lit LONDON*

'Brings London to life past and present in a way no conventional guide book could ever achieve.'

Tarquin Hall, author of **Salaam Brick Lane**

'For those visitors to London who seek to do more than bag Big Ben and Buckingham Palace this is the ideal guide, a collection of writings that expose not only the city's secret places but its very soul. The topography, culture and unquenchable spirit of this extraordinary city are brought sparklingly to life by some of the finest writers imaginable, past and present, among whom I am proud to be included. I can't imagine a more perfect travelling companion than this wonderful anthology.'

Clare Clark, author of **The Great Stink**

'This treasure trove of a book consists of a diverse collection of literary excerpts that provide a unique way to explore the ever-changing landscape of the city, through the voices of those that know it intimately.'

Rachel Lichtenstein, author of **On Brick Lane**

'The second volume in this enticing new series includes extracts from the work of 60 wonderfully diverse writers, including Will Self, Monica Ali, Alan Bennett, Dostoyevsky, and yes, Barbara Cartland (writing about a West End ball)'

Editor's Pick, **The Bookseller**

Editor's Note

Putting together an anthology on your own city is like trying to paint a picture of a lover: the more you try to capture it, the more it seems to escape definition. But it makes you appreciate as never before London's 'infinite variety', its slipperiness and diversity, its varying moods and modulations.

The portrait I've ended up with is in part a personal one: some editors would have chosen less by Jan Morris, and I make no excuse for the several appearances of Virginia Woolf, one of the most significant London writers. But I've also tried to present the capital through others' eyes – whether tourists, immigrants, temporary workers, or visitors from other parts of the United Kingdom, the very old and the very young. Also a scattering of 'standards' – like the London fog of Dickens. And along the way I've acquired some new favourites: Alan Bennett's good-natured portrait of the Queen as she suddenly discovers 'reading'; a piece of journalism by a very young Maeve Binchy; and Will Self's wonderful creation of a London cabbie in *The Book of Dave*.

Hope you enjoy the tour.

Heather Reyes

Contents

Contents

Contents

London Transport

Whatever the weather

And the rest is history ...

Introducing London ...
by PETER WATTS

I don't really know London. This despite having lived and worked within the collar of the M25 for my entire life, something that is simultaneously a source of great pride and creeping shame. I've explored it, sure. I've gazed down at dawn on drowsy Londoners from atop a thirteenth-century church tower in darkest Hackney. I've listened to the hum of traffic passing overhead from deep within the buried Fleet River beneath Holborn Circus. I've walked the Thames from St Paul's to Hampton Court, been to the end of more than half the tube lines, sniffed Billingsgate Market's early-morning buzz and fed the black-tongued giraffes at London Zoo. I've even travelled every bus from 1 to 50 in numerical order, a task that's taken me to every point of the compass from Debden in the north-east to Fullwell in the south-west (no, I'd never heard of them before I started, either). But I still don't know London. Not really. There are vast tracts of its urban geography that are a total mystery to me, a no-man's land, vacant lots, blank space in my internal A-Z.

This is not an unusual condition. Indeed, it might even be a necessity for living a sane, balanced London life because most of the city's residents seem to suffer from it, some quite contentedly, perfectly happy to stay within the few square miles where they live and the West End where they work. This could be because there is simply too much London to handle – too many streets, too many people, too much history, too many inconsistencies. The London cabby, scientists say, has developed a larger-than-average hippocampus – the part of the brain that processes navigation – simply to cope with all the information. One of them, Fred Housego, even won 'Mastermind' in 1980.

Most of us don't even try to deal with all this geographical sludge. In *Soft City*, Jonathan Raban's charismatic study of the modern city from 1974, he noted: 'The Greater London Council is responsible for a sprawl shaped like a rugby ball about twenty-five miles long and twenty miles wide; my London is a concise kidney-shaped patch within that space, in which no point is more than seven miles from any other ... I hardly ever trespass beyond those limits, and when I do, I feel I'm in foreign territory, a landscape of hazard and rumour. Like any tribesman hedging himself in behind a stockade of taboos, I mark my boundaries with graveyards, terminal transportation points and wildernesses. Beyond them, nothing is to be trusted and anything might happen.'

This is a common way of behaving, retreating within self-imposed borders and putting up the fences to the darkness on the other side. It's captured in this volume by Tarquin Hall's passage from 'Salaam Brick Lane' and the stark single-line confession: 'Most of London, the city of my birth, was as foreign to me as Prague'. The bard of Cricklewood, Alan Coren, explores a related theme in a typically whimsical extract in which he imagines his intended tour of all the London landmarks he has never actually visited – the Tower of London the Monument and the Serpentine – having decided to leave that sort of thing to the tourists.

No wonder and no shame. If you're born in Harrow, what should you understand of Harlow? If you live near Crystal Palace Park, why would you need to know Hampstead Heath? How many Londoners have ever toured the Houses of Parliament or been into the Whispering Gallery of St Paul's? The greatest area of neglect is the City – if you don't work within that glorious square mile that contains all history from the Romans to the Credit Crunch why would you ever have a reason to go there? Londoners leave it to tourists and bankers.

And then there are the contradictions. This is the city that features some of the wealthiest real estate within some of the most deprived boroughs in the United Kingdom; the city whose ships helped spread English around the world but is now home to more than 250 different languages and has schools where the native tongue is barely spoken; the city that when recently called upon to appoint a new mayor, replaced a left-wing, working-class, car-hating socialist with a right-wing, public-school educated, neo-Thatcherite motoring correspondent, two iconoclasts who seemed to have nothing in common bar a quick wit and mutual contempt for orthodoxy. Who can get their head round that?

So, how can you learn to master this metropolis, the first great city of the modern age and still the world leader in art and commerce? Well, you could follow in the footsteps of Phyllis Pearsall, the creator of the single greatest London book – and one that is understandably omitted from this anthology – 'The A-Z'. In the 1930s, Pearsall is said to have walked every one of London's 23,000 streets – that's around

3,000 miles of serious perambulation – in her determination to produce the most comprehensive map of London that is humanly possible. Alternatively, you could save on leatherwear and consult some of the other classics of London literature, those writers who have made it their business to understand the city, or at least their particular patch of it. After all, will anybody ever show off Soho like Colin McInnes, or capture Camden like David Thomson? Virginia Woolf's West End is so beautifully developed, so perfectly drawn, so hyper-real, it almost dwarfs the genuine article. And Monica Ali's Brick Lane places it as firmly on the tourist map as Big Ben and the Wheel, so you can tell yourself that there really isn't any need to check it out for yourself.

London books allow you to travel in time as well as space. McInnes's Soho is the good one, the one we've all heard about from the 1950s, when it was still raw, neon-lit, jazz-fuelled and edgy rather than a shallow cluster of over-priced restaurants and drunken daytrippers wondering where all the loucheness has gone (it's still there, just, in secret drinking clubs and members' bars hidden behind nameless Georgian façades). And Thomson's Camden is one on the verge of massive change, a working-class district of pubs and markets that is about to experience the first invasion by the middle-classes that will recondition the area beyond all recognition, setting off a chain reaction of gentrification around London's inner suburbs from Notting Hill to Islington. For those of us who only know these places in their current incarnation, this stuff has an extraordinary archaeological value that their authors could never have intended, like the background of family photographs that show furniture and fittings everybody forgot about long ago because they never bothered to record them.

But that's not to say things were so much better in the old says. Indeed, one of the most important things about this volume is that it emphasises the current prodigious strength of London writing. Yes, there's Dickens and Woolf and Conrad and Wilde and Conan Doyle – as there should be – but there's also Ackroyd and Sinclair and Self, the titanic trinity of contemporary London writing. These three create a London in which all of the past is present in today, one in which the lines between what counts as history and what counts as modern are blurred, and one in which London's reality is as evocative as their powerful imaginations. Since the 1980s they have done more to resurrect the concept of London writing as a standalone genre than anybody since the Victorian era, when London, the New Jerusalem, was seen to embody the contradictory values of Empire and became a rich source of fiction and journalism. They have encouraged the rediscovery of some of the lost classics of London literature and fostered the climate in which anthologies like this one can flourish. In their wake, modern classics have followed, from Justin Cartwright's snappy satirical novel *Look At It This Way* to Sukhdev Sandhu's invaluable nocturnal jaunts into the belly of sleeping London in *Night Haunts*. This regained respect for London writing also allows the voice of the new Londoner to be heard – the 27.1 per cent of the population that the 2001 census considered to be non-native-born – through authors such as Xiaolu Guo, with her faux-naïve extracts from *A Concise Chinese-English Dictionary for Lovers*. In Rebecca Taylor's 'London Lives' we even meet one of these recent arrivals in the form of a young brother and sister who travel to London from Poland to begin their new lives, part of the huge wave of Eastern European immigration that has transformed the city in recent years.

It is authors from this final category who could provide some of the finest and boldest London writing of the twenty-first century, because they will come to the city with a fresh mind and open eye, prepared to live and work in those parts of London that are closed by personal choice to most natives. None of them, of course, will ever really get on top of London, even if they choose to stay here for the rest of their lives – but every little bit helps. And if you put all the fragments together, you may one day get something close to the full picture, the London that we all love, even if it's not the one we know.

PETER WATTS is *Time Out London*'s features writer and edits the 'Big Smoke' section.

"Maybe it's because I'm a Londoner … "

A famous old music-hall song begins with the words "Maybe it's because I'm a Londoner that I love London so", and if the best writers on the city are anything to go by, this seems to be true: most Londoners do love their sprawling, vibrant, contradictory, sometimes ugly but often beautiful, ever-changing, history-laden capital. The great Dr Johnson once remarked, 'The happiness of London is not to be conceived but by those who have been in it', so let's fly in with travel writer Jan Morris.

One of the flight-paths to London Airport, Heathrow, goes straight over the middle of the capital, east to west. The city does not look much at first: just a drab sprawling mass of housing estates, terraces and industrial plants, nibbled at its edges by a fairly grubby green – just mile after mile of the ordinary, splodged here and there with the sordid.

Presently, though, the route picks up the River Thames, sinuously sliding between the eastern suburbs, and one by one landmarks appear that are part of the whole world's consciousness, images familiar to every one of us, reflecting the experience of half mankind. The Tower of London squats brownish at the water's edge. Buckingham Palace reclines in its great green garden. The Houses of Parliament, of all famous buildings the most toylike and intricate, stand like an instructional model beside Westminster Bridge. There are the swathes of London parks, too, and the huge Victorian roofs of the railway terminals, the cluttered hub of Piccadilly, the big new block of Scotland Yard, and always the river itself, twisting and turning through it all, out of the city centre into the western purlieus, until the first of the country green appears again on the other side, with gravel pits and motorways. Windsor Castle appears tremendous on its hillock, and the aircraft, slightly changing its tone of voice, tilts a wing over Slough and begins the last descent to the airport.

It is the city of cities that we have flown over. Like it or loathe it, it is the daddy of them all. If New York is ethnically more interesting, Moscow or Peking ideologically more compelling, Paris or Rome more obviously beautiful, still as a historical phenomenon London beats them all. It has been itself, for better or for worse, for a thousand years, unconquered by a foreign army since William the Norman was crowned King of England in Westminster Abbey in 1066. It has spawned and abandoned the greatest empire known to history. It was the first great industrial capital, the first parliamentary capital, the arena of social and political experiments beyond number. It is a city of terrific murders and innumerable spies, of novelists, auctioneers, surgeons and rock stars. It is the city of Shakespeare, Sherlock Holmes, Dr Johnson, Churchill, Dick Whittington, Henry VIII, Florence Nightingale, the Duke of Wellington, Queen Victoria, Gladstone and the two Olivers, Cromwell and Twist. Mozart wrote his first symphony in London, and Karl Marx began *Das Kapital*. London has five great symphony orchestras, eleven daily newspapers, three cathedrals, the biggest subway on earth and the most celebrated broadcasting system. It is the original world capital of soccer, cricket, rugby, lawn tennis and squash. It is where Jack the Ripper worked. It is the home of the last great monarchy of all, the House of Windsor, likely to be outlived only, in the expert judgement of the late King Farouk of Egypt, by the Houses of Hearts, Diamonds, Clubs and Spades. London is nearly everything. If you are tired of London, Dr Johnson once remarked, you are tired of life.

Jan Morris, *A Writer's World*

✳ ✳ ✳

In The Groundwater Diaries, *Tim Bradford also recalls Dr Johnson's most famous words about London, then adds his own quirky list of the city's attractions.*

London is beautiful. Samuel Johnson, in the only quote of his anyone can really remember, said, 'When a man is tired of London, he is tired of life.' He may have been a fat mad-as-a-hatter manic depressive in a wig, but there is something in his thesis. London's got its fair share of nice parks and museums, but I love its underbelly, in fact its belly in general – the girls in their first strappy dresses of the summer, the smell of chips, the liquid orange skies of early evening, high-rise glass office palaces, the lost-looking old men still eating at their regular caffs even after they've been turned into Le Café Trendy or Cyber Bacon, the old shop fronts, the rotting pubs, the cacophony of peeling and damp Victorian residential streets, neoclassical shopping centres, buses that never arrive on time, incessant white noise fizz of gossip, little shops, big shops, late-night kebab shops with slowly turning cylinders of khaki fat and gristle in the window, the bitter caramel of car exhaust fumes, drivers spitting abuse at each other through the safety of tinted electric windows, hot and tightly packed tubes in summer, the roar of the crowd from Highbury or White Hart Lane, dog shit on the pavements, psychopathic drunken hard men who sit outside at North London pub tables. London has got inside me. I've tried to leave. But I always come back. It's love, y'see.

Tim Bradford, *The Groundwater Diaries*

✻　✻　✻

And as a complete contrast, Virginia Woolf's middle-aged Mrs Dalloway gets high on the beauty of a glorious summer morning in the city.

For having lived in Westminster – how many years now? over twenty, – one feels even in the midst of the traffic, or waking at night, Clarissa was positive, a particular hush, or solemnity; an indescribable pause; a suspense (but that might be her heart, affected, they said, by influenza) before Big Ben strikes. There! Out it boomed. First a warning, musical; then the hour, irrevocable. The leaden circles dissolved in the air. Such fools we are, she thought, crossing Victoria Street. For Heaven only knows why one loves it so, how one sees it so, making it up, building it round one, tumbling it, creating it every moment afresh; but the veriest frumps, the most dejected of miseries sitting on doorsteps (drink their downfall) do the same; can't be dealt with, she felt positive, by Acts of Parliament for that very reason: they love life. In people's eyes, in the swing, tramp, and trudge; in the bellow and the uproar; the carriages, motor cars, omnibuses, vans, sandwich men shuffling and swinging; brass bands; barrel organs; in the triumph and the jingle and the strange high singing of some aeroplane overhead was what she loved; life; London; this moment of June.

Virginia Woolf, *Mrs Dalloway*

✻　✻　✻

At the beginning of the eighteenth century, London wasn't always good for the health – open sewers, contaminated drinking water, a refuse problem, high infant mortality, tuberculosis and smallpox rife – but

> *it was nevertheless a beautiful and energetic city to*
> *which many young people flocked, attracted by its*
> *high wages. (Sound familiar? ...)*

London in 1700 was the most magnificent city in Europe. It took its beauty from Wren's skyline of churches, especially as viewed from the river. Dominating the city, the new St Paul's rested on its hilltop nearing completion. Only the dome was outstanding, prompting the wag Ned Ward's analogy, 'As slow as a Paul's workman with a bucket of mortar'. The River Thames was the artery of the metropolis, the wide thoroughfare dotted with thousands of pleasure craft and red and green passenger boats plying their trade. London Bridge with its density of houses and souvenir shops was the only bridge linking the north and south banks. And below it at the Port of London the ships lined up like a floating forest to unload their cargoes from the furthest corners of the world. Only a few miles away the hills of Hampstead and Highgate provided a reassuring rural backdrop to the thriving metropolis at their feet.

The capital dominated the kingdom to an extent that it has never done before or since. It was home to at least 530,000 people – one in nine of the entire population – while the second city, Norwich, had a population of 30,000. Not only did so many of William III's subjects live in London, but the city impinged on the lives of many more. It was a magnet to all classes. Aristocracy and gentry flocked to London to be seen at court, to attend parliament, to settle their legal affairs, to enjoy the season and arrange marriages for their children, and to shop. London was a shopper's paradise, a great emporium of goods for its hungry consumers. The booming newspaper industry in Grub Street found a ready market in London's coffee-houses where everything was up for discussion. London was the centre of a lively publishing trade, the theatre and music. Visitors absorbed its ideas and culture and disseminated them to all parts of the kingdom.

Maureen Waller, 1700: Scenes from London Life

Although the protagonist of Joseph Conrad's famous novel, The Secret Agent, *runs a seedy shop in Soho where political extremists meet, even he seems transformed as he steps out into a lovely London morning ...*

Such was the house, the household, and the business Mr Verloc left behind him on his way westward at the hour of half past ten in the morning. It was unusually early for him; his whole person exhaled the charm of almost dewy freshness; he wore his blue cloth overcoat unbuttoned; his boots were shiny; his cheeks, freshly shaven, had a sort of gloss; and even his heavy-lidded eyes, refreshed by a night of peaceful slumber, sent out glances of comparative alertness. Through the park railing these glances beheld men and women riding in the Row, couples cantering past harmoniously, others advancing sedately at a walk, loitering groups of three or four, solitary horsemen looking unsociable, and solitary women followed at a long distance by a groom with a cockade to his hat and a leather belt over his tight-fitting coat. Carriages went bowling by, mostly two-horse broughams, with here and there a victoria with the skin of some wild beast inside and a woman's face and hat emerging above the folded hood. And a peculiarly London sun – against which nothing could be said except that it looked bloodshot – glorified all this by its stare. It hung at a moderate elevation above Hyde Park Corner with an air of punctual and benign vigilance. The very pavement under Mr Verloc's feet had an old-gold tinge in that diffused light, in which neither wall, nor tree, nor beast, nor man cast a shadow. Mr Verloc was going westward through a town without shadows in an atmosphere of powdered old gold.

Joseph Conrad, *The Secret Agent*

❋ ❋ ❋

The opening of Ian McEwan's novel, Saturday, *describes neurosurgeon Henry Perowne rising before dawn and, from his bedroom window in Fitzrovia, looking out over a typical London square and contemplating the beauty and success of London.*

He opens the second shutter, letting it concertina into the casement, and quietly raises the sash window. It is many feet taller than him, but it slides easily upwards, hoisted by its concealed lead counterweight. His skin tightens as the February air pours in around him, but he isn't troubled by the cold. From the second floor he faces the night, the city in its icy white light, the skeletal trees in the square, and thirty feet below, the black arrowhead railings like a row of spears. There's a degree or two of frost and the air is clear. The streetlamp glare hasn't quite obliterated all the stars; above the Regency façade on the other side of the square hang remnants of constellations in the southern sky. That particular façade is a reconstruction, a pastiche – wartime Fitzrovia took some hits from the Luftwaffe – and right behind is the Post Office Tower, municipal and seedy by day, but at night, half-concealed and decently illuminated, a valiant memorial to more optimistic days.

And now, what days are these? Baffled and fearful, he mostly thinks when he takes time from his weekly round to consider. But he doesn't feel that now. He leans forwards, pressing his weight onto his palms against the sill, exulting in the emptiness and clarity of the scene. His vision – always good – seems to have sharpened. He sees the paving stone mica glistening in the pedestrianised square, pigeon excrement hardened by distance and cold into something almost beautiful, like a scattering of snow. He likes the symmetry of black cast-iron posts and their even darker shadows, and the lattice of cobbled gutters. The overfull litter baskets suggest abundance rather than squalor; the vacant benches set around the circular gardens look benignly expectant of their daily traffic – cheerful lunchtime office crowds, the solemn, studious boys from the Indian hostel, lovers in quiet raptures or crisis, the crepuscular drug dealers, the ruined old lady with her wild, haunting calls. Go away! she'll shout for hours at a time, and squawk harshly, sounding like some marsh bird or zoo creature.

Standing here, as immune to the cold as a marble statue, gazing towards Charlotte Street, towards a foreshortened jumble of façades, scaffolding and pitched roofs, Henry thinks the city is a success, a brilliant invention, a biological masterpiece – millions teeming around the accumulated and layered achievements of the centuries, as though around a coral reef, sleeping, working, entertaining themselves, harmonious for the most part, nearly everyone wanting it to work.

Ian McEwan, *Saturday*

✻ ✻ ✻

Aldous Huxley's novel, Antic Hay, *also finds a gentleman enjoying a London square from his balcony, though in a less salubrious part of the city.*

Gumbril Senior occupied a tall, narrow-shouldered and rachitic house in a little obscure square not far from Paddington. There were five floors, and a basement with beetles, and nearly a hundred stairs, which shook when any one ran too rudely down them. It was a prematurely old and decaying house in a decaying quarter. The square in which it stood was steadily coming down in the world. The houses, which a few years ago had all been occupied by respectable families, were now split up into squalid little maisonettes, and from the neighbouring slums, which along with most other unpleasant things the old bourgeois families had been able to ignore, invading bands of children came to sport on the once-sacred pavements.

Mr Gumbril was almost the last survivor of the old inhabitants. He liked his house, and he liked his square. Social decadence had not affected the fourteen plane-trees which adorned its little garden, and the gambols of the dirty children did not disturb the starlings who came, evening by evening in summertime, to roost in their branches.

On fine evenings he used to sit out on his balcony waiting for the coming of the birds. And just at sunset, when the sky was most golden, there would be a twittering overhead, and the black, innumerable flocks of starlings would come sweeping across on the way from their daily haunts to their roosting-places, chosen so capriciously among the tree-planted squares and gardens of the city and so tenaciously retained, year after year, to the exclusion of every other place. Why his fourteen plane-trees should have been chosen, Mr Gumbril could never imagine. There were plenty of larger and more umbrageous gardens all round; but they remained birdless, while every evening, from the larger flocks, a faithful legion detached itself to settle clamorously among his trees. They sat and chattered till the sun went down and twilight was past, with intervals every now and then of silence that fell suddenly and inexplicably on all the birds at once, lasted through a few seconds of thrilling suspense, to end as suddenly and senselessly in an outburst of the same loud and simultaneous conversation. [...]

... darkness came down, and the gas-lamps round the square lit up the outer leaves of the plane-trees, touched the privet bushes inside the railings with an emerald light; behind them was impenetrable night; instead of shorn grass and bedded geraniums there was mystery, there were endless depths. And the birds at last were silent.

Aldous Huxley, *Antic Hay*

* * *

One of the most beautiful and popular strolling places for Londoners is Hampstead Heath. In Helen Simpson's novel, Constitutional, *a school teacher makes the most of her lunch-hour by taking her regular walk around the Heath, enjoying the views and the snippets of conversation overheard from other walkers.*

'I just think she's a bit passive-aggressive,' said the woman to her friend. 'In a very sweet way. D'you know what I mean?'

This is so much the sort of thing you hear on the Heath that I couldn't help smiling, straight from Stella's funeral though I was, standing aside to let them past me on to the pavement. Even five minutes later, almost at the ponds, I'm smiling, but that could be simple relief at being outside in some November sun.

The thing about a circular walk is that you end up where you started – except, of course, that you don't. My usual round trip removes me neatly from the fetid staffroom lunch-hour, conveniently located as the school is on the very edge of the Heath. […]

Because I know exactly how long I have – quick glance at my watch, fifty-three minutes left – and exactly how long it takes, I can afford to let my mind off the lead. Look at the sparkle of that dog's urine against the dark green of the laurel, and its wolfish cocked leg. In the space of an hour I know I can walk my way back to some sort of balance after my morning-off's farewell distress before launching into sexual reproduction with Year Ten at five past two.

When the sun flares out like this, heatless and long-shadowed, the tree trunks go floodlit and even the puddles in the mud hold flashing blue snapshots of the sky. You walk past people who are so full of their lives and thoughts and talk about others, so absorbed in exchanging human information, that often their gaze stays abstractedly on the path and their legs are moving mechanically. But their dogs frisk around, curvetting and cantering, arabesques of pink tongues airing in their broadly smiling jaws. They bound off after squirrels or seagulls, they bark, rowrowrow, into the sunshine, and there is no idea anywhere of what comes next.

This walk is always the same but different, thanks to the light, the time of year, the temperature and so on. Its sameness allows me to sink back into my thoughts as I swing along, while on the other hand I know and observe at some level that nothing is ever exactly the same as it was before.[…]

Forty-nine minutes. From that hill up there to my left it's possible to see for miles, all over London, and on a clear day I'm pretty sure I can pinpoint my road in Dalston. A skipper on the Thames looked up here at the northern heights three centuries ago and exclaimed at how even though it was midsummer the hills were capped with snow. All the Heath's low trees and bushes were festooned with clean shirts and smocks hung out to dry, white on green, this being where London's laundry was done.[...]

As I overtake an elderly couple dawdling towards the ponds, these words drift into my ears – ' ... terrible pain. Appalling. They've tried this and that but nothing seems to help. Disgusting ... ' The words float after me even though I speed up and leave the two of them like tortoises on the path behind me. [...]

Thirteen minutes. It always surprises me how late in the year the leaves stay worth looking at. November gives the silver birches real glamour, a shower of gold pieces at their feet and still they keep enough to clothe them, thousands of tiny lozenge-shaped leaves quaking on their separate stems. That constant tremor made them unpopular in the village where I grew up – palsied, they called them.

Trees live for a long time, much longer than we do. Look at this oak, so enormous and ancient standing in the centre of the leaf-carpeted clearing [...] They have been known to live for a thousand years, oak trees, and there are more really old ones growing on the Heath than in the whole of France. Look at it standing stoutly here, all elbows and knees. When the weather is stormy, they put up signs round here – 'Beware of falling limbs'. [...] Four minutes to go, and I'm nearly there. Walking round the Heath on days like this when there is some colour and sun, I can feel it rise in me like mercury in a thermometer, enormous deep delight in seeing these trees with their last two dozen leaves worn like earrings, amber and yellow and crimson, and in being led off by generously lit paths powdered silver with frost. It must be some form of benign forgetfulness, this rising bubble of pleasure in my chest, at being here, now, part of the landscape and not required to do anything but exist. I feel as though I've won some mysterious game.

Helen Simpson, *Constitutional*

"Maybe it's because I'm a Londoner ... "

✻ ✻ ✻

A love of the city – particularly the area along the Thames – is captured in this short but energetic extract from Colin McInnes' Absolute Beginners.

Whoever thought up the Thames embankment was a genius. It lies curled firm and gentle round the river like a boy does with a girl, after it's over, and it stretches in a great curve from the parliament thing, down there in Westminster, all the way north and east into the City. Going in that way, downstream, eastwards, it's not so splendid, but when you come back up along it – oh! If the tide's in, the river's like the ocean, and you look across the great wide bend and see the fairy advertising palaces on the south side beaming in the water, and that great white bridge that floats across it gracefully, like a string of leaves. If you're fortunate, the cab gets all the greens, and keeps up the same steady speed, and looking out from the upholstery it's like your own private Cinerama, except that in this one the show's never, never twice the same. And weather makes no difference, or season, it's always wonderful – the magic always works. And just above the diesel whining of the taxi, you hear those *river* noises that no one can describe, but you can always recognize. Each time I come here for the ride, in any mood, I get a lift, a rise, a hoist up into joy. And as I gazed out on the water like a mouth, a bed, a sister, I thought how, my God, I love this city, horrible though it may be, and never ever want to leave it, come what it may send me. Because though it seems so untidy, and so casual, and so keep-your-distance-from-me, if you can get to know this city well enough to twist it round your finger, and if you're its son, it's always on your side, supporting you – or that's what I imagined.

Colin MacInnes, *Absolute Beginners*

✻ ✻ ✻

16

Back to Jan Morris. Having lived most of her adult life abroad, she admits to being something of a stranger in her own capital. Here she describes spending a very happy morning wandering around the city with which she was 'innocently infatuated'.

The day was very early when I began my morning's affair with London, and I started, as determined lovers should, with a nourishing English breakfast, the most potent of aphrodisiacs. The first watery sunshine was glimmering as I walked into the streets of Covent Garden, and the noble façade of the Opera House stood there above the vegetable-wagons pale and romantic. The alleys were stodgy with lorries, and the pavements were bustling with porters, and a fine old lady in black strode by with a tray of cabbages on her head. In the shade of a classical portico some union propagandist had pinned a notice suggesting disagreeable methods of dealing with strike-breakers. Hanging, it observed, was too good for such vermin.

There was a public house around the corner. Licensed for the porters of the market, it was the one pub in London where you could get beer at that time of the morning, so I sat down to a brown ale, three smoking golden sausages, and a slice of toast – a princely breakfast. Two extremely stout men shared my table and swapped an incessant flow of badinage. Their Cockney was proud and undiluted, and every now and then one of them winked blearily at me, to put me at my ease. I put lots of mustard on my sausages and tried hard to enjoy the ale. London is a rich and saucy city, for all its espresso-bar veneer, and its heart still thrives on beer and bangers and such old stalwarts of the palate.

Presently the sun, like a timid tippler, appeared through the glass of the saloon bar door: so I said goodbye to those two portly jokers and made my way east to Billingsgate. London Bridge was almost empty when I arrived there, and as I climbed down the gloomy staircase to the fish market my footsteps echoed desolately away beneath the bridge: but when I emerged from the tunnel into Lower Thames Street there before me was all the blast and colour and virility of Billingsgate, against one of the most glorious city settings on earth.

Away to the east stood the bastions of the Tower, like misty cardboard replicas; and behind me there arose the mountainous hump of Cannon Street Station, grandly cavernous; and beside me, hunched against an office block, there stood the fine old church of Magnus Martyr, with its 'inexplicable splendour of Ionian white and gold'; and to my left a mesh-work of city lanes, Fish Street and Pudding Lane, Botolph Lane and St. Mary at Hill, clambered up the slope around the Monument; and everywhere there were the fish-men, in their white coats and queer leather hats, barging and pushing their way from the refrigerator trucks to the market, splashed with mud and gusto and fishy liquids. There was grandeur, and humour, and vivacity, and brutality to this compelling scene: and in the middle of it all stood the City policemen, like holy men, writing things down in little black notebooks.

Across the river on Bankside no such noble turmoil animated the wharves. A hush lay over the alleyways and warehouses, and only a few early dockers were coughing and talking throatily on the barges moored alongside. As I wandered, though, I could feel the rising animation of the place as the city woke to the day; and soon there approached me down an empty lane a figure whose eager stride and sharp decisive footfalls were the very epitome of morning purpose. It was dressed all in black, and as it advanced down the shadowy canyon of the warehouses I saw that its legs were sheathed in gaiters. I stopped in my tracks, overcome by this pungent confrontation of the commercial, the medieval, and the ecclesiastical. 'Magnificent!' said I. 'Well, er, yes,' said the clergyman, 'it always is lovely at this time of the morning, and if you go a little farther you'll see the new house they've just built for me next to Christopher Wren's, thus enabling me to be the first Provost of Southwark to live on the spot since my cathedral was founded some, let me see, yes,

some *one thousand, three hundred* years ago: Good morning!'
– and the Provost strode off to his cathedral.

But even London's chain of associations is sometimes broken,
and when one of the old landmarks is destroyed, replaced or
made redundant, then you may feel the melancholy of the place,
and realize how heavily it leans upon the grandeurs of the past.
You may sense this nostalgia beside the forgotten India Office, or
outside an Admiralty that is no longer the world's final arbiter,
or beside Buckingham Palace, where Queen Victoria gazes
bleakly across an empire that has vanished: or you may do as
I did that morning, cross by Blackfriars Bridge, meander down
an awakening Fleet Street, turn into Kingsway, and pause for a
moment to watch them pulling down the old Stoll Theatre. [...]
By now the day had burst, so I took a bus to Harley Street: for
there on any weekday morning, parked in lordly comity, you
may inspect the best selection of Rolls-Royces in the world.

Jan Morris, *A Writer's World*

* * *

*And the last word on that very special affection for
the capital comes from well-known humourist Alan
Coren.*

I'm off to the Dome, me. Any minute now. Just a few things
to be sorted out first, and then I'm away to Greenwich. That is
the joy of living in London, it is not like living in Runcorn or
Bute, you do not have to engage in major long-term plans and
serious expenditure if you want to take in the sights, you do
not have to pore over timetables or work out complex routes,
you do not have to book expensive hotels or give advance
notice to employers or arrange with neighbours to feed the cat
and water the pot plants, you do not have to turn off the gas
and notify the police of keyholders, or pack for unpredictable
meteorological contingencies, you just walk out of your gate
and, a short bus ride away, there it all is – ships, towers, domes,

theatres and temples lie, open unto the fields and to the sky, all bright and glittering in the smokeless air. Any time you choose, you can go. Everything is always there.

Like the Tower of London. It has been there since 1038. As early as 1947, I nearly went, my sandwiches were packed, the Tizer was in my satchel, the school bus was ticking over at the corner of Cecil Road, but then I sneezed a couple of times, and she was always a worrier, my mother. But no matter, the Tower would always be there, the Crown Jewels, the ravens, the Beefeaters, the Traitor's Gate, a terrific day out, and I shall certainly get around to it any day now. I have of course seen it many times and not just driving past, either: I stopped once, got out, and had a look in the moat. It is a really knockout moat. It made me more determined than ever to do a proper visit, sometime.

I could do it on the day I visit the Monument, it is a stone's throw away, you could kill two birds with that stone, it is merely a matter of deciding whether to go up the Monument first or afterwards. There is an amazing view from the top, tourists come from all over the globe, but you have to climb 365 steps to get to it, and that could take time. I might be too knackered for the Tower, after that. I intended to go with David Collingwood in 1951, the year we didn't go to the Festival of Britain; I actually had a golf ball in my pocket, we were going to drop it off the Monument to see how high it would bounce, but we went to the pictures instead. I'm not even sure I could do 365 steps now, it would be a bit embarrassing to drop dead at step 189, it is a spiral staircase, the emergency services would have a hell of a job getting a stretcher all that way up and down, they might have to lug me to the top and lower me on a rope. An undignified way to go. Not nice for the family.

St Paul's would be a safer bet. There is only one flight of steps up to the famed Whispering Gallery. God knows what's held me back all these years, but I shall of course go, as soon as

I've thought of something a bit special to whisper. A man in my position can't whisper any old rubbish. The smart thing to do would be to practise in Guildhall, it doesn't have an echo; at least, I don't think it does, but it'd be a doddle to find out, it is only a half-hour bus ride from Cricklewood and you would also get to see the world's most magnificent municipal building. Still, it's been there since 1430, it is unlikely to fall down over the next few days, there's no rush, I could go after I've visited Westminster Abbey, which has poets underneath it. You can stand on Chaucer. Better still, I could make a day of it by walking from the abbey across Horse Guards Parade on the day Her Majesty was Trooping the Colour, it looks terrific on television, and then visit Buckingham Palace, open to the public now, and an absolute must. I just hope the Millennium Wheel is working by June, it is a mere stroll from the Palace, it'd be crazy to miss the opportunity, the bit of the wheel you can see from my roof looks stunning. You can also see the Post Office Tower and Canary Wharf, both essential to go to the top of for unparalleled views of the world's greatest city, which I eagerly look forward to, even if you can't see Peter Pan's statue, one of my top priorities. I shall visit it very soon, also the Serpentine, which I've often nearly seen, only to be irritatingly thwarted by having to fasten my seat-belt and make sure my tray-table was safely stowed.

And, after all that, the Dome awaits. Why my heart leaps within me at the very prospect, who can say? Maybe it's because I'm a Londoner.

Alan Coren, *The Cricklewood Tapestry*

Take the Tour

Big Ben, Buckingham Palace, Westminster Abbey, The British Museum, Madame Tussaud's, the great London parks ... And what better company in which to visit them than that of writers – in person or through their fictional characters. We take a tour of some of the standard 'sights', and go a little further afield, too. Hampstead Heath, Keats' House, Highgate Cemetery and Kew Gardens are among the stopping-off points. First, here's Canadian novelist Margaret Atwood remembering her first visit to London and putting herself through a punishing programme of sight-seeing.

The truth is that I didn't have much idea of what I was really doing. Certainly, I had almost no idea at all of where I was really going, and how much it had changed since I'd last checked in via the pages of Charles Dickens. Everything was so much smaller and shabbier than I had imagined. I was like the sort of Englishman who arrives in Canada expecting to find a grizzly bear on every street corner. 'Why are there so many *trucks*?' I thought. There were no trucks in Dickens.

There weren't even many in T.S. Eliot. 'I did not know Death had undone so many,' I murmured hopefully, as I made my way across Trafalgar Square. But the people there somehow refused to be as hollow-cheeked and plangent as I'd expected. They appeared to be mostly tourists, like myself, and were busy taking pictures of one another with pigeons on their heads.

My goal, of course, was Canada House, the first stop of every jet-stunned, impecunious young Canadian traveller in those days. [...]

Fashion-wise, 1964 was not really my year. Beatniks had faded, and I hadn't discovered the romantic raggle-taggle gypsy mode; but then, neither had anyone else. Jeans had not yet swept all before them, and for ventures to such places as churches and museums, skirts were still required; grey-flannel jumpers with Peter-Pan-collared blouses were my uniform of choice. High heels were the norm for most occasions, and about the only thing you could actually walk in were some rubber-soled suede items known as Hush Puppies.

Lugging my suitcase, then, I Hush-Puppied my way up the imposing steps of Canada House. At the time it offered – among other things, such as a full shelf of Geological Surveys – a reading room with newspapers in it. I riffled anxiously though the Rooms To Let, since I had no place to stay that night. By pay telephone, I rented the cheapest thing available, which was located in a suburb called Willesden Green. This turned out to be about as far away from everything as you could get, via the London Underground, which I promptly took (here at last, I thought, looking at my intermittently-bathed, cadaverous and/or dentally-challenged fellow passengers, were a few people Death had in fact undone, or was about to). The rooming-house furnishings smelled of old, sad cigarette smoke, and were of such hideous dinginess that I felt I'd landed in a Graham Green novel; and the sheets, when I finally slid between them, were not just cold and damp, they were wet. ('North Americans like that kind of thing,' an Englishwoman said to me, much later. 'Unless they freeze in the bathroom they think they've been cheated of the English experience.')

The next day I set out on what appears to me in retrospect a dauntingly ambitious quest for cultural trophies. My progress through the accumulated bric-a-brac of centuries was marked by the purchase of dozens of brochures and postcards, which I collected to remind myself that I'd actually been wherever it was I'd been. At breakneck speed I gawped my way through Westminster Abbey, the Houses of Parliament, St Paul's Cathedral, the Tower of London, the Victoria and Albert Museum, the National Portrait Gallery, the Tate, the houses of Samuel Johnson, Buckingham Palace, and the Albert Memorial. At some point I fell off a double-decker bus and sprained my foot, but even this, although it slowed me down, did not stop me in my headlong and reckless pursuit. After a week of this, my eyes were rolling around like loose change, and my head, although several sizes larger, was actually a good deal emptier than it had been before. This was a mystery to me. [...]

When not injecting myself with culture, I was looking for something to eat. In England in 1964, this was quite difficult, especially if you didn't have much money. I made the mistake of trying a hamburger and a milkshake, but the English didn't yet have the concept: the former was fried in rancid lamb fat, the latter fortified with what tasted like ground-up chalk. The best places were the fish-and-chip shops, or, barring that, the cafés, where you could get eggs, sausages, chips, and peas, in any combination. Finally, I ran into some fellow Canadians, who'd been in England longer than I had, and who put me onto a Greek place in Soho, which actually had salads, a few reliable pubs, and the Lyons' Corner House on Trafalgar Square, which had a roast-beef-all-you-can-eat for a set price. A mistake, as the Canadian journalists would starve themselves for a week, then hit the Lyons' Corner House like a swarm of locusts. (The Lyons' Corner House did not survive.)

It must have been through these expatriates that I hooked up with Alison Cunningham, whom I'd known at university and who was now in London, studying modern dance and sharing a second-floor flat in South Kensington with two other young women. Into this flat, Alison – when she heard of my wet-sheeted Willesden Green circumstances – generously offered to smuggle me. 'Smuggle' is appropriate; the flat was owned by aristocratic twins called Lord Cork and Lady Hoare, but as they were ninety and in nursing homes, it was actually run by a suspicious dragon of a housekeeper, so for purposes of being in the flat I had to pretend I didn't exist.

In Alison's flat I learned some culturally useful things that have stuck with me through the years: how to tell a good kipper from a bad one, for instance; how to use an English plate-drying rack; and how to make coffee in a pot when you don't have any other device. I continued with my tourist programme – stuffing in Cheyne Walk, several lesser-known churches, and the Inns of Court – and Alison practised a dance, which was a reinterpretation of *The Seagull*, set to several of the Goldberg Variations as played by Glenn Gould. I can never hear that piece of music, without seeing Alison, in a black leotard and wearing the severe smile of a Greek caryatid of the Archaic period, bending herself into a semi-pretzel on the South Kensington sitting-room floor.

Margaret Atwood, *Curious Pursuits*

✳ ✳ ✳

A less exhausting way, these days, of getting the measure of London, without also getting sore feet, is to take a trip on the London Eye – like the narrator of Joseph O'Neill's Netherland.

While Cardozo rushes by Underground to Sloane Square and his fiancée-to-be, I stroll across Waterloo Bridge with my jacket suspended from a hooked finger. I am happy to be walking. Although it's early evening, it's still very warm: this is, after all, the summer of the great heatwave. The English summer is actually a Russian doll of summers, the largest of which is the summer of unambiguous disaster in Iraq, which immediately contains the summer of the destruction of Lebanon, which itself holds a series of ever smaller summers that lead to the summer of Monty Panesar and, smallest of all perhaps, the summer of Wayne Rooney's foot. But on this evening at the end of July, it feels like summer simpliciter, and it's with no real thought of anything that I detach myself from the mass whose fate is Waterloo Station and go down the steps to the riverbank. It's a scene of good cheer on the esplanade, where the wanderers are in receipt of that peculiar happiness a summer river bestows, a donation of space, of light and, somehow, of time: there is something regretful in Big Ben's seven gongs. I go under Hungerford Bridge and its sunny new walkways and am overwhelmingly confronted by the London Eye, in profile. Here, by the tattered lawn of Jubilee gardens, is where I've arranged to meet wife and son. Rather than crane up at the Eye, I pass ten minutes watching the waters of the Thames. It's hard to believe this is exactly the stretch where, in January, with television helicopters buzzing overhead and millions watching its every sinking and surfacing, a whale swam. Chuck the birder taught me the term for such a creature: a vagrant, to be distinguished from a migrant.

My son's voice calls out. Daddy! Turning, I see my family and its super-long shadows. We are all beaming. Reunions in unfamiliar places have this effect, and maybe the great wheel itself is infectious: the stupendous circle, freighted with circumferential eggs, is a glorious spray of radiuses. In due course a security guard waves his wand over our possessions; an egg hatches Germans; and a gang of us boards. According to officialdom, we are flying counterclockwise at less than two miles an hour. Jake, beserk with excitement, quickly befriends a six-year-old boy who speaks not a word of English. As we rise over the river and are gradually presented with the eastern vista, the adults also become known to one another: we meet a couple from Leeds; a family from Vilnius

(Jake's pal is one of these); and three young Italian women, one of whom has dizziness and must stay seated.

As a Londoner, I find myself consulted about what we're all seeing. At first, this is easy – there's the NatWest tower, which now has a different name; there's Tower Bridge. But the higher we go, the less recognisable the city becomes. Trafalgar Square is not where you expect it to be. Charing Cross, right under our noses, must be carefully detected. I find myself turning to a guidebook for help. The difficulty arises from the mishmashing of spatial dimensions, yes, but also from a quantitative attack: the English capital is huge, huge; in every direction, to distant hills – Primrose and Denmark and Lavender, our map tells us – constructions are heaped without respite. Riverbank traffic aside, there is little sign of life. Districts are compacted, in south London especially: where on earth are Brixton and Kennington and Peckham? You wonder how anyone is able to navigate this labyrinth, which is what this crushed, squashed, everywhere-spreading city appears to be. 'Buckingham Palace?' one of the Lithuanian ladies asks me, and I cannot say. I notice, meanwhile, that Jake has started to race around and needs to be brought to order, and that Rachel is standing alone in a corner. I merely join my wife. I join her just as we reach the very top of our celestial circuit and for this reason I have no need to do anything more than put an arm around her shoulder. A self-evident and prefabricated symbolism attaches itself to this slow climb to the zenith, and we are not so foolishly ironical, or confident, as to miss the opportunity to glimpse significantly into the eyes of the other and share the thought that occurs to all at this summit, which is, of course, that they have made it thus far, to a point where they can see horizons previously unseen, and the old earth reveals itself newly. Everything is further heightened, as we must obscurely have planned, by signs of sundown: in the few clouds above Ealing, Phoebus is up to his oldest and best tricks. Rachel, a practical expression all of a sudden crossing her face, begins to say something, but I shush her. I know my wife: she feels an urge to go down now, into the streets and into the facts. But I leave her with no choice, as willy-nilly we are lowered westward, but to accept her place above it all. There is to be no drifting out of the moment.

Joseph O'Neill, *Netherland*

✳ ✳ ✳

Big Ben is probably as famous as the Eiffel Tower, but while most people know that the icon of Paris is called after the engineer who built it, even Londoners themselves may be hard pushed for an answer as to why Big Ben is called Big Ben. There are two theories ...

Big Ben is one of London's oddest buildings and the story of how it came to be built is typical of the eccentric way in which things tend to get done in London. Like the rest of the Palace of Westminster, it was built by Charles Barry (1795–1860) and Augustus Pugin (1812–1852) after a nationwide competition to find a new design for the seat of government after the disastrous fire of 1834.

The late Georgian passion for Gothic gave the Barry design a head start and after duly winning the competition, he began building the clock tower we see today, but when it was first built it wasn't known as Big Ben at all – the name Big Ben refers to the huge bell on which the hours are struck.

All the statistics to do with St Stephen's Tower (as Big Ben is really known) and its great clock are astonishing: the tower is nearly three hundred and twenty feet high; it took almost nineteen years from laying the first foundation stone to getting the clock going, largely because no one could agree about who should make it.

The job was first offered to Benjamin Vulliamy, the Queen's clockmaker, who was based in Pall Mall. His design was attacked as absurd and incompetent by another clockmaker, J. Dent, and after a huge fight with letters banging to and fro and *Times* leaders thundering out various opinions, the commissioners charged with organising the work gave in and launched a competition to design and build the new clock. The contract finally went to Dent amid much acrimony, in 1852. […]

There are two theories about the origins of the name 'Big Ben': around the time the clock was due to be completed, the prizefighter and publican Ben Caunt went sixty rounds with the best bare-knuckle boxer in the country, Nat Langham. The bout was declared a draw but it made both men national heroes. Ben Caunt was a huge man and one story has it that the great bell was named after him. The other story attributes the name to Benjamin Hall, the chief commissioner of works, who was addressing the House on the subject of a name for the new bell tower when, to great laughter, someone shouted 'Call it Big Ben!'

Perhaps the most remarkable thing about the clock is that even by the standards of today's atomic timepieces it is wonderfully accurate. When the commissioners launched their competition to design it they stipulated that it must be accurate to within one second an hour – most clock makers at the time agreed that this was impossible but that's how accurate the clock still is today. If it does get slightly out of time, a tiny coin, kept especially for the purpose, is placed on the huge pendulum and the weight of the coin is enough to adjust the clock by a fraction of a second.

Tom Quinn, *London's Strangest Tales*

✼ ✼ ✼

This short extract from Mrs Dalloway *combines a perceptive glimpse of Buckingham Palace, through the eyes of Richard Dalloway, with the sound of Big Ben striking the hour.*

As for Buckingham Palace (like an old prima donna facing the audience all in white) you can't deny it a certain dignity, he considered, nor despise what does, after all, stand to millions of people (a little crowd was waiting at the gate to see the King drive out) for a symbol, absurd though it is; a child with a box of bricks could have done better, he thought; looking at the memorial to Queen Victoria (whom he could remember in her horn spectacles driving through Kensington), its white mound, its billowing motherliness; but he liked being ruled by the descendant of Horsa; he liked continuity; and the sense of handing on the tradition of the past. It was a great age in which to have lived. Indeed, his own life was a miracle; let him make no mistake about it; here he was, in the prime of life, walking to his house in Westminster to tell Clarissa that he loved her. Happiness is this, he thought.

It is this, he said, as he entered Dean's Yard. Big Ben was beginning to strike, first the warning, musical; then the hour, irrevocable.

Virginia Woolf, *Mrs Dalloway*

✳ ✳ ✳

Though residents of London, Chanu and his family – in Monica Ali's best-selling novel, Brick Lane *– become 'tourists' on an unforgettable day out …*

The avenue that swept down to Buckingham Palace was wide as forty bullock carts and it was the grandest of roads. It was not black or grey. Nor was it brown or dusty yellow. It was red. It was fit for a queen. The tall black railings that guarded the palace were crowned with spikes of gold. Nazneen held on to a rail and surveyed the building. After a couple of seconds she looked behind her. The pavement was rife with tourists. Young couples, joined at the hip; tour groups, homogenized by race and tourist equipment; small bands of teenagers, who smoked or chewed gum or otherwise engaged their mouths in ferocious displays of kissing. Many people looked at the palace. Nazneen looked back at the building. It was big and white and, as far as she could see, extraordinary only in its size. The railings she found impressive but the house was only big. Its face was very plain. Two pillars (in themselves plain) sat at the main doorway, but there was little else in the way of decoration. If she were the queen she would tear it down and build a new house, not this flat-roofed block but something elegant and spirited, with minarets and spires, domes and mosaics, a beautiful garden instead of this bare forecourt. Something like the Taj Mahal.

Chanu had found his page in the guidebook. 'Buckingham Palace has been the official residence of British sovereigns since 1837. The palace evolved from a town house owned from the beginning of the eighteenth century by Dukes of Buckingham.' [...] 'Queen Victoria added a fourth wing to the building because of an absence of nurseries and too few bedrooms for visitors. Marble Arch had to be relocated to the north-east corner of Hyde Park.' Chanu took off his cap and wiped his forehead. He noticed his daughter leaning against the rails. 'Have a look, Shahana. Look at this beautiful building.'

Nazneen regarded the palace. 'Oh yes,' she said, 'it is very clever of your father to bring us here. It is a good choice.' Some of the windows were hung with net curtains, like the windows on the estate. She wanted to ask questions so that Chanu would answer them. What came to her mind was unsuitable. How many cleaners do they have? How long does it take to change all the beds? How does one family find each other in all that space? Eventually she asked, 'Which is the biggest room, and what is it used for?'

Chanu was pleased. 'The ballroom is one hundred and twenty-two feet long, sixty feet wide and forty-five feet high. When it was built it was the largest room in London. It is used for all sorts of big functions. The Queen, you see, must entertain many people. It is part of her duty to the country. Most British people know someone who has, at one time or another, been a guest at a palace tea party. This is how she maintains the affection and loyalty of her subjects.' [...]

Two hundred yards down the Mall was a cart with a big tin drum of hot caramelized peanuts. Nazneen, pursuing her campaign for enjoyment, became animated. 'Mmm,' she said, and clasped a hand to her chest. 'That smells delicious. Will you buy some for me?' Chanu patted his money belt. 'I have made provision for treats.'

They sat on some steps opposite the entrance to the park and ate the nuts from paper twists with the smell of burnt sugar in their nostrils. Nazneen ate and talked and laughed and asked as many questions as she could. After a while, when Chanu began an answer and she laughed again, he stopped and looked at her with his head to one side. 'Are you feeling well? Too much sun, perhaps?' She flushed, and she laughed again. She was laughing too much, but now that she had started this laughing business it was difficult to keep it under control. [...]

'Well now,' said Chanu. He swelled with pride at how marvellously he had managed the day. 'It is a lot of fun.'

They walked on the other side of the road, following St James's Park, back towards Buckingham Palace. The girls went in front, with a carrier bag each, still holding hands. 'That is the best of all sights,' Chanu told Nazneen, and she stumbled and grabbed his arm.

They had to return to the palace because Chanu wanted to try out the panoramic-view camera. It should be possible, he explained, to come close to the building and still fit the whole thing in one shot. He fiddled around with the little cardboard box for several minutes. 'It's a disposable camera,' said Shahana. 'What's he got to fiddle around for?' But when he had finished with that camera, the situation grew worse. He searched for the other camera and announced that he had been robbed. He proposed to tell the Guards who stood in little black boxes inside the palace forecourt. 'They have guns, they could shoot the bastard.' Nazneen suggested he empty all his pockets. 'God,' he said, 'I'm not a child.' He emptied all his pockets and found the camera, and then the girls had to pose.

Monica Ali, *Brick Lane*

* * *

Another tourist 'must see' is Westminster Abbey. As well as gazing at the tombs of famous monarchs, one goes there to pay tribute to Britain's great writers. Among those interred and commemorated at Poet's Corner is the famous London-lover, poet and essayist, Dr Samuel Johnson. At the end of her novel According to Queeney, *Beryl Bainbridge gives a brief but moving description of Johnson's funeral.*

Twenty-four coaches followed the funeral carriage to Westminster Abbey. It being a Monday and the streets crowded, several officials of the abbey went ahead to clear the way. Snow fell, but gently, as though to draw a veil across the heavens.

Sir Joshua Reynolds was chief mourner, followed by Francis Barber; the exalted importance afforded to the latter caused Sir John Hawkins considerable irritation.

The burial service was conducted by Dr Taylor of Ashbourne at one o'clock in the south close. Edmund Burke and Mr Langton were among those who bore the lead coffin. James Boswell was not present.

Dr Taylor lost strength of voice on two occasions, upon which he dabbed at his eyes with the cuff of his gown. He had drunk heavily the night before and was conscious that his own end could not be long delayed.

A hole had been dug close by the remains of David Garrick. The coffin lowered into the damp darkness, a flagstone was set in place inscribed with the words:

Samuel Johnson, L.L.D.
Obiit XIII die Decembris
Anno Domini MDCCLXXXIV
Ætatis suæ LXXV

The expenses for the funeral amounted to forty-four pounds six shillings and seven pence, excluding the sum of thirteen shillings and fourpence paid separately to the bellringers.

Beryl Bainbridge, *According to Queeney*

✳ ✳ ✳

And for those who prefer their celebrities looking more life-like than the stone effigies in Westminster Abbey, there's always Madame Tussaud's. Here's Czech writer Karel Capek writing home about a lesson learnt during a visit to the waxworks.

Madame Tussaud's is a museum of the famous, or rather of their wax-effigies. The Royal Family is there (also King Alphonso, somewhat moth-eaten). Mr. MacDonald's Ministers, French Presidents, Dickens and Kipling, marshals, Mademoiselle Lenglen, famous murderers of the last century and souvenirs of Napoleon, including his socks, his belt and his hat; then, in a place of dishonour, are Kaiser Wilhelm and Franz Josef, still dapper-looking for his years. Before one particularly life-like effigy of a gentleman in a top-hat I paused to peruse and find out who it was, when suddenly the top-hatted gentleman moved and walked away. It was dreadful! A little while later, two young ladies consulted the catalogue to see who *I* was. At Madame Tussaud's I made a rather unpleasant discovery: either I am absolutely incapable of assessing human faces, or else physiognomies are deceiving. For example, I was attracted, on a first glance, by a seated gentleman with a goatee beard, No. 12. In the catalogue I read: '12. Thomas Neill Cream, hanged in 1892. Poisoned Matilda Glover with strychnine. He was also found guilty of murdering three other women.' And in fact his face is highly suspicious. No. 13, Franz Müller, murdered Mr. Biggs on a train. Mm. No. 20, a clean-shaven gentleman, of more-or-less admirable appearance: Arthur Devereux, hanged 1905, known as the 'trunk murderer,' because he hid his victims' corpses in trunks. Horrible. No. 21 – no, this worthy priest just can't be

'Mrs. Dyer, the Reading baby murderess.' I now realise that I have got the pages of the catalogue mixed up, and have to correct my judgements: the seated gentleman, No. 12, is only Bernard Shaw; No. 13 is Louis Blériot, and No. 20 is just Guglielmo Marconi.

Never again will I judge people by their looks.

Karel Capek, *Letters from England*
translated by Anya Clark

❋ ❋ ❋

Among London's famous, architect Sir Christopher Wren is of the first rank. Apart from designing and overseeing the building of St Paul's Cathedral and many other churches, afte r the destruction of the Great Fire in 1666, he was inadvertently responsible for the design of our traditional wedding cake – or 'bride' cake – thanks to St Bride's.

St Bride's Church in Fleet Street is a fund of wonderfully odd stories. Its lightning conductor was designed and fitted by the great American republican and inventor Benjamin Franklin (1706–1790) but only after a huge row about whether blunt-ended conductors (seen as American) should be used or British pointed-end conductors.

The church steeple, designed by Christopher Wren, was used by a local baker, Mr Rich, as the inspiration for the bridal cake design that we now take for granted – St Bride's didn't get its name from the cake, the cake design copied the church and Rich became very rich indeed as a result of his new cake which, as we all know, survives to this day.

The remains of seven previous churches have been found during excavations at St Bride's and among more recent monuments are two that are very special indeed. On a wall close to the front there is a small memorial to Virginia Dare, whose claim to fame is that she was the first English child to be born in America. There is also a memorial – an unusually light-hearted one – to the man who built the church. We don't know the name of the author but it begins:

> Clever men like Christopher Wren
> Only occur just now and then.
> No one expects
> In perpetuity
> Architects of his ingenuity.
> No – never a cleverer dipped his pen
> Than clever Sir Christopher, Christopher Wren.

Tom Quinn, *London's Strangest Tales*

❊ ❊ ❊

From Westminster Abbey, a stroll up Whitehall will take you to Trafalgar Square and one of the world's greatest art collections, in the National Gallery. (And it's free.) The humorous opening of Julian Barnes' early novel, Metroland, *gives us two teenage boys hanging around the Gallery, less for the art than for observing people's responses to it.*

There is no rule against carrying binoculars in the National Gallery.

On this particular Wednesday afternoon in the summer of 1963, Toni had the notebook and I had the glasses. So far, it had been a productive visit. There had been the young nun in men's spectacles who smiled sentimentally at the Arnolfini Wedding, and then, after a few moments, frowned and made a disapproving cluck. There had been the anoraked girl hiker, so transfixed by the Crivelli altarpiece that we simply stood on either side of her and noted the subtlest parting of the lips, the faintest tautening of skin across the cheek bones and the brow ('Spot anything on the temple your side?' 'Zero' – so Toni wrote down *Temple twitch; LHS only*). And there had been the man in the chalk-stripe suit, hair precisely parted an inch above his right ear, who twitched and squirmed in front of a small Monet landscape. He puffed out his cheeks, leaned back slowly on his heels, and exhaled like a discreet balloon.

Then we came to one of our favourite rooms, and one of our most useful pictures: Van Dyck's equestrian portrait of Charles I. A middle-aged lady in a red mackintosh was sitting in front of it. Toni and I walked quietly to the padded bench at the other end of the room, and pretended interest in a tritely jocund Franz Hals. Then, while he shielded me, I moved forward a little and focussed the glasses on her. We were far enough away for me to be able to whisper notes to Toni quite safely; if she heard anything, she'd take it for the usual background murmur of admiration and assent.

The gallery was fairly empty that afternoon, and the woman was quite at ease with the portrait. I had time to impart a few speculative biographical details.

'Dorking? Bagshot? Forty-five, fifty. Shoppers' return. Married, two children, doesn't let him fug her any more. Surface happiness, deep discontent.'

That seemed to cover it. She was gazing up at the picture now like an icon-worshipper. Her eyes hosed it swiftly up and down, then settled, and began to move slowly over its surface. At times, her head would cock sideways and her neck thrust forward; her nostrils appeared to widen, as if she scented new correspondences in the painting; her hands moved on her thighs in little flutters. Gradually, her movements quietened down.

'Sort of religious peace,' I muttered to Toni. 'Well, quasi-religious, anyway; put that.'

I focussed on her hands again; they were now clasped together like an altar-boy's. Then I tilted the binoculars back up to her face. She had closed her eyes. I mentioned this.

'Seems to be recreating the beauty of what's in front of her; or savouring the after-image; can't tell.'

I kept the glasses on her for a full two minutes, while Toni, his biro raised, waited for my next comment.

There were two ways of reading it: either she was beyond the point of observable pleasure; or else she was asleep. [...]

We hunted emotions. Railway termini gave us weepy farewells and coarse recouplings. That was easy. Churches gave us the vivid deceptions of faith – though we had to be careful in our manner of observation. Harley Street doorsteps gave us, we believed, the rabbit fears of men about to die. And the National Gallery, our most frequent haunt, gave us examples of pure aesthetic pleasure – although, to be honest, they weren't as frequent, as pure, or as subtle as we'd first hoped. Outrageously often, we thought, the scene was more appropriate to Waterloo or Victoria; people greeted Monet, or Seurat, or Goya as if they had just stepped off a train – 'Well, what a nice surprise. I knew you'd be here, of course, but it's a nice surprise all the same. And my, aren't you looking just as well as ever? Hardly a day older. No really ... '

Our reason for constantly visiting the Gallery was straightforward. We agreed – indeed, no sane friend of ours would bother to argue – that Art was the most important thing in life, the constant to which one could be unfailingly devoted and which would never cease to reward; more crucially, it was the stuff whose effect on those exposed to it was ameliorative. It made people not just fitter for friendship and more civilised (we saw the circularity of *that*), but *better* – kinder, wiser, nicer, more peaceful, more active, more sensitive. If it didn't, what use was it? Why not just go and suck cornets instead? *Ex hypothesi* (as we would have said, or indeed *ex vero*), the moment someone perceives a work of art he is in some way improved. It seemed quite reasonable to expect that the process could be observed.

Julian Barnes, *Metroland*

* * *

W. Somerset Maugham is probably best known for his stories set in far-flung and exotic places. But here he is, as a young man, describing a more familiar location.

Piccadilly before dawn. After the stir and ceaseless traffic of the day, the silence of Piccadilly early in the morning, in the small hours, seems barely credible. It is unnatural and rather ghostly. The great street in its emptiness has a sort of solemn broadness, descending in a majestic sweep with the assured and stately ease of a placid river. The air is pure and limpid, but resonant, so that a solitary cab suddenly sends the whole street ringing, and the emphatic trot of the horse resounds with long reverberations. Impressive by reason of their regularity, the electric lights, self-assertive and brazen, flood the surroundings with a harsh and snowy brilliance; with a kind of indifferent violence they cast their glare upon the huge silent houses, and lower down throw into distinctness the long evenness of the park railings and the nearer trees. And between, outshone, like an uneven string of discoloured gems, twinkles the yellow flicker of the gas jets.

There is silence everywhere, but the houses are quiet and still, with a different silence from the rest, standing very white but for the black gaping of the many windows. In their sleep, closed and bolted, they line the pavement, helplessly as it were, disordered and undignified, having lost all significance without the busy hum of human voices and the hurrying noise of persons passing in and out.

W. Somerset Maugham, *A Writer's Notebook*

* * *

In the company of another night bird, we visit a Hyde Park abandoned to the dark by tourists and Londoners alike ... well, most of them.

On this north front of the Hyde, the terraces are great white monsters, like the shots you see in films of hotels at the Côte de France. There's the terraces for miles, like cliffs, then the Bayswater speedway with its glare lights and black pools, and the great dark green-purple park stretching on like a huge sea. The thing about the park is, in day time they're all innocence and merriment, with dogs and perambulators and old geezers and couples wrapped up like judo performers on the green. But soon as the night falls, the whole scene reverses – into its exact opposite, in fact. In come the prowlers and the gropers and the cops and narks and whores and kinky exhibition numbers, and the thick air is filled with hundreds of suspicious, peering pairs of eyes. Everyone is seeking someone, but everyone is scared to meet that him or her they're looking for. If you're out of it, you want to go inside to see, and once you're in, you're very anxious to get out again. So I went. [...]

I got on a stretch of curving roadway that was so dam black I kept walking off it, and getting tangled up in the whatsits that they put there to say please-keep-off-the-thing. A light shaft suddenly appeared from nowhere, and by me there flashed a pair of mad enthusiasts in track-suits, puffing and groaning and looking bloody uncomfortable and virtuous. Good luck to them! 'God bless!' I shouted after.

Then unexpectedly I came out on a delightful panorama of the Serpentine, lit up by green gas, and by headlamps from the cars whining across the bridge. I picked my way down by the water, and trod on a lot of ducks, they must have been, who scattered squawking sleepily. 'Keep in your own manor, where you belong,' I told them, chasing the little bastards down into the lake.

I was now beside the waves, and I could just make the sign out, 'Boats for Hire', and saw them moored fifteen feet away from me out there. So thinking, why not? anything to relieve the agony, I sat on the grass, and took off my nylon stretch and Itie clogs, and rolled up my Cambridge blues, and stepped into the drink like King Canute.

Colin MacInnes, *Absolute Beginners*

* * *

A good many visitors like to pay tribute to the intellectual history of London by visiting the British Museum Reading Room, now a key 'exhibit' but once – before the building of the new British Library near King's Cross Station – as hard to enter as Fort Knox. It was here that great thinkers and writers from far and wide thought their thoughts and wrote their writings. The Museum and Reading Room feature in Virginia Woolf's novel Jacob's Room. *We join the young Jacob Flanders, after a day's 'research', as he waits for his walking-stick, deposited in the cloakroom, and follow his thoughts about the British Museum and the Reading Room.*

There is in the British Museum an enormous mind. Consider that Plato is there cheek by jowl with Aristotle; and Shakespeare with Marlowe. This great mind is hoarded beyond the power of any single mind to possess it. Nevertheless (as they take so long finding one's walking-stick) one can't help thinking how one might come with a note-book, sit at a desk, and read it all through. A learned man is the most venerable of all – a man like Huxtable of Trinity, who writes all his letters in Greek, they say, and could have kept his end up with Bentley. And then there is science, pictures, architecture – an enormous mind.

They pushed the walking stick across the counter. Jacob stood beneath the porch of the British Museum. It was raining. Great Russell Street was glazed and shining – here yellow, here, outside the chemist's, red and pale blue. People scuttled quickly close to the wall; carriages rattled rather helter-skelter down the streets. Well, but a little rain hurts nobody. Jacob walked off much as if he had been in the country; and late that night there he was sitting at his table with his pipe and his book.

The rain poured down. The British Museum stood in one solid immense mound, very pale, very sleek in the rain, not a quarter of a mile from him. The vast mind was sheeted with stone; and each compartment in the depths of it was safe and dry. The night-watchmen, flashing their lanterns over the backs of Plato and Shakespeare, saw that on the twenty-second of February neither flame, rat, nor burglar was going to violate these treasures – poor, highly respectable men, with wives and families at Kentish Town, do their best for twenty years to protect Plato and Shakespeare, and then are buried at Highgate.

Stone lies solid over the British Museum, as bone lies cool over the visions and heat of the brain. Only here the brain is Plato's brain and Shakespeare's; the brain has made pots and statues, great bulls and little jewels, and crossed the river of death this way and that incessantly, seeking some landing, now wrapping the body well for its long sleep; now laying a penny piece on the eyes; now turning the toes scrupulously to the East. Meanwhile, Plato continues his dialogue; in spite of the rain; in spite of the cab whistles; in spite of the woman in the mews behind Great Ormond Street who has come home drunk and cries all night long, 'Let me in! Let me in!'

Virginia Woolf, *Jacob's Room*

❋ ❋ ❋

Many of London's intellectual élite have lived in Hampstead – and some still do. But for Iqbal Ahmed the place and its residents remain elusive and less than friendly.

I travelled by bus from Camden Town to Hampstead Heath. The green and grey bus gained height before reaching the fountain by South End Green. When I got off the bus and walked towards the Heath, I caught the sight of woodland and meadow for the first time in London. It was like a homecoming for me after drifting through the various neighbourhoods of London in search of work. It was a Saturday afternoon in July and many people were arriving for a picnic in the park. The first pond opened in my field of vision like the landscape in George Seurat's *Sunbathers*. A group of tramps was making merry by the next pond. One of them was playing the guitar and another was dancing on tottering feet. A woman in the group was feeding a dog from the palm of her hand. The path inclined after the second pond, and I could see many people on top of a hill trying to locate landmark buildings in London.

The second time I visited this area, I travelled by tube to Hampstead High Street. The train shed its load at Camden Town, and the conversations of the passengers became distinct and clear after the train had passed Chalk Farm. Two middle-aged women were talking about Sargent and Constable. I wondered why they were so fascinated by an army officer and a policeman. The tube station was located on a hill. There was a jovial guide waiting outside the station holding a placard for a walking tour of Hampstead village. I walked downwards towards the Heath. The High Street looked very nice with its boutiques and brasseries. The men sitting in the bars and cafés wore shorts and hats, but looked rather self-conscious in their casual gear. I stopped for a cup of coffee in one of the cafés. The toilet sign was spelt as 'toilette' to make the café look more chic. Without a book or newspaper, I found the atmosphere in the café very oppressive. So I left soon after finishing my coffee. An artist displayed a few paintings on the pavement for sale while he worked on a fresh canvas. Close by, a homeless woman sold copies of a magazine to raise money for food. Two nannies were pushing strollers up the hill, engaged in conversation. I cut through Devonshire Hill to reach Hampstead Heath. In this road, a stockbroker was operating from a solitary shop with a baroque interior, in which computer screens on desks looked most incongruous. A wine bar was named after a nineteenth-century poet, its tables laid with brilliant white cloths. Where the road branched into two, someone asked me directions for Keats' House, unaware that I was also new to the neighbourhood.

I found my first job in London in a corner shop in South End Road. A year later, I rented a room in a house on South Hill Park. I spent two thirds of my meagre wages on rent. I had heard about Hampstead for the first time in E. M. Forster's *A Passage to India*, in which an Englishman tells Dr Aziz that Hampstead is 'a thoughtful little suburb of London'. [...]

It was the Heath which offered me consolation while living a solitary life in South Hill Park. There was a passageway leading to the Heath from there. I took a longer route through the Heath to the corner shop in the mornings. The weekends brought picnickers, but on weekdays I caught sight of other solitary people – an Italian woman with a poodle, a French woman with a spaniel who bought a copy of *Le Figaro* and a pack of Gauloises from me in the corner shop. The summer months were like a fiesta, with funfairs and open-air concerts. I spent my first few months in Hampstead in such diversions.

South Park Hill had a row of trees, which I could not name, on each side of the road. Sometimes a piano would break into a tune as I passed by a certain bay window on my way home. There were many creative people living in this neighbourhood. I felt as if God has made their hearts cold in return for creativity. I was trying to build friendships on the quicksand of the indifference of the people living in Hampstead. [...]

When winter set in, the Heath looked forlorn and barren. I took a walk as usual up to the Highgate ponds, which had been painted by melancholy artist, Howard Hodgkin, in vivid colours. These ponds looked desolate in winter light. Sometimes I would carry on walking until I reached a cemetery where George Eliot was buried. I had mistaken her name for a male writer, a misapprehension that was reinforced when I saw her picture. I pondered over my own isolation while passing by the catacombs of the cemetery.

I would take Highgate Road on my way back to the Heath. I had stayed in a hostel in this road during my second week in London. One day, I walked into this hostel again to use its cafeteria. It was empty. I sat in one corner with my nose in a book. A few minutes later, an American woman asked me if I minded her joining me. I didn't mind at all, but I was taken aback by her request. People in Hampstead Heath find it excruciating to share a table with someone else in a café, preferring to wait for a table to become available. It would amount to incivility to ask a Hampsteadian to share a table with him or her in a café when other tables were unoccupied. It would be enough to make them leave the place immediately. I had once made the mistake of asking a woman, whom I saw often in the corner shop, if I could join her at a table in a café in Hampstead. The woman seemed puzzled and looked pointedly at the empty tables. I realized my folly and rushed to a table at the far end of the café. [...]

If I ever had to go to the tube station in Hampstead High Street, I walked up Willow Road and turned into Flask Walk to reach it. One evening, I drifted into a labyrinth of alleyways near Flask Walk until I reached an estate which looked like old-fashioned blocks of council flats. A man was lying on the ground playing an acoustic guitar; another man was rolling up tobacco in cigarette paper. A woman was braiding the hair of a long-bearded man. In this neighbourhood of unsociable people, it looked like a veritable commune. [...]

The people who live in Hampstead have remained elusive to me during the ten years that I have lived in this area. It is the proximity of Hampstead to Central London that makes life bearable for me in this neighbourhood. I often travel by bus to the West End to spend my evenings. I have never entered The Freemason's Arms or Spaniards Inn in Hampstead to drown my sorrows. [...]

One could be living a tormented life while breathing the pure air on Mount Tyndall in Hampstead, and it was possible to live a joyous existence in the marshes of East London. One could also be beggarly even after owning a mansion in Hampstead. My life in Hampstead resembled that patch of the Heath that grows nettles in it for unknown reasons.

Iqbal Ahmed, *Sorrows of the Moon*

❊ ❊ ❊

A rather different view of Hampstead comes from Virginia Woolf. Apart from a walk on the Heath, with its wonderful views across the capital, any visit to Hampstead must take in Keats' House – a moving experience for anyone who loves the poet's work.

If houses have their voices and places their seasons, it is always spring in Hampstead as it is always February in Cheyne Row. By some miracle, too, Hampstead has always remained not a suburb or a piece of antiquity engulfed in the modern world, but a place with a character peculiar to itself. […] Its bow windows still look out upon vales and trees and ponds and barking dogs and couples sauntering arm in arm and pausing, here on the hill-top, to look at the distant domes and pinnacles of London, as they sauntered and paused and looked when Keats lived here. For Keats lived up the lane in a little white house behind wooden palings. Nothing has been much changed since his day. But as we enter the house in which Keats lived some mournful shadow seems to fall across the garden. A tree has fallen and lies propped. Waving branches cast their shadows up and down over the flat white walls of the house. Here, for all the gaiety and serenity of the neighbourhood, the nightingale sang; here, if anywhere, fever and anguish had their dwelling and paced this little green plot oppressed with the sense of quick-coming death and the shortness of life and the passion of love and its misery.

Yet if Keats left any impress upon his house it is the impression not of fever, but of that clarity and dignity which come from order and self-control. The rooms are small but shapely; downstairs the long windows are so large that half the wall seems made of lights.

46

Two chairs turned together are close to the window as if someone had sat there reading and had just got up and left the room. The figure of the reader must have been splashed with shade and sun as the hanging leaves stirred in the breeze. Birds must have hopped close to his foot. The room is empty save for the two chairs, for Keats had few possessions, little furniture and not more, he said, than one hundred and fifty books. And perhaps it is because the rooms are so empty and furnished rather with light and shadow than with chairs and tables that one does not think of people, here where so many people have lived. The imagination does not evoke scenes. It does not strike one that there must have been eating and drinking here; people must have come in and out; they must have put down bags, left parcels; they must have scrubbed and cleaned and done battle with dirt and disorder and carried cans of water from the basement to the bedrooms. All the traffic of life is silenced. The voice of the house is the voice of leaves brushing in the wind; of branches stirring in the garden. Only one presence – that of Keats himself – dwells here. And even he, though his picture is on every wall, seems to come silently, on the broad shafts of light, without body or footfall. Here he sat on the chair in the window and listened without moving, and saw without starting, and turned the page without haste though his time was so short.

There is an air of heroic equanimity about the house in spite of the death masks and the brittle yellow wreaths and the other grisly memorials which remind us that Keats died young and unknown and in exile. Life goes on outside the window. Behind this calm, this rustling of the leaves, one hears the far-off rattle of wheels, the bark of dogs fetching and carrying sticks from the pond. Life goes on outside the wooden paling. When we shut the gate upon the grass and the tree where the nightingale sang we find, quite rightly, the butcher delivering his meat from a small red motor van at the house next door. If we cross the road, taking care not to be cut down by some rash driver – for they drive at a great pace down these wide streets – we shall find ourselves on top of the hill and beneath shall see the whole of London lying below us. It is a view of perpetual fascination at all hours and in all seasons. One sees London as a whole – London crowded and ribbed and compact, with its dominant domes, its guardian cathedrals; its chimneys and spires; its cranes and gasometers; and the perpetual smoke which no spring or autumn ever blows away. London has lain there time out of mind scarring that stretch of earth deeper and deeper, making it more uneasy, lumped and tumultuous, branding it for ever with an indelible scar. There it lies in layers, in strata, bristling and billowing with rolls of smoke always caught on its pinnacles. And yet from Parliament Hill one can see, too, the country beyond. There are hills on the further side in whose woods birds are singing, and some stoat or rabbit pauses, in dead silence, with paw lifted to listen intently to rustlings among the leaves. To look over London from this hill Keats came and Coleridge and Shakespeare, perhaps. And here at this very moment the usual young man sits on an iron bench clasping to his arms the usual young woman.

Virginia Woolf, *The London Scene*

❊ ❊ ❊

While in the Hampstead area, the visitor with a taste for the quirky should take a look at the great Victorian cemetery of Highgate – the London equivalent of the Père-Lachaise cemetery in Paris. Among its stone angels of every conceivable design can be found the great, grizzled head of Karl Marx.

All cemeteries are places of reflection, but Highgate is unique, with a spirit all its own. A fusion of brooding Neo-gothic architecture and ivy-shrouded masonry, it lies 400 feet above St Paul's, looking out over one of the most mysterious and fascinating cities in the world. Perhaps there is something about the very location of Highgate which contributes to the cemetery's magical atmosphere. Even today, it is full of hidden beauty and eccentricity, a haven from the strange disease of modern life. In his introduction to a collection of essays,

John Betjeman refers to Highgate as the Victorian cemetery *par excellence*, the 'Victorian Valhalla'. This is a wonderful description, combining as it does the pagan imagery and Dickensian atmosphere of Highgate. [...]

Highgate was already fashionable – a trendy spot for promenading Londoners. A purpose-built cemetery adjacent to the new church on the west side of Swain's Lane and in such a sought-after part of London, was inevitable – and in 1839 it became a reality.

In 1836, Stephen Geary (1797–1854) founded the London Cemetery Company. An entrepreneur, architect and surveyor, Geary had turned his attention to cemetery design after witnessing the success of the General Cemetery Company at Kensal Green. [...]

In his capacity as a founder, chairman and architect of the London Cemetery Company, Geary could act as his own client. His task was to design the cemetery, and he did so in his own idiosyncratic way. While he may have been inspired by the *commercial* success of Kensal Green, Geary was determined to use the most progressive architectural style of the day – which he then imposed on a Classical model. Two chapels flank a gateway on Swain's Lane, which bear the words LONDON CEMETERY and features impressive iron gates. The twin chapels (one for Anglicans, one for Dissenters), situated on either side of the entrance, comply with the Classical rules of symmetrical design. The curved walls enclose the entrance forecourt in the same way as those at Blenheim and Castle Howard. However, once the Classical layout was *in situ*, Geary was free to play around with his own interpretation of Gothic Revival, one which can only be described as 'Tudorbethan'. The octagonal chapels feature spiral staircases, stained-glass bay windows, lancet windows (as used by archers to repel invaders), steep gables and bristling pinnacles.

Geary's original plans incorporated St Michael's Church. [...] The plan was abandoned when David Ramsay was appointed landscape gardener. Together, he and Geary created a picturesque landscape of avenues and plantations intersected by winding gravel paths, reminiscent of those at Père Lachaise, ingeniously leading from one level to the next without any need for steps, thus performing the dual function of allowing easy access to the graves, while also creating an illusion of spaciousness in the cemetery's twenty acres. [...]

Geary now created a magnificent series of features intended to confirm Highgate's reputation as London's principal cemetery. The first of these, the Egyptian Avenue, pandered to the craze for Egyptiana inspired by the funereal specimens brought back to the British Museum by nineteenth-century explorers [...] Egyptiana offered magnificent potential for memorial art. It seems appropriate that the Victorians, with their fascination with mortality, should turn for inspiration to another culture that was equally obsessed by death, and incorporate the pagan symbolism of Egypt into familiar rituals of Anglican burial.

The Egyptian Avenue is essentially a street of the dead, created by excavating twelve feet deep into the steepest part of the hillside. One enters beneath a colossal arch, flanked by columns featuring a lotus-bud motif and leading to a tunnel. The dead were interred in a line of sixteen family vaults, which resemble a street of terraced houses. Each vault was brick-lined, with enough shelf-room for twelve coffins. In front of each door was an inverted torch – the symbol of life extinguished. [...]

Beyond the Egyptian Avenue stood a huge Cedar of Lebanon, an original feature of the Ashurst garden, already over 150 years old when Geary was planning the cemetery. He constructed a circle of twenty catacombs around the tree, each with an Egyptian-style pediment. These were so popular that forty years later an outer circle of sixteen was constructed facing into the circle.

Above the Circle of Lebanon was Highgate's third great feature, the Terrace catacombs, which consisted of an underground gallery beneath the terrace; it was more than 80 yards long and contained

840 recesses, each big enough to take a single coffin. Known as *loculi*, the catacombs were roofed with asphalt and featured glass apertures, which admitted light into the tombs below. [...]

Soon Highgate Cemetery was a tourist attraction in its own right. [...]

Highgate Cemetery's most famous inhabitant is Karl Marx, who managed to cause controversy long after his death. Demonstrations arranged to mark the centenary of his birth in 1918 were banned by the Home Office, and only those carrying wreaths were admitted. In 1924, the Russian Communist Party petitioned the Home Office to remove his remains to Russia. This was opposed by the British Communist Party, which claimed Marx belonged to the world, not just to Russia. Marx's grave was moved from the south of the New Ground in 1954, and the distinctive grizzled head was sculpted by Lawrence Bradshaw and unveiled in 1956. [...]

After the war, London's great Victorian cemeteries went into terminal decline. [...]

And then, suddenly, rescue arrived in the form of Sir John Betjeman. A writer, Victorian enthusiast and architectural expert, Betjeman spearheaded the conservation movement in Britain, campaigning for endangered buildings. [...]

In 1957, the Friends of Highgate Cemetery was formed. Dedicated to clearing brambles and opening access to graves, the organization subsequently obtained the freehold of the Cemetery and began an impressive programme of restoration.

Catherine Arnold, *Necropolis*

* * *

For those with the time and determination to explore the outer reaches of London and who prefer their 'Nature' a little more controlled than it is on Hampstead Heath, a trip to Kew Gardens can make a delightful day out – though it doesn't meet with the complete approval of Chinese visitor Xiaolu Guo ...

guest *n* person entertained at another's house or at another's expense; invited performer or speaker; customer at a hotel or restaurant

A new day. You call me. At once I know your voice. You ask if I want visit Kew Gardens.

'Queue Gardens?'

'Meet me at Richmond tube station,' you say. 'R–i–c–h–m–o–n–d.'

Is beautiful weather. What a surprise. And so peaceful in the grassy space. So green. Cherry blossoms is just coming out and you tell me about your favourite snowdrops. We see there is different small gardens with different theme. Africa garden are palm trees. North America garden are rocks. South America garden are cactus. And there is too Asia gardens. I so happy Manager not forgetting Asia gardens.

But I so disappointing after we walk in. Lotuses and bamboos is growing in India garden, plum trees and stone bridge is growing in Japanese garden. Where is my Chinese garden?

'Doesn't look like they've made a Chinese garden,' you say to me.

'But that very unfair,' I say in angry voice. 'Bamboos belongs to China. Panda eats bamboos leafs in China, you must hear, no?'

You laugh. You say you agree. They should move some plants from India and Japan garden to make Chinese garden.

The meadow asking us to lie. We rest beside each other. I never do that with a man. Juice from grass wetting my white shirt. My heart melting. Sky is blue and airplane flying above us, low and clear. I see moving shadows of the plane on the meadow.

'I want see where you live,' I say.

You look in my eyes. 'Be my guest.'

Xiaolu Guo, *A Concise Chinese – English Dictionary for Lovers*

❊　❊　❊

Visitors don't just come from abroad: in his autobiographical A Start in Life, *the Nottingham-born novelist Alan Sillitoe (best known for* Saturday Night and Sunday Morning*) describes the pleasures and excitement of a young man from 'The North' exploring London for the first time.*

It was a raw morning, and though it was foul I liked it because it was in London. At the nearest newsagent's I bought a street atlas and a copy of the local paper, two pieces of literature to see me through the day. It felt good to have my legs working again, and I was determined to walk them back into shape, for they'd grown soft in the glorious weeks of having a car. At Russell Square the ache was so sharp at my calves that I considered jumping a tube to Soho, but gritted my toes and traipsed on, pausing now and again for a flip at the map. [...]

The smell of the city was like Brilliantine and smoke, chicken and iron filings, and I fed on it as I walked along, even smiling at the curses of a taxi driver when I nipped too sharply on to a pedestrian crossing. You couldn't take your rights too much for granted here, I thought, and was even glad of such cold comfort, for my backbone was made of optimism. [...]

That first day I walked and re-walked the whole middle area of London, and by the end of it, when I headed back in the direction of the hotel, I knew that it wasn't as big as I'd always heard it was. The next day I did the City, and for a fortnight, till my money was near enough done for, I got familiar with most of the sprawl. At first the far-off places were known only from the tube scheme. If I was at Bond Street and wanted to go to Hampstead I looked at the underground map and said to myself: 'I'll get on the Central Line, to Tottenham Court Road, then turn left on the Northern Line, and go up until I see Hampstead on the station label.' Often I'd fiddle my way down by bus until, eventually, if some foreigner (or even Londoner) stopped me in the street and asked where a certain place was I'd be able to tell them in five cases out of ten. [...]

Exploring this gigantic and continuous prairie of buildings during the day, and wandering around the West End like the Phantom of the Opera until late at night, didn't leave much time or energy for serious speculation. In other words I was living the full life because I felt no real connection to what went on around me. If I had, or began to, I should become buried in it and wouldn't be able to see anything at all. Which was why I clung as long as possible to my arduous free wandering.

Alan Sillitoe, *A Start in Life*

* * *

London from the air at night has its own special beauty, as Sukdhev Sandhu discovers when he accompanies those who patrol the city's skies between nightfall and dawn.

The streets of London are made from gold. But only at night time and only from the sky. They lie there glimmering like a Hatton Garden window display. Jewelled necklaces winking at us. At Piccadilly Circus and along Oxford Street the refracted neon gives them a ruby-red and emerald-green lustre. "Cracking night, Sukhdev," pipes the pilot, but I am too awestruck by the city's beauty to reply. This is the panoptic sublime.

The helicopter flies in orbit. It wiggles and tilts. At time it feels as if the pilot has lost control, an outdoor tightrope walker about to fall to earth. The stomach-nausea is accompanied by bursts of landmark glee: there, in the distance, is Wembley Stadium with cranes and machines perched over it like basketball players primed to slamdunk; there the Fabergé ruby ball of the Swiss Re Tower.

Politicians and demographers often assert that London is overloaded, crammed to the hilt, but from the sky it appears far from congested. The concrete jungle is nowhere to be seen. Even the most built-up areas are punctuated by large expanses of dark forest, empty parts of the city's night-canvas. The capital is an endless origami unfolding, stretching out horizontally rather than vertically. Its residential buildings are so crabbed and timid that any sticking out appear both heroic and lonely.

The sky is constantly lit up as private planes carrying Russian billionaires to vital soccer fixtures start their descent, and a whole queue of commercial airliners begin stacking to come into Heathrow; the effect is that of a corporate quasar game as lights continually strafe the darkness. Things invisible at ground level suddenly rear into view: industrial parks – there seem to be hundreds of them. And while, even from Primrose Hill or Greenwich Park, the city melds into one largely unindividuated flatscape, at night time it becomes more composite in character, a loose and disconnected set of Lego pieces. [...]

It's overcast tonight. The clouds we skim and fly through are disorientating. They make it seem as if smoke is rising, as if the city is ablaze. We hover briefly above a mist-obscured St Paul's Cathedral and for a moment I feel I have been transported back to World War Two and the scene of that iconic photograph of Blitz London in which Christopher Wren's dome is surrounded by acres of bloodied devastation. [...]

Flying over a city, especially at night time, allows a brief glimpse of freedom. It is to be liberated from the stress and murk of terrestrial life. Towards the end of their shifts, the darkness slides almost imperceptibly towards dawn, the avian police start to fly back to Lippitt's Hill Camp. Their heads ache and their backs are sore, but though they're at a low-ebb physically, for a few minutes they relax a little and let their minds wander. They think of their families and of past loves. They look at the line of pollution that hangs above the city, so thick they could walk on it, and wish it could be disappeared. They look at the city twitching into motion below them and are touched by its fragility. How beautiful Hampstead looks as it rises out of the mist.

A pilot, his operational lingo replaced by dreamy reverie, reflects on his working life in London:

"When I was working on the ground I certainly didn't like the city. Quite the opposite. But everywhere's lovely from the air. Even the worst bits look good. Like King's Cross: I never noticed the architecture of St Pancras before – all the stations and the buildings are fantastic. To be honest, I'd rather spend more time in the air than on the ground."

Sukhev Sandhu, *Night Haunts*

✳ ✳ ✳

And to finish with, here's all of London's statuary coming to life in a wonderful sequence from Will Self's The Book of Dave.

Achilles was getting off his plinth; first one big foot then the other tore from its base with a tortured screech. He cut at the rags of mist with his short sword and brandished his shield at the Hilton Hotel. A couple of early-bird tourists who had been posing for a snap in front of the statue – male pecking with camera, female with wings neatly folded – were struck to the ground by one of Achilles's bulldozing greaves, as he clunked by them heading for Apsley House. He did not waver – he had no quarrel with them. He took no issue either with the cars he kicked as he strode across the roadway and on to the traffic island. Seven metres of bronze against two-millimetre thicknesses of steel – there was no contest; in the statue's wake smashed vehicles lay on their sides, their engines racing and groaning.

Lit by the rising sun, fingernails of opalescent cloud scratched contrails on the sky. Achilles stood beneath Constitution Arch and beat shield with sword. With a bang, then a spatter of stony fragments, the four horses atop the arch came alive, tossing their leaden heads. The boy holding the traces struggled to control them. Peace, erect in her chariot, her robe coming off her shoulder in rigid folds, flicked the reins and the whole, mighty quadriga rose, banked sharply and came crunching down. Peace threw her laurel wreath like a Frisbee, and Achilles caught it on his sword.

The other statues on the traffic island were animating: the Iron Duke spurred down his horse, Copenhagen; the bronze figures that attended him – Guard, Dragoon, Fusilier and Highlander – wrenched themselves free from the polished granite and fell in behind their commander-in-chief. On the Royal Regiment of Artillery memorial the dead gunner rose up from under his petrified greatcoat and joined his comrades. Together they unlimbered their stone field gun. David, tall, svelte and naked, shimmied from the Machine Gun Corps memorial – sword in one hand, Bren gun in the other. These terrible figures stood apart, turning to face down Piccadilly, Knightsbridge, Grosvenor Place and Park Lane, undecided what to do now movement had been bestowed upon them. The few pedestrians who were abroad at this early house scattered like rabbits, tearing between the trees of Green Park, discarding briefcases and umbrellas as they ran, while those drivers not violently impinged on remained oblivious, their heads clamped in their own metal tumult. The company of statues formed up, with Achilles in the van and Peace to the rear. They marched off down Constitution Hill, feet striking sparks as they clanked over the kerbs.

All across London, as the statues came to life, they were at first bemused – then only with reluctance purposeful. Clive of India jumped from his plinth and took the stairs down to Horse Guards skipping. Lincoln at first sat down, surprised, then, struggling up from his chair in Parliament Square, crossed over to the menhir bulk of Churchill, took his arm and assisted him to walk. Earl Haig led his mount alongside Montgomery, who was preposterous in his dimpled elephantine trousers. In Knightsbridge, Shackleton and Livingstone stepped out from their niches in the Royal Geographic Society. Golden Albert squeezed between the gilded stanchions of his memorial, and those blowzy ladies Europe, Africa, Asia and America formed a stony crocodile in his train. In Waterloo Place, Scott strolled up and down the pavement, striking a few attitudes, modelling his Burberry outfit.

In Chelsea, Thomas More stood up abruptly, his golden nose flashing; while across the river the droopy-eared Buddhas were stirring in their pagoda. Up in Highgate Cemetery the colossal head of Marx wobbled, then rolled downhill over the mounds of freshly dug graves. They were all heading for Trafalgar Square, where five-metre-high Nelson was gingerly shinnying down his own column, while Edith Cavell tripped past St Martin-in-the-Fields, her marble skirts rattling against the pedestrian barriers.

Not only human figures were on the move but animals as well: packs of stone dogs and herds of bronze cattle. Guy the Gorilla knuckle-walked out of London Zoo and around the Outer Circle; the dolphins slithered from the lamp-posts along the Thames and flopped into town. Mythical creatures joined the throng closing in on Trafalgar Square: riddling sphinxes, flying griffins and even the ill-conceived Victorian dinosaurs came humping overland from Crystal Palace. The whole mad overwrought bestiary arrived ramping and romping. The Landseer lions rose up to meet them, stretched and soundlessly roared.

Multiples of monarchs: doughty Williams, German Georges, dumpy Victorias. Presses of prime ministers, scrums of generals and colonial administrators, flying bees of viceroys, gaggles of writers and artists, cohorts of Christs – from façades and niches, plinths and pediments, crucifixes and crosses, the statues of London tore themselves free, until the whole centre of the city was a heaving hubbub of tramping bronze, clanking cast-iron, grating granite and marble. These graven images, these tin-pot gods! They had no more uniformity of purpose than they did of style, substance or scale – giant warmongers and diminutive deities, they were distorted embodiments of their creators' confused and ever-changing priorities. They didn't mean to cause any damage or distress – but they just did. They left pediments bare and cornices crumpling, domes imploded, porticos and bridges slumped, colonnades collapsed. They didn't mean to hurt the soft little people, but they were so big and hard that skins were split and skulls were crushed wherever they went.

Standing on the steps of Nelson's Column, Achilles beat sword on shield, trying to gain the statues' attention. It was pointless – these hunks could make no common cause, they knew nothing, felt nothing – only the rage of eternal sleepers robbed of their repose. Greek gods and goddesses stood about in profile; Saint Thomas à Becket writhed in his death agony; Baden-Powell scouted out the terrain. Slowly – lazily even – the statues began to fight one another. Marble clanged on iron, granite on bronze, as the maddened effigies battled with the incomprehensibility of their own sentience. What were they? Nothing. So sightlessly stared through for so very long that they had no more significance than a dustbin or a postbox – less perhaps.

Then there was a diversion – some dumb cabbie had managed to wrestle his vehicle free from the jam on the Charing Cross Road, and now he was trying to turn around in the roadway beneath the National Gallery. He backed and filled, knocking fauns, cherubs and caryatids over like ninepins. Achilles leaped down from his vantage and strode over. He leaned down, and his disproportionately tiny cock rasped along the cab's roof, shattering the 'For Hire' sign ...

Will Self, *The Book of Dave*

"Old Father Thames ... "

Over the river by Westminster Bridge, the Thames alive with light, sparkling green in the autumn sunshine, and the sight of it did me good.

Patrick McGrath, *Spider*

* * *

A breeze had got up. It played down the length of the river so that the water was chased into little overlapping waves. As the moon slid out from behind a shawl of cloud, casting a pale silver light on the water, they glistened and squirmed. A gigantic black sea monster, Rose thought, that was the Thames, slithering through the city's ditch towards its lair beneath the open seas. A grotesque beast that devoured and half-digested the waste of the largest city in the world, its open maw ceaselessly swallowing its rotting vegetation, its excrement, its dead. Its appetite was voracious, indiscriminate, its tentacles stretching even into the city's bowels to lick at their squalid deposits.

Clare Clark, *The Great Stink*

* * *

*Like London itself, the great river that divides the north
of the capital from the south has many sides to it – the
mere sight of it on a bright autumn day can lift the spirits,
while its great, black, night-time body can send a shiver
through the hardiest Londoner, even now when its waters
are less threatening that at the time of the Great Stink
(the summer of 1858 when the city was overwhelmed
by smell from the general 'sewer' that the Thames had
become). The river's contradictory nature is also felt in
this excerpt from Sukhdev Sandhu's* Night Haunts.

Londoners take the Thames for granted. They may walk across its
bridges, but they rarely sail across the water itself. To them, just
as to the location scouts who make sure that every Hollywood
movie set in the capital has at least one shot in which A-list star-
crossed lovers wander its banks with a view of St Paul's Cathedral
behind them, it's seen as a place of lazy fun. The bargers, though
they love the river dearly, are closer in opinion to H.V. Morton
who believed the Thames at night was the most mysterious thing
in the whole of the capital: "So much part of London, yet so
remote from London, so cold, so indifferent ... "

For the bargers know that if they listen carefully they will
hear the cries of thousands of stricken Londoners sinking into
the turbulent waters: Elizabethan lightermen whose boats fell
apart; eighteenth-century African slaves jumping overboard
to avoid being deported back to plantation servitude; the six
hundred passengers who drowned in 1878 when the paddle
steamer *Princess Alice* collided with another ship at Galleons
Reach, the victims of the *Marchioness* disaster in 1989.

The river is a place of death and disappearance. Bargers have
been known to curse eco-vandals who fling bags of rubbish into
the water, only to realise that those bags were human bodies.
They have seen drunken revellers shout 'Wa-hey!' and leap into
low water with the result that their feet got trapped in the mud
and they drowned still standing. They tell of down and outs,

misery-sodden tramps and OD-ing kids jumping into the river, unspotted by bystanders, so that their weed-entangled bodies are only found many days later. [...]

As we move towards Greenwich, and then to St Paul's, new apartments dazzle with gay-liberation and graffiti-bright colours. The city's skyline has changed, the church spires and cathedral domes that gave it spiritual elevation supplanted by blobs and beehives and trout-pouted constructions seemingly imported from Legoland. The bridges gleam like candelabras. The Dome, built on poisonous junkspace from toxic strata of acid, coal and asbestos, still looks paralysed and absurd, an upturned crab unable to move. Canary Wharf, still and bemoneyed, its uptight verticality in contrast to the river's shifting, curving horizontality, blazes out light: a bonfire of London's soul. [...]

We are tired and quiet, but as dawn leaks into view, it is impossible not to be beguiled by the river. There are no traffic jams, no road works closing off access: just a long, sun-glazed vista that stretches for miles.

Sukhdev Sandhu, *Night Haunts*

✻ ✻ ✻

The fog and murkiness often associated with London has gone, along with the pollution of its river: salmon have been back since the 1970s. For Jan Morris, one of the best views of the now (relatively) unpolluted city is to be had from the middle of London Bridge.

Ever since the Industrial Revolution the nature of London has been masked by fog and murk. It has been a city of black suggestiveness, choked often in impenetrable mists off the river, against which the splendours of the kingdom were paraded in pungent contrast. The very name London used to sound echoing and foggy, and every Hollywood film about the place had it thick with murderous fog.

Now the smoke has gone, and with it some of the romantic mystery, the camouflage. The city has been steam-cleaned all over.

The river has been so brilliantly cleared of pollution that in 1977 the first salmon ran upstream through London from the sea. There is a new glint to London now, and its clarity tells a truer story than the swirls and opacities of old. The best place to look at London is not in the Mall after all, where the Queen rides by, and certainly not in Knightsbridge or Lewisham Way, but half-way across London Bridge – *new* London Bridge. The previous one now resides in Arizona, the one before that – the one with the shops, houses and turrets on it, and the malefactors' heads dripping blood at its gates – having been pulled down in 1832.

It is in fact the fourth London Bridge we are going to, completed only a few years ago, but still spanning the Thames in exactly the same spot as the ford by which, two thousand years ago, the Romans crossed to found their Londinium on the north bank. It is always, of course, an intensely busy place. The road is busy above, the river below. Distorted loud-speaker voices echo from beneath the bridge as the tourist launches chug their way to Greenwich or the Tower. Dirty squat tugs with lines of barges labour against the tide toward the Isle of Dogs. Downstream lies the superannuated cruiser *Belfast*, speckled with the unseamanlike pinks and yellow of tourists, while upstream indistinct flotillas of small craft seem to be milling purposelessly about in the distant haze of Westminster. But when we reach the middle of the bridge, and discover the north bank spread there before us, the Thames seems hardly more than a country stream, a pleasure pond, beside the gleaming vulgarity, the harshness, the concentration of the new City of London, the square mile that is the financial heart of the capital and its true core of constancy.

Jan Morris, *A Writer's World*

* * *

Peter Ackroyd, too, pays homage to London Bridge.

The most celebrated of all Thames bridges, however, must be London Bridge. It is the most frequented of all bridges, the great highway of the city; if we may speak in an Aboriginal sense of a songline, or dreamline, of London then it is represented by this path across the river. It is a great cord of humanity. It creates the great stream of human beings, contracted and innumerable, which in itself becomes a river echoing the Thames. For a brief passage the vehicles and the people are brought into relation with the push and flow of the sea. The wind and the dust, the noise of the traffic and the cry of the gulls, are brought together.

There are no buildings upon it, as there were in past ages of the bridge. Now the pedestrians are outlined against the sky and framed by the water beneath their feet; they are caught between immensities. They become frail and evanescent, a pilgrimage of passing souls suspended between the elements. Over the bridge cross all the varieties of human character with no complicity, or community of interest, between them. They are together but alone; they evince expressions of endurance or of merriment, of suffering or of abstraction. It is the most suggestive of all bridges. It has evoked, in many writers and artists, phantasmal or oneiric images.

Peter Ackroyd, *Thames: Sacred River*

❖ ❖ ❖

In Stella Duffy's novel The Room of Lost Things, *it is Hungerford Bridge – linking Charing Cross Station and the Festival Hall – that provides the good views ... and the site for an extraordinary little ceremony.*

The air is crisp, the early-afternoon sun half-set already, and, though her shopping bags are weighing her down, she makes a detour across Covent Garden, down to Waterloo Bridge, the stop for the 59 is a little out of her way, but she'd rather walk over the river whenever possible, and she has Audrey's Christmas present to leave. Since Audrey died eight years ago, Marilyn has used the Thames for memorial. For the first year, she threw yellow roses into the river, anniversary Pooh-sticks, twenty-five roses floating down to Tilbury, catching on the rubbish barges low in the water. Marilyn does not believe her mother is in the water, any more than she thinks the real Audrey is in that rose garden up at Norwood, but if she's anywhere at all, she is more likely to be found in the middle of London, in the wide brown river that separates the centre from the South. To Marilyn's right, Hungerford Bridge is a dream spider's web, sticky iron filaments holding up a toy train as it crosses south to north; she looks through the white threads of the bridge to the chocolate box Houses of Parliament and Big Ben. To her left, St Paul's is diminished by a Christmas-lit city crane, directly ahead, the National Theatre squats in great chunks of illuminated concrete. Walking further over the bridge, the angle of the wheel becomes so acute it is a single green cat's eye, turning slowly above the water, and every ripple below, every wave, is a Christmas sparkle in the slanting western light. Ten yards further on, and the sand on the southern shore becomes a humpbacked whale, waves idly sloping in to a mudflat beach. Behind the Festival Hall is a new building wrapped in scaffolding, like a Christmas gift or a sick patient hiding behind its screens, Marilyn can't tell which. As with so much of her city's incessant reconstruction, it will take the removal of the building works to decide.

Standing in a scimitar wind off the bend of the river, she reaches into a Selfridge's bag to offer the gift. The conversation in her head has Audrey horrified by the expense and Marilyn giggling at the extravagance. She throws her gift, tossing love and gratitude to the water, and hurries off to catch the 59, there's a lot to get on with this afternoon, as well as a nice half bottle of non-vintage champagne to keep her company at the stove. A bus pulls up fifteen feet from the stop and Marilyn runs to the door. Behind her, on the water, the seagull that alights on the soggy 'Authentic Individual Panettone' can't believe its luck ...

Stella Duffy, *The Room of Lost Things*

✳ ✳ ✳

Waterloo Bridge runs in close to the National Theatre on the South Bank. In a diary entry from National Service, *Richard Eyre (Director of the National Theatre from 1987 to 1997) records walking over the bridge and remembering a particularly downbeat description of London in Dickens'* Our Mutual Friend.

13th February I was walking over Waterloo Bridge, and I saw a police launch circling a bloated body floating face up in the river, and it reminded me of the opening of *Our Mutual Friend*. It seemed like an omen, that Christopher and I should and would make the film of it. I've just finished the novel – I haven't read it since I studied it, although I've been championing it for years and we've talked for years about the film. I remembered the book as richer and more vivid and darker and more pessimistic. It seemed to be full of holes and loose ends with some really wonderful passages in between. This is London: 'Such a bleak, shrill city, combining the qualities of a smoking home and a scolding wife; such a gritty city; such a hopeless city, with no rent in the leaden canopy of its sky; such a beleaguered city, invested by the great Marsh Forces of Essex and Kent.'

Richard Eyre, *National Service*

✻ ✻ ✻

The Millenium links St Paul's Cathedral with the Tate Modern art gallery and the Globe Theatre. The southern end of the bridge is also very close to a small, old house through whose story Gillian Tindall explores various aspects of the area's history.

What were originally the 'mean streets' and 'dirty dark alleys' of waterside Thames are now extremely expensive real-estate, a cosmopolitan ribbon worlds away from the drab hinterlands behind them. In this ribbon, 49 Bankside, with its old-fashioned lamp, stands at night like a forgotten cottage in a children's story.

Below the raised walkway and the fairylike Millennium Bridge, the dark tides come and go as ever, now largely unregarded. Here and there, at the sites of a few of the old water stairs, concrete steps descend to the river floor, but they are little used. Sometimes, when the water at Bankside is very low, it uncovers the foundations of ancient wooden jetties, places where boats tied up on the gravelly strand before the Cardinal's Hat was even rebuilt into number 49. Every so often another find – a handmade nail, a copper coin, the sole of a medieval shoe – is dredged from the mud where it has been lying whilst generations came and went above. [...]

You can reach the house a number of different ways. It will still be the same, an inconspicuous but remarkable survivor in a landscape where almost everything else has changed. And changed. And changed again.

You may approach it from London Bridge, as people did when it was a new house, because that was then the only route from the opposite bank of the Thames, on foot, on horseback or on wheels. There was already a bridge there under the Roman occupation, and a later one was constructed in wood on the remains of the Roman stone work. The song that is still sung in our nurseries today commemorates this wooden bridge: it was burnt down in the Danish wars about a thousand years after the Roman invasion. Subsequent bridges on the site also suffered from fire, or were broken down by gales and flood tides. '*Sticks and stones will wash away ...* '

Then, in the last quarter of the twelfth century, another stone one was constructed, a triumph of engineering with nineteen arches. This bridge, with intermittent accidents and modifications, carried Londoners back and forth for the next six hundred and fifty years; till the time came when accumulating complaints about its antique inconvenience, followed by decades of discussion, finally decided the Corporation of London to replace it.

Shortly before Victoria became Queen, when the new London Bridge was at last opened with flags, fire-works, balloon ascents, royalty and massed bands, the house across the water from St Paul's was one hundred and twenty years old already.

You could also take a route a little further west, over Southwark, Blackfriars or Waterloo Bridges. The house saw all these built too. From any of these bridges you can walk to the house along the river, where today a continuous, broad pedestrian path has superseded the old quays. What you cannot readily do, however, since the quays were swept away along with their many mooring points and water stairs, is what people did for hundreds of years: reach Bankside by crossing from the north shore in a boat.

Bankside, where the house stands, derives its name from being one of the earliest pieces of embanking done of the edge of the sprawling Thames, providing a solid shore for men and goods to land in a low-lying, marshy area. But today Bankside's long and intimate working relationship with the river seems to be over. The Thames, which throughout history has bound London and Southwark informally together, linking the north and south banks in waterborne commerce, is now little more than a great, airy space which separates them, a ribbon of changing light, a view.

To counteract this separation one more very recent bridge has been built, with the declared intention of linking Bankside to the heart of London. The Millennium Bridge, the footway on the axis of St Paul's cathedral, now crosses the water to meet the almost equally large bulk of the Power Station-turned Tate Modern on the other side. But a bridge at this point, usually a full-scale traffic one, has been hanging ghostly in the air for more than three hundred years. First suggested soon after the Restoration, the idea was revived at intervals through the eighteenth century but never quite got carried out. In the year of the Great Exhibition, in the mid-nineteenth century, it was proposed again with much fervour, and continued to be intermittently during the decades that followed. It nearly got itself built in the years just before 1914, but the Great War supervened and by the 1920s the sheer cost of the enterprise, including the amount of compensation that by then would have had to be paid to City property owners, meant that the plan lapsed again. This was fortunate, for the St Paul's Bridge as dreamed by its most enthusiastic promoters was a massive affair, complete with a winged goddess driving a two-horse chariot, and double pedestrian staircases surmounted by turrets at either end. Whatever social cachet its construction might have imparted to the warehouses and wharves which by then crowded on Bankside, one thing is sure: built where the present airy, slim pedestrian bridge now spans the river, St Paul's Bridge would have caused the destruction of a broad swathe of riverside building including the house which we are now approaching. As things are, by one of those chances which obliterate so much and yet sometimes idiosyncratically preserve, the newest bridge across the river misses the house but leads to within fifty yards of its door.

Viewed from the footbridge today the house, and the two smaller rebuilt ones adjoining it, look like miniatures that have strayed into the wrong construction-model. The house is three storeys high, plus an attic, but the modest scale of this quintessential English domestic architecture is dwarfed by two giants. On one side of it stands the industrial pile of the ex-Power Station, and on the other the reconstructed Globe Theatre with its combination of Disneyland fantasy and genuine sixteenth-century building methods. These two exceptional buildings are strange company for the house to keep. Long ago, it was one of a whole line of houses, many of them rather like itself or at any rate built to the same dimensions. Then, people would have passed it by without a second glance.

Now, as it stands almost alone in its white-stuccoed traditionalism, the guides on the passing tourist boats single it out:

'– And on your left,' the loud-speakers proclaim, 'we are just passing the house that was lived in by Sir Christopher Wren while he was building St Paul's, directly opposite.' Heads swivel, cameras snap, starting images of the house on journeys to the ends of the earth, promulgating the myth. It is not actually true. Wren can never have watched the dome of his cathedral take shape from those twelve-paned windows, since the house was not built till about 1710 when only the final touches remained to be put to St Paul's and Wren himself was nearing eighty. [...]

People passing the house on foot, treading the brief stretch of cobbles, now hemmed in by the walkway, that is the remaining vestige of the Bankside quays, stop to look at the plaques. If you sit in the house's first-floor front room, the room where Wren is said to have gazed out on his works, the sound of the words being read aloud and commented on in a variety of tongues reaches you from below. After several hundred years of resounding to the noise of laden wheels on cobbles, this river bank has been returned to the era of the footstep and human voice.

Occasionally strangers will be brave enough to tug the ancient bell-pull, which jangles a bell within on the end of a wire, and enquire if the house is a museum that can be visited. They are politely turned away.

Before the door is shut again they will get a glimpse of a panelled room and an arched doorway, rugs and a longcase clock, perhaps a whiff of logs smouldering on a pile of soft ash in an open fireplace. Here, surely, is the past, on which the door has fleetingly opened?

Gillian Tindall, *The House by the Thames*

✳ ✳ ✳

How many paintings are there of London? ... of the Thames? The river and the views of the city from its banks and bridges have inspired whole armies of artists (good and bad). But Iain Sinclair regrets that relatively few of them are ever seen in public.

Photographs, however tactfully composed, cannot do justice to the civic prospect. The kick of visionary rapture outreaches Wordsworth on the roof of his coach as he jolted over Westminster Bridge: "The river glideth at his own sweet will ... And all that mighty heart is lying still!" Mendacious and masculine, the khaki Thames is as much present on this day, as it was for the Cumberland poet: a mirror of clouds and shadows. The span of Thomas Page's cast-iron bridge doubles into a rank of caves. The low tide reveals steep gravel beaches. Bruised blue pebbles, flints, glinting bottle-tops against the fleshy pink of the bridge's paintwork. Poets can snatch at it, carry away their hasty illuminations for revision in tranquillity. Painters are forced to take their time, let the subject work them over. The poets don't realise, until it's too late, that they've been gulled. They've been programmed to celebrate all these domes and balconies by a peculiarly seductive electromagnetic field. Painters fall prey to epiphanies of light on stone. They bend and twist the shapes at the margin until the river is squeezed out of the composition, until it's a slash of reflected sky. [...]

The river moves through time, obsessively painted and sketched, shifts of light captured, so that it retains its special status as a ribbon of memory: a journey through a collection of these images becomes the best way of travelling back, discovering what we have done to ourselves. And yet how many of the Tate Gallery's dozens and dozens of river-scapes have we been permitted to see? [...] The Thames has been diverted into an underground channel, the darkness and obscurity of the reserve collection. A greater acreage of London views hangs in government departments, in elegant offices, than in all the refurbished salons of the Tate Gallery. A virtual reality river, in framed panels of oil and watercolour, has been broken up, suborned to flow across the stucco of Whitehall like a private trout stream.

Iain Sinclair, *Lights Out for the Territory*

* * *

One of the most atmospheric and memorable descriptions of the Thames comes at the opening of Joseph Conrad's novel, Heart of Darkness.

The sea-reach of the Thames stretched before us like the beginning of an interminable waterway. In the offing the sea and the sky

71

were welded together without a joint, and in the luminous space the tanned sails of the barges drifting up with the tide seemed to stand still in red clusters of canvas sharply peaked, with gleams of varnished spirit. A haze rested on the low shores that ran out to sea in vanishing flatness. The air was dark above Gravesend, and farther back still seemed condensed into a mournful gloom, brooding motionless over the biggest, and the greatest, town on earth. […] The day was ending in a serenity of still and exquisite brilliance. The water shone pacifically; the sky, without a speck, was a benign immensity of unstained light; the very mist of the Essex marshes was like a gauzy and radiant fabric, hung from the wooded rises inland, and draping the low shores in diaphanous folds. Only the gloom to the west, brooding over the upper reaches, became more sombre every minute, as if angered by the approach of the sun.

And at last, in its curved and imperceptible fall, the sun sank low, and from glowing white changed to a dull red without rays and without heat, as if about to go out suddenly, stricken to death by the touch of that gloom brooding over a crowd of men.

Forthwith a change came over the waters, and the serenity became less brilliant but more profound. The old river in its broad reach rested unruffled at the decline of day, after ages of good service done to the race that peopled its banks, spread out in the tranquil dignity of a waterway leading to the uttermost ends of the earth. We looked at the venerable stream not in the vivid flush of a short day that comes and departs for ever, but in the august light of abiding memories. And indeed nothing is easier for a man who has, as the phrase goes, 'followed the sea' with reverence and affection, than to evoke the great spirit of the past upon the lower reaches of the Thames. The tidal current runs to and fro in its unceasing service, crowded with memories of men and ships it had borne to the rest of home or to the battles of the sea. It had known and served all the men of whom the nation is proud, from Sir Francis Drake to Sir John Franklin, knights all, titled and untitled – the great knights-errant of the sea. It had borne

72

all the ships whose names are like jewels flashing in the night of time, from the *Golden Hind* returning with her round flanks full of treasure, to be visited by the Queen's Highness and thus pass out of the gigantic tale, to the *Erebus* and *Terror*, bound on other conquests – and that never returned. It had known the ships and the men. They had sailed from Deptford, from Greenwich, from Erith – the adventurers and the settlers; kings' ships and the ships of men on 'Change; captains, admirals, the dark 'interlopers' of the Eastern trade, and the commissioned 'generals' of East India fleets. Hunters for gold or pursuers of fame, they all had gone out on that stream, bearing the sword, and often the torch, messengers of the might within the land, bearers of a spark from the sacred fire. What greatness had not floated on the ebb of that river into the mystery of an unknown earth! ... The dreams of men, the seed of commonwealths, the germs of empires.

The sun set; the dusk fell on the stream, the lights began to appear along the shore. The Chapman lighthouse, a three-legged thing erect on a mud-flat, shone strongly. Lights of ships moved in the fairway – a great stir of lights going up and going down. And farther west on the upper reaches the place of the monstrous town was still marked ominously on the sky, a brooding gloom in sunshine, a lurid glare under the stars.

'And this also,' said Marlow suddenly, 'has been one of the dark places of the earth.' [...]

His remark did not seem at all surprising. It was just like Marlow. It was accepted in silence. No one took the trouble to grunt even; and presently he said, very slow –

'I was thinking of very old times, when the Romans first came here, nineteen hundred years ago – the other day ... Light came out of this river since – you say Knights? Yes; but it is like a running blaze on a plain, like a flash of lightning in the clouds. We live in the flicker – may it last as long as the old earth keeps rolling! But darkness was here yesterday. Imagine the feelings of a commander of a fine – what d'ye call 'em? – trireme in the Mediterranean, ordered suddenly to the north; run overland across the Gauls in a hurry; put in charge of one of these craft the legionaries – a wonderful lot of handy men they must have been, too – used to build, apparently by the hundred, in a month or two, if we may believe what we read. Imagine him here – the very end of the world, a sea the colour of lead, a sky the colour of smoke, a kind of ship about as rigid as a concertina – and going up this river with stores, or orders, or what you like. Sand-banks, marshes, forests, savages – precious little to eat fit for a civilized man, nothing but Thames water to drink. No Falernian wine here, no going ashore. Here and there a military camp lost in a wilderness, like a needle in a bundle of hay – cold, fog, tempests, disease, exile, and death – death skulking in the air, in the water, in the bush. They must have been dying like flies here.'

Joseph Conrad, *Heart of Darkness*

* * *

And as an antidote to Conrad, here's Virginia Woolf's energetic and multifarious appreciation of the great river.

With the sea blowing its salt into our nostrils, nothing can be more stimulating than to watch the ships coming up the Thames – the big ships and the little ships, the battered and the splendid, ships from India, from Russia, from South America, ships from Australia coming from silence and danger and loneliness past us, home to harbour. But once they drop anchor, once the cranes begin their dipping and their swinging, it seems as if all romance were over. If we turn and go past the anchored ships towards London, we see surely the most dismal prospect in the world. The banks of the river are lined with dingy, decrepit-looking warehouses. They huddle on land that has become flat and slimy mud. The same air of decrepitude and of being run up provisionally stamps them all. If a window is broken, broken it remains. A fire that has

74

lately blackened and blistered one of them seems to have left it no more forlorn and joyless than its neighbours. Behind the masts and funnels lies a sinister dwarf city of workmen's houses. In the foreground cranes and warehouses, scaffolding and gasometers line the banks with a skeleton architecture. [...]

As we go on steaming up the river to London we meet its refuse coming down. Barges heaped with old buckets, razor blades, fish tails, newspapers and ashes – whatever we leave on our plates and throw into our dust bins – are discharging their cargoes upon the most desolate land in the world. The long mounds have been fuming and smoking and harbouring innumerable rats and growing a rank coarse grass giving off a gritty, acrid air for fifty years. The dumps get higher and higher, and thicker and thicker, their sides more precipitous with tin cans, their pinnacles more angular with ashes year by year. But then, past all this sordidity, sweeps indifferently a great liner, bound for India. She takes her way through rubbish barges, and sewage barges, and dredgers out to sea. A little further, on the left hand, we are suddenly surprised – the sight upsets all our proportions once more – by what appear to be the stateliest buildings ever raised by the hand of man. Greenwich Hospital with all its columns and domes comes down in perfect symmetry to the water's edge, and makes the river again a stately waterway where the nobility of England once walked at their ease on green lawns, or descended stone steps to their pleasure barges. As we come closer to the Tower Bridge the authority of the city begins to assert itself. The buildings thicken and heap themselves higher. The sky seems laden with heavier, purpler clouds. Domes swell; church spires, white with age, mingle with the tapering, pencil-shaped chimneys of factories. One hears the roar and the resonance of London itself. This is the knot, the clue, the hub of all those scattered miles of skeleton desolation and ant-like activity. Here growls and grumbles that rough city song that has called the ships from the sea and brought them to lie captive beneath its warehouses.

Now from the dock side we look down into the heart of the ship that has been lured from its voyaging and tethered to the dry land. The passengers and their bags have disappeared; the sailors have gone too. Indefatigable cranes are now at work, dipping and swinging, swinging and dipping. Barrels, sacks, crates are being picked up out of the hold and swung regularly on shore. Rhythmically, dexterously, with an order that has some æsthetic delight in it, barrel is laid by barrel, case by case, cask by cask, one behind another, one on top of another, one beside another in endless array down the aisles and arcades of the immense low-ceiled, entirely plain and unornamented warehouses. Timber, iron, grain, wine, sugar, paper, tallow, fruit – whatever the ship has gathered from the plains, from the forests, from the pastures of the whole world is here lifted from its hold and set in its right place. A thousand ships with a thousand cargoes are being unladen every week.

Virginia Woolf, *The London Scene*

* * *

Historian Maureen Waller focuses on the watermen of the Thames in this passage from her portrait of London in the year 1700.

The hub of London life was the Thames itself, the great thoroughfare dotted with thousands of red and green boats. Like many visitors before and since, César de Saussure loved this sight:

You cannot see anything more charming and delightful than this river. Above the bridge it is covered with craft of every sort; round about London there are at least 15,000 boats for the transport of persons, and numbers of others for that of merchandise. Besides these boats there are others called barges and galleys, painted, carved, and gilt. Nothing is more charming and attractive than the Thames on a fine summer evening; the conversations you

76

hear are most entertaining, for I must tell you that it is
the custom for anyone on the water to call out whatever
he pleases to other occupants of boats, even were it to
the King himself, and no one has a right to be shocked.

The language of the watermen as they indulged in the tradition
of shouting insults across the water was 'coarse and dirty'.
It was all very confusing to a newcomer. Ned Ward joked
that when he was first approached by watermen shouting,
'Scholars, scholars, will you have any hoars?' he was shocked,
until his companion explained that the watermen distinguished
themselves by the titles of Oars and Scullers.

River transport was essential, partly because the streets
were so congested and also because the bone-shaking jolting of
hackneys was unendurable. [...]

London Bridge was still the only bridge across the Thames.
Von Uffenbach remarked that 'one does not take it for a bridge
because it has on both sides large and handsome houses, the
lower storeys of which are shops. Well over half way across
the bridge towards Southwark is a single place about eight feet
long where there is not a house and the Thames can be seen
through the iron palings.' Compressed among the pillars of
the bridge, the water was a deep, roaring torrent. It was so
treacherous that many boat passengers preferred to disembark
and re-embark on the other side of the bridge.

Maureen Waller, *1700: Scenes from London Life*

* * *

For Ed Glinert, the energy of London is concentrated
in its trade – and thus in the river that, for most of the
city's history, has carried that trade.

Energy made London the world's greatest port. Energy to trade
and open new trade routes. Energy to tame the river and make

it work for those transporting goods. Energy to tame the sea and make it work for the merchant adventurer. Energy to build bigger, better boats that could bring more goods back to London. Energy to construct more accurate compasses and chronometers. Energy to make London the world's busiest port from 1800 to 1970.

No city has ever witnessed such dynamic riverside activity. At its peak tens of thousands of dockers, stevedores, samplers, boiler-smiths, custom officers, cargo superintendents, yardmasters, winch-men, lightermen and lumpers worked the tens of thousands of ships bringing the world's produce to London's seven sets of docks – four in the East End – which covered 720 acres and 35 miles of quayside servicing the most vibrant empire the world had ever known.

Ed Glinert, *East End Chronicles*

✤ ✤ ✤

But all that energy and activity in a densely populated city produced vast amounts of waste of every kind. Here's a little more detail about what happened in the mid- nineteenth century, at the time of the Great Stink, before 'waste disposal' became the organised and scientific activity that it is today and the number one priority of any properly functioning city.

At the beginning of the century, each household had disposed of its waste into a private cesspool in its cellar which was regularly emptied by nightsoil men. However, as the population of the capital grew this system was decried as impractical and unsanitary. Instead all cesspools were to be connected to a local sewer which would conduct the flow, by way of a main sewer to drain directly into the river. In the rotting and inadequate sewers, human excrement mixed with refuse from the slaughterhouses and knackers' yards, and waste from the tanneries and factories. Every day it drained into the Thames. It was not long before the river itself became the great cesspool of the city. At low tide the effluvium clung to the pillars of bridges or piled itself into stinking mudbanks and fermented.

London, the largest metropolis in the world, was poisoning itself. That was the consensus reached by doctors and scientists as the century passed its midpoint. As the filth pooled and putrefied in local sewers, many of which were hardly more than open ditches, it exhaled highly poisonous gases. When these poisons were diffused into the atmosphere and carried by corrupted air and water into the lungs and stomach, they entered directly into the blood, spreading deathly disease. In twenty years London had been ravaged by three brutal epidemics of the cholera. Each time the disease had attacked the city most savagely in the places where the air and the water was foulest. No one doubted that something would have to be done.

Clare Clark, *The Great Stink*

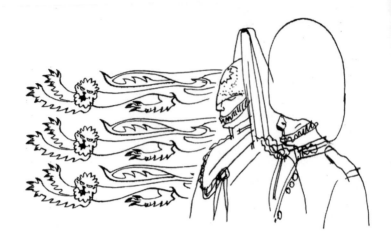

Pomp and Circumstances

Nowhere does pageantry like London. From the daily 'changing the guard' to the State Opening of Parliament and all the full-scale pomp of a coronation or royal funeral, the Monarchy is at the heart of all the uniforms and ceremonies forming part of the spectacle that visitors expect – a strange fantasy world of golden coaches and soldiers on horseback and arcane symbolism. All a bit silly? ... A canny marketing tool? ... Or a symptom of something 'theatrical' deep in the British psyche?

It is a gift of London, or rather a technique, that through the dingy and the disagreeable, the fantastic habitually looms. Illusion breaks in! Its principal agency is that monarchy whose heraldic lions, unicorns, crowns, roses, thistles and Norman mottos are as inescapable in this city as Leninist quotations in Moscow.

Monarchy in London is part religion, part diplomacy, part make-believe; if the gleaming standards above the royal residences are like prayer flags or talismans, the ramrod soldiers stamping and strutting between their sentry boxes are pure Sigmund Romberg. The mystique of London's royal presence, the fetish feel, the mumbo jumbo, colours the sensations of this peculiar city, and often makes it feel like a place of pilgrimage, a Lourdes or a Jerusalem, or more exactly, perhaps, like one of those shrines where a familiar miracle is regularly re-attested, the saintly blood is annually decongealed or the hawthorn blossoms each Christmas morning. The world flocks in to witness the mystery of London, enacted several times a year in the ceremonial thoroughfare called the Mall. The pavements then are thick with foreigners, and far away up Constitution Hill the tourist buses, emblazoned with the emblems and registration plates of all Europe, stand nose to nose in their shiny hundreds. The guardsmen lining the Mall are like the acolytes at the shrine; the patrolling policemen, sacristans.

The beat of a drum is the start of the ritual, somewhere up there in the blur of gold, grey and green that is Buckingham Palace. The beat of a drum, the blare of a band, and presently a procession approaches slowly between the plane trees. A drum major leads, in a peaked jockey cap and gilded tunic, as impassive on his tall white horse as a time drummer on a slave galley. Then the jangling, clopping, creaking, panting cavalry, black horses, brass helmets, plumes, anxious young faces beneath their heavy helmet straps, the skid and spark of hoofs now and then, the shine of massive breastplates, sour smells of horse and leather. Three strange old gentlemen follow, weighed down beneath fat bearskin hats, with huge swords bouncing at their sides; they ride their chargers rheumatically stooped, as though they have been bent in the saddle like old leather.

Another plumed squadron ... a pause ... a hush over the crowd ... and then, bobbing high above the people, almost on a level with the flags, the familiar strained and earnest face of the mystery itself, pale beneath its heavy makeup. It is like the Face on the Shroud, an image-face. Everybody in the world knows it. It is a lined and diligent face, not at all antique or aristocratic, but it possesses its own arcanum. The crowd hardly stirs as it passes,

81

and the murmur that runs down the pavement is a tremor less of astonishment or admiration than of compassion. It is as though a martyr is passing by. She rides, she bleeds, for us!

There is something fatalistic about the spectacle. The ritual is so old, so very old, so frozen in so many conventions and shibboleths. The Queen bobs away with her guards, her captains and her bands towards whatever elaborate and meaningless ceremonial her major-domos have prepared for her beyond the trees, but she leaves behind something stale. Her martyrdom is the suffering of a tired tradition, and if the royal flummery is the saving fantasy of London, it is the city's penance too. London seems often to be labouring beneath the weight of its own heritage – year after year, century upon century, the same beat of the drum-major's drum, the same jangle of the harnesses, the same bent old courtiers on their chargers lurching generation after generation down the Mall.

Jan Morris, *A Writer's World*

✽ ✽ ✽

The hub of London's ceremonial life is Buckingham Palace, of course ... and everyone knows that when the flag flies above it, the Queen is 'in'. Most Londoners, as well as tourists, have their initiation into royal ceremonies by being taken to see the changing of the guard ... though it's sometimes the four-legged participants who get the attention.

We went to see the changing of the guard. I parked the car near the Foreign Secretary's neglected house and we walked down the huge granite stairs beneath a statue of George VI towards the palace. There is a country feel here – overhanging chestnut trees with a few wet leaves, squirrels racing about and horsemen trotting grandly to their military duties. The Scots Guards came down from their barracks in full flower; we followed their wild noise and their mascot, a goat, to their appointment. The bagpipes played a lament, with only the kettle-drums accompanying them quietly, it was very moving. Gemma tried to keep abreast of the goat. It was the leader of this strange band of men in skirts and bearskins, she could see that. We marched down the Mall, level with the caprine commander, our ears filled with the plangent cries of the Highlands – deforested, depopulated, despoiled by the Hanoverians – towards whose pile the Guards were marching, not to exact revenge for these outrages, but to amuse the tourists gathered by the railings and around the monument which dominated the view with the same Victorian overkill.

I have been inside Buckingham Palace myself, for the reception for George Bush. The vast stairway was peopled by Life Guards with breastplates and drawn swords, and the long reception rooms were decorated with glorious paintings by Rubens, Van Dyck, Constable and Rembrandt. (I don't remember seeing any Landseers.) The palace was draughty. I would have liked to see where they watched television and played whist. The Queen spoke to me. She was very small and quite plump and her face had a lot of powder on it close to, like my mother's did. I also chatted to a major-general in the British army who was fascinated by the old-fashioned wiring.

'Look. She's in. The Queen's at home. See that flag there, that's the royal standard. That means she's at home,' I said.

'I like goats. Can we have a goat? What does he get for his dinner?'

The goat wore a small regimental overcoat. With its long white beard and pale eyes it looked like Trotsky. It tried to eat the orderly's kilt as the soldiers went through their rituals, and the bagpipes cheered up.

Justin Cartwright, *Look At It This Way*

* * *

In Alan Bennett's hugely witty, perspicacious but generous-spirited little novel, The Uncommon Reader, *we see things from the other side of the carriage window. Based on the premise that Her Majesty suddenly becomes an avid reader (thanks to a mobile library and a servant called Norman), the following incident is the kind of thing that tends to happen as a result of her newly-discovered passion for literature.*

One of the Queen's recurrent royal responsibilities was to open Parliament, an obligation she had never previously found particularly burdensome and actually rather enjoyed: to be driven down the Mall on a bright autumn morning even after fifty years was something of a treat. But not any more. She was dreading the two hours the whole thing was due to take, though fortunately they were in the coach, not the open carriage, so she could take along her book. She'd got quite good at reading and waving, the trick being to keep the book below the level of the window and to keep focused on it and not the crowds. The duke didn't like it one bit, of course, but goodness it helped.

Which was all very well, except it was only when she was actually in the coach, with the procession drawn up in the palace forecourt and ready for the off, that, as she put on her glasses, she realised she'd forgotten the book. And while the duke fumes in the corner and the postillions fidget, the horses shift and the harness clinks, Norman is rung on the mobile. The Guardsmen stand at ease and the procession waits. The officer in charge looks at his watch. Two minutes late. Knowing nothing displeases Her Majesty more and knowing nothing of the book, he does not look forward to the repercussions that must inevitably follow. But here is Norman, skittering across the gravel with the book thoughtfully hidden in a shawl, and off they go.

Still, it is an ill-tempered royal couple that is driven down the Mall, the duke waving viciously from his side, the Queen listlessly from hers, and at some speed, too, as the procession tries to pick up the two minutes that have been lost.

At Westminster she popped the offending book behind a cushion in the carriage ready for the journey back, mindful as she sat on the throne and embarked on her speech of how tedious was the twaddle she was called on to deliver and that this was actually the only occasion when she got to read aloud to the nation. 'My government will do this … my government will do that.' It was so barbarously phrased and wholly devoid of style and interest that she felt it demeaned the very act of reading itself, with this year's performance even more garbled than usual as she, too, tried to pick up the missing couple of minutes.

It was with some relief that she got back into the coach and reached behind the cushion for her book. It was not there. Steadfastly waving as they rumbled along, she surreptitiously felt behind the other cushions.

'You're not sitting on it?'

'Sitting on what?'

'My book.'

'No, I am not. Some British Legion people here, and wheelchairs. Wave, for God's sake.'

When they arrived at the palace she had a word with Grant, the young footman in charge, who said that while ma'am had been in the Lords the sniffer dogs had been round and security had confiscated the book. He thought it had probably been exploded.

'Exploded?' said the Queen. 'But it was Anita Brookner.'

The young man, who seemed remarkably undeferential, said security may have thought it was a device.

The Queen said: 'Yes. That is exactly what it is. A book is a device to ignite the imagination.'

Alan Bennett, *The Uncommon Reader*

* * *

When Richard Eyre goes to the Palace to receive his knighthood for services to the theatre, his diary shows the event to be somewhat less impressive than one might have expected …

5th March The laying on of the sword at Buckingham Palace. We have a kneeling rehearsal in an ante-chamber before the ceremony.

We all self-consciously test out the kneeling procedure on a little kneeling-rostrum with a small rail that looks like a prop exiled from a production of *The Yeoman of the Guard*. I don't know any of my fellow knights and dames, but I talk to Barbara Mills, who I think runs the DPP, and the man who runs the Marines. He's wearing a very tight dark-blue uniform with a red stripe down the trouser leg. I told him how much I liked his costume, and he looked at me as if I was about to ask him to take it off. Massive sense of bathos in the ceremony: it's all pure D'Oyly Carte – wildly unglamorous, devised by a Victorian clerk, in desperate need of a designer, director and writer. The military string band played stridently out of tune, selections from *Lilac Time* and *My Fair Lady*. My conversation with HMQ was brief and to the point:

HMQ: So you're at the National Theatre.
ME: Yes, indeed.
HMQ: How interesting.

Then the handshake which turned into a mild shove to deter me from persisting in the lively interchange. In the evening I saw the Queen on the News opening a school computer centre wearing a purple hat that looked like a flying saucer: 'I have great pleasure in opening the royal website.'

Richard Eyre, *National Service*

❋ ❋ ❋

Jan Morris, too, sees the funny side of a ceremonial event viewed from the Vistors' Gallery of the House of Lords.

I went one day to the installation of a new member in the House of Lords, the upper chamber of the British Parliament. He was a prominent politician ennobled for his party services, and I was taken to the ceremony by another peer, of more literary distinction. We were late and hurried through the vast, florid halls of the Palace of Westminster, past multitudinous busts and forbidding portraits ('my great-great-great-grand-father', panted Lord J. as we passed William III, 'illegitimately, of course') down interminable carpeted corridors, through chambers enigmatically labelled, until up a winding stone staircase, through a creaking oak door, he shoved me precipitately into the visitors' gallery.

Inside a dream was in progress. The rest of the peers and peeresses indeed looked mundane enough on their benches below: thick-set party reliables, jowly former ministers, a handful of flinty and talkative women, a bishop with heavy-rimmed spectacles and a resolutely ecumenical expression. But slumped eerily with his back to me, the Lord Chancellor of England sat like a dummy on his woolsack, the big woollen bag which has for 600 years and more sustained the Chancellorian rump. Dark robes blurred the shape of him, a black tricorn hat was perched on top of his judicial wig, and he suggested to me the presiding judge of some sinister hearing, with a hint of that magisterial caterpillar with his hookah, on top of the mushroom in *Alice*.

Just as I entered, the new peer, appearing silently out of nowhere, approached this daunting figure. He was dressed in red and ermine, escorted by two colleagues and preceded by a functionary in black knee breeches holding a silver wand. Spooky things ensued in the silence. The three peers sat down, but almost at once they rose again, in dead silence, and in unison bowed toward the woolsack, simultaneously removing their hats. The Lord High Chancellor removed his in return, adjusting his posture on his sack and bowing slightly, almost frigidly, in their direction. Twice more, without a sound, the ritual was repeated – down, up, hats off, bow, hats on, down – while we in the galleries, perhaps even the other peers and peeresses in their benches below, watched almost aghast, so arcane was the spectacle.

This was not a charade. This was a contemporary political occasion, London style. As soon as it ended I hastened out of the gallery and down the steps in time to bump into Lord J. emerging from the chamber below. 'Good gracious me,' I could

not help saying, 'however long have they been doing that?' 'I
believe it began,' he replied quite seriously, 'with the Druids.'

Jan Morris, *A Writer's World*

* * *

*Vita Sackville-West, writer and close friend of Virginia
Woolf, was herself a member of the aristocracy, but in
this account of a coronation in Westminster Abbey, in
her novel* The Edwardians, *she pokes gentle fun at the
whole elaborate charade.*

Sebastian's coach drew up with commendable swagger at the West
Door of the Abbey. […] Within the Vestibule all was quiet and
dignity. Such business as reigned was conducted in the hush that
befitted so august an occasion and so venerable a fane. Some officer,
detailed for the job, approached Sebastian, received his name, and
instantly preceded him, soft-footed, to the allotted place. Sebastian
looked around, and nodded to the men he knew. He no longer felt
so self-conscious in the company of other men attired as he himself
was attired. He straightened his shoulders beneath the heavy cloak.
He even felt inadequately dressed, in so far as these men – older
men – all displayed the insignia of some Order, which he, by his
youth, was denied. There was the Duke of Northumberland with
the Garter; Lord Waterford with the Star of St. Patrick. They were
all men of a certain age and experience; Sebastian either knew
them personally, or he had heard them speaking in the House of
Lords. He felt apologetic for his youth, and for the rank which
entitled him to a place in their midst. Young boys, their pages, in
white and scarlet dress, clung closely behind them; and Sebastian
himself felt that such a role would have become him better than the
active role he had to play. His own page joined him; a little cousin,
an Eton boy; joined him with evident relief at his arrival, and took
his coronet from him, tucking it under his arm much as he might
have secured a passed ball at football. Sebastian smiled at him with
sympathy. He was a shiny-cheeked little boy, more delighted by the

special permission which had released him from school than by the privilege of attending the Coronation.

Sebastian looked round again as he waited. There on the table lay the Regalia; there stood the great Officers of State; there stood the Archbishops of Canterbury and York, and seven bishops with their great lawn sleeves; many peers, and a number of Gentlemen-at-Arms. They were waiting for the moment when the pieces of the Regalia should be delivered to them, passing first from the hands of the Lord Chamberlain of the Household to the hands of the Lord High Constable, and from the hands of the Lord High Constable to the hands of the Lord Great Chamberlain, and from the hands of the Lord Great Chamberlain to the hands of the peer or prelate destined to bear them in the procession. The crown of Edward the Confessor lay there; the orb, the sceptre; the golden spurs; the swords of justice; Curtana, the sword of mercy. They seemed to Sebastian to hold about as much significance as the staves of a Tarot pack, yet something within him responded to these strange emblems of centuries and sovereignty. […]

In the body of the Abbey, the assembled congregation passed the time as best they might by watching the arrival of the distinguished guests. They saw the Royal Representatives escorted to their seats in the Choir; the German Crown Prince and Princess were there, the Archduke Charles Francis Joseph of Austria, the Grand Duke Boris Vladimirovitch, Prince Chakrabhongs of Pitsanulok, and Dejasmatch Kassa of Ethiopia. The Ethiopian wore a bristling lion's mane swathed about his head-dress, which tickled the face of his neighbour in the next choir-stall every time he turned his head to observe the movements of some fresh dignitary taking up his position. This misfortune, however, was concealed from the gaze of the smaller fry in the body of the Abbey. It was revealed only to the privileged few assembled in the Royal Box and the Transepts. These privileged few beguiled the time likewise by observing the arrival, the hushed and almost stealthy arrival, of the forerunners of the main ceremony. They had, indeed, need of something to beguile the time. Most of them had been in their places since eight o'clock. They were already beginning to look dubiously at the little greasy packets of sandwiches that they had brought with them. They were already beginning to wonder about the practicability of other, more intimate, arrangements. Meanwhile, they could solace themselves by taking in the details of those preparations which had closed the Abbey for so many days while carpenters in their aprons went about, and the vast space, now murmurous with the strains of the organ, had echoed only to the tap of hammers on tin-tacks. The light at first was dim, falling only from the high windows of the clerestory; some hours passed before the golden lights in the candelabra began to pale and the shadows to lesson, revealing many motionless figures, such as those of the Yeomen of the Guard in the nave, who hitherto had gone almost unperceived. There was indeed much to notice, and the eye strayed alternately from the overhead architectural splendours of the vault and column to the tiny figures moving across the floor, stiff as dolls in their multi-coloured robes. The blue-and-silver of the velvet hangings, the blue mantle of the Prince of Wales, the grey heron-plumes in his cap, the silks of the Indian princes, the lozenges on a herald's tabard, the crimson of the peers and peeresses massed in the transepts, the motley of a jewelled window, the silence of the Throne, the slight stir, the absence of voices, the swell of the organ, the hushed arrivals, the sense of expectancy – all blended together into one immense and confused significance. It is to be doubted whether one person in that whole assembly had a clear thought in his head. Rather, words and their associations marched in a grand chain, giving hand to hand: England, Shakespeare, Elizabeth, London; Westminster, the docks, India, the Cutty Sark, England; England, Gloucestershire, John of Gaunt; Magna Carta, Cromwell, England. Vague, inexplicable epithets flitted across the mind, familiar even in their unfamiliarity: Unicorn Pursuivant, Portcullis, Rouge Dragon, Black Rod, [...]

So thought Sebastian, bearing his little mediæval object in the train of the King. Somewhere in the galleries above him was a choir five hundred strong, shouting, "Vivat! Vivat Rex Georgius!" as the procession came up the narrow path of the blue carpet and paused for a moment before the empty thrones. There was the King, in his Robe of State, the Cap of State upon his head, escorted by Bishops, his train borne by eight young pages, flanked by twenty Gentlemen-at-Arms, and assisted – indeed, he had need of assistance, thought Sebastian – by the Master of the Robes. There was the tiny figure of Lord Roberts, and the towering figure of Lord Kitchener. There were the Standards, hanging limp on their poles. There was the Queen – [...]

Meanwhile, the pageant went superbly forward from rite to rite. The undoubted King of this Realm had been presented to his people at each point of the compass, and at each point of the compass had been recognised with loud and repeated acclamations and with the blare of trumpets echoing against the stones from the pavement to the roof. The waiting Altar had received the Bible, the paten, and the chalice. Zadok the priest and Nathan the prophet had been invoked and the crowning of Solomon recalled. Four Knights of the Garter had raised a canopy of cloth of gold over the King. Oil from the Ampulla, poured from the beak of the little golden eagle, had anointed his head, his breast, and his hands. His hands had been dried with cotton-wool. The white tunic of the Colobium Sindonis and the golden pall of the Supertunica had replaced his robes of state, revealing the mark of sunburn at the back of his neck. The golden spurs had touched his heels; the Armill had been flung about his shoulders; the Sword had been girded on and redeemed with one hundred shillings in a red velvet bag; the Orb, the Ring, and the Sceptres had been delivered to him; the Lord of the Manor of Worksop had offered a glove. The Crown had been placed upon his head, the trumpets and drums had sounded, the people had cried God save the King.

And at the moment when the Queen was crowned the peeresses had likewise put on their coronets, in a single gesture of exquisite beauty, their white arms rising with a sound like the rushing of birds' wings and a proud arching like the arching of the neck of a swan. Then out came the little mirrors, and with furtive peeps in that cluster of femininity, hands had stolen upwards again to adjust, to straighten. Many dowagers, looking down from the galleries above, tut-tutted. In their day, they said, ladies were not in the habit of producing mirrors in public. It was easy to see, they said, that the reign of Edward the Seventh was over and the days of decent behaviour ended.

Everybody streamed out of the Abbey, greatly relieved. They were tired, but how impressive it had been! And, thank heaven, no one had thrown a bomb.

Vita Sackville-West, *The Edwardians*

❋ ❋ ❋

And finally a wry look at a royal wedding – that of Princess Anne to Captain Mark Philips – from the pen of a then very young Irish journalist, Maeve Binchy, who went on to become a best-selling novelist.

The ushers were simply delighted to see me. 'Splendid,' they said, 'absolutely splendid. Let's have a little look. Oh, yes; seat number 17 this way. Super view, and just beside the telly, too. Super!' They could have been brothers of my dearest friends instead of members of Mark Philips' regiment examining the press ticket, which had cost £23.

Westminster Abbey was lit up like an operating theatre, the light from the chandeliers was only like candlelight compared to the television lights. Well, since 500 million people, including the Irish, were meant to be looking in, I suppose you had to have it bright enough to see something.

There was plenty to see from the top of a scaffolding over the north transept. Grace Kelly staring into space, looking like she always looked, kind of immaculate. Rainier has aged a bit oddly and looks like Marlon Brando in the 'Godfather'. Harold Wilson, all smiles and straightening his tie, his wife looking as if she were about to compose the final poem on the occasion. Jeremy Thorpe was all giggles and jauntiness, Heath looked like a waxwork. [...]

There were a lot of people whose faces I thought I knew, but it was no help asking for advice on either side. The man from the *Manchester Evening News* seemed to be writing an extended version of *War and Peace* in a notebook and on my right an agency reporter was transcribing a file of cuttings.

And then the royals started to arrive. We could see them on the television set – which was six inches from me – leaving Buckingham Palace in their chariots, and like characters stepping out of a film, they suddenly turned up a hundred feet below our seats. The Queen Mother looked the way she has ever looked – aged 56 and benign. The Queen looked thin and unhappy in a harsh blue outfit. [...]

The Dean of Westminster, who is a very civilised, cheerful sort of man, was sort of happy about it all, and so was the Archbishop of Canterbury. They beamed all round them and extracted a few return grins from the nervous-looking lot in the V.I.P. seats. The choirboys looked suitably angelic and uncomfortable in their ruffs. One of them got his fingers caught behind his neck and had to have them released.

The trumpeters were noble and rallying, and the Beefeaters were traditionally beefy. Everything was as it should be in fact, as we waited for the bride.

About three seconds after the glass-coach had left Buckingham Palace with Anne and her father we were all handed two pages of strictly embargoed details about the wedding dress: it would have threatened national security to have had it before, apparently. Journalists all around me were devouring it and writing the details of seed pearls and 1,000 threads of 20-denier silk to every inch of the garment. When she arrived at the door of the Abbey there was a bit of excitement about arranging the train and adjusting the tiara, and the bride looked as edgy as if it were the Badminton Horse Trials and she was waiting for the bell to gallop off.

Up at the altar all the royals looked out as eagerly and anxiously as if they thought the Duke of Edinburgh and his only daughter might have dropped off for a pint on the way. The Queen actually smiled when they got into sight, and Mark gave a matinee-idol shy, rueful smile. Princess Margaret read her programme of the wedding service as if it were the latest Agatha Christie that she had promised to finish before lunchtime.

The Duke of Edinburgh went and sat beside his wife and mother-in-law, and seemed to have a far greater control over his sword than did Prince Charles, who carried his as if it were an umbrella. I was waiting for half his relatives to have their legs amputated but there must have been some kind of plastic top on it because nobody seemed to be maimed or anything when they were leaving.

The Service went as planned, and the young voices were clear and loud, as everyone remarked approvingly afterwards, no coyness or nervous stutters. There were a lot of hymns, and I saw the Queen singing her head off, but gloomily, and the Phillips parents sang, too, nervously on their side.

Then, off they galloped down the aisle and it was over. [...]

It was a very well-produced show, no-one could deny that, but then the actors are getting slightly above Equity rates.

Maeve Binchy, 'Pageantry and Splendour at Westminster for Royal Wedding', early journalism collected in *My First Book*

East Enders

London, like all big cities, being a place of infinite variety and contrasts, what could be more appropriate than leaving the world of the Monarchy and its pageantry for a visit to the famous – and sometimes infamous – East End.

Bernie had a great idea for a musical. It's based on his childhood in the East End. To me, despite the refurbishment, the yuppie mice nibbling at the edges of the huge stale cheese, the East End is a solidly blank, depressing place of crumbling, weeping buildings and exhausted little shops selling third-rate goods. Its inhabitants seem equally tired; if they are white, they are crushed by the realisation that they will never be able to afford to get out, and if they are Asian, they are exhausted after the struggles of emigrating from Bangladesh. Bangladesh seems to be under water most of the time, so perhaps the East End with its (merely) damp and suppurating buildings appears a haven of stability, the proverbial high ground, to Bangladeshis.

Anyway, as we powered along the Commercial Road, there was a surprising amount of traffic in the pre-dawn gloom: newspaper trucks and vans, refrigerator trucks, out-of-town buses and rusted cars. This is the time of day when cleaners and dustmen and street sweepers and construction workers and shift workers are about. At bus stops, little, dispirited groups of Asian women waited, whether on the way home from work or on the way to work I could only speculate. Against this not very colourful backdrop, gliding by, Bernie told me the idea – the big concept which was going to free him both from bit parts and humiliation at the hands of producers. I hadn't told Bernie that the car was bought with the proceeds of our American Eagle commercial. After all he had a far more labour-intensive part than I did. If Marx is correct about the plus factor of labour in any industrial compact, then Bernie should have been paid more than me.

Strangely enough, I hardly needed to listen to Bernie to know the plot. Against all the evidence, musicals celebrate the triumph of the individuals over the system, in all sorts of improbable ways. I was ahead of Bernie. Before his large elastic mouth got there, I could see the tenement buildings, the market traders, the fish porters, the not-so-lovable bobbies, the raggedy (lovable) children, the beautiful Lady Bountiful, the synagogue in Bacon Street, the doomed love affair, the heartbreak, the disturbing social ructions, the scene in the Salvation Army hostel, the swaggering blackshirts, the camaraderie of poverty (as nothing, in my experience, to the chumminess of wealth), the chorus line of washerwomen and fishwives (contralto and soprano), the barrels of jellied eels, the pubs frequented by boxers and criminals, the whores with hearts of gold, and so on. And so it proved. The twist is that Bernard Koppel rises from the ashes of the Blitz to become a famous entertainer. In this case life is definitely lagging some way behind art, but Bernie is quite prepared to give life the necessary kick up the backside.

'Up the Khyber, know what that means?'

'No,' I say, although of course I do.

'Rhyming slang. Khyber pass, arse, gottit?'

I glanced at him. For a potential world-beater, the Chaplin *de nos jours* (or even something less ambitious), he needs to do something about his nasal and aural hair. It's growing like rhubarb. Also his breath is none too good at this time of day. (Whose is?) Perhaps Bernie lives on jellied eels. Certainly there's a whiff of the sea – or more specifically the riverbed – adorning his early-morning monologue.

Bernie can see the romance in anything. His wife died twenty years ago, worn out, I should imagine, by his optimism. This gloomy East End whizzing by with its saree importers, its Eldorado Night Clubs and Golden Gate Bingo clubs, its second-hand car dealers (Japanese minibuses a speciality), its massage parlours, its grimy tower blocks, its pubs advertising Australian lager, its litter, its squalor – this will become in Bernie's retelling, a fabulous wonderland of plucky little Cockney folk, fighting cheerfully against the odds until Hitler, Uncle Adolf himself, sends his buzz-bombs and whizz-bangs screaming over the narrow, cold Channel to obliterate the workhouses, the almshouses, the bawdyhouses, the public houses and the rest; buildings on which the sun never shone, out of a sky without a rent in its leaden canopy. Nothing will crush their spirit; certainly the weather hasn't a hope where Adolf and Hermann (who had no balls at all) failed.

'You've got to look on the bright side, rise above it, ain'tcher?'

Justin Cartwright, *Look At It This Way*

✻ ✻ ✻

Part of the East End's reputation for cheery stoicism comes from newsreel footage of war-time London and thinly disguised propaganda films. During the Blitz there was, of course, a great deal of genuine spirit, defiance and bravery among those who lived with the daily traumas of bombings, but Ed Glinert challenges the general truth of this image with some hard facts.

When the planes appeared in the sky on Sunday 8 September, a crowd surged from Spitalfields towards Liverpool Street tube station, and were shocked to find it shut, with troops protecting the entrance. Panic-stricken, they refused to disperse. After much heated argument the authorities let them in the station. Once inside, the shelterers decided they were staying; that this subterranean sanctuary was now their home. More people came to Liverpool Street, bringing with them bedding, flasks of tea, sandwiches, packs of cards, books and wirelesses. The police, ordered to move on anyone who looked as if they were about to bed down for the night in the station, were powerless.

The government soon changed its mind about not using tube stations – it had little choice, after all – and began supplying bunk beds and toilets. Rules were set. Before 7.30 in the evening shelterers had to keep behind a line drawn eight feet from the edge of the platform. From 9 to 10.30 they could encroach as far as the second line, four feet from the edge, and when the trains stopped running, the lights dimmed and the current in the rail was cut, they could make use of the entire platform.

By the end of September nearly 200,000 people were using the stations. They had created another London, a city obscured from light, an underground world with its own capricious social order and unrelenting angst. Many became trapped psychologically. They went down but were afraid to leave; they had acquired deep-shelter mentality. […] The war created another East End myth: the myth of the Blitz. An idealized vision of a burning, bombed-out Stepney gallantly defended by the plucky East Ender endures in British society. Less publicized are the stories of how East End criminals worked largely undisturbed while the Blitz raged. One gang obtained an ambulance, painted on the appropriate civil defence logos, put stretchers inside and journeyed round London lifting not injured bodies, but broken material – anything that was worth a bob or two. Looting was rife. Some was the seemingly innocent work of carefree children rummaging excitedly through the rubble; some was more concerted and veered over the blurred edge between helping oneself and stealing. Food shops whose windows had been blown in were prime targets. Rings and jewellery were torn from dead bodies.

Ed Glinert, *East End Chronicles*

* * *

The East End has changed drastically over the last half century as the latest waves of immigrants have taken over this poor part of the city, unable to afford more salubrious areas – just like Tarquin Hall who, having grown up in some very pleasant parts of London, finds a tight budget obliging him to settle for the East End.

'You won't get a shoebox in Dagenham on your budget, sir,' one estate agent told me on Barnes High Street when I'd gone in search of a place to live.

It was a similar story in Chiswick, Kew, Putney, Richmond – all the areas I had known intimately as a child and thought of as home. Even Sheen, where my parents had lived when I was an infant (then still a working-class neighbourhood where the neighbours kept carrier pigeons), was leagues out of my price range.

Reluctantly, over the past fortnight, I had started looking elsewhere. Searching through the *Evening Standard* classifieds, I had travelled the length and breadth of the capital. And in the process, I had had a revelation. Most of London, the city of my birth, was as foreign to me as Prague.

The East End in particular was one huge blank spot. Until a week ago, I had never so much as set foot east of the City – but then again, I'd never had any desire to do so. The borough of Tower Hamlets, which today encompasses the East End proper, might as well have been marked on the map with a large skull and crossbones. My impression of the place was still coloured by childhood images of fog-bound streets stalked by Jack the Ripper,

Bill Sykes, and the notorious Kray Twins, who drove black Sedans and buried their victims in the foundations of motorways. At home and at school, I had been taught that the people of the East End were different. My parents and teachers had made the Cockneys sound like a distinct race – cheery, perhaps, like Eliza Doolittle's father, but tougher, wilier and never wholly to be trusted. They even had their own language, Cockney rhyming slang, which – it was said – they had developed to fool policemen.

My father and his father before him had never set foot in the East End either. Their world had been Chelsea and Knightsbridge (where my grandmother did all her shopping at Harrods) and later, the villagey suburbs of south-west London. During my childhood, my parents had rarely travelled beyond these borders, except to go to the theatre in the West End or to visit Hampstead where, compared to Barnes, their friends were distinctly bohemian. The closest we had ever come to the East End was during a day trip to Greenwich. Standing on the Meridian, we had looked out over the Thames to the badlands beyond, a grim cityscape of gasworks and disused cranes, abandoned warehouses and crumbling wharves, and we had counted ourselves lucky that we didn't live there.

By the time I reached Whitechapel it was nearly four o'clock and already dusk was falling. The neon signs above the shopfronts seared the gathering darkness like branding irons, while the main road, still slick with rain, began to glisten beneath the headlights of passing vehicles. I crossed over Whitechapel Road and entered the warren of narrow streets behind the East End mosque where Bangladeshi children in white skullcaps played football between rows of parked cars. Not for the first time during the past few days, I found that I was the only white face on the street. Everyone else was from Afghanistan, Bangladesh, India, Pakistan, Somalia. As I passed by, I caught snippets of conversation in some of the estimated 102 languages spoken in the East End. Only occasionally did I hear a word or two in English – and only then amid a babble of Somali or Urdu.

The area was mostly residential, the streets filled with the sounds of Talvin Singh blaring from open windows, and the enticing aromas of businesses too, all of them immigrant-owned. A halal butcher here, an old warehouse packed with rows of people working behind sewing machines there. And on one corner, an Islamic paraphernalia shop selling everything from leather-bound Korans to prayer mats with sew-in compasses, designed to ensure that the twenty-first-century Muslim never fails to locate Mecca.

Looking up at the street signs, I noticed they were written in Bengali, as were the posters plastered on the lamp-posts and walls. The illusion of being back in South Asia was almost complete. But as I reached the next main road, the sight of a red double-decker bus hurtling past reminded me that this was London – just not the London I knew.

Tarquin Hall, Salaam Brick Lane

✱ ✱ ✱

But immigration is nothing new to the East End. Today's immigrants are in a long line stretching back to the first century BC.

Immigration has long shaped the East End. The Belgae, who came to the area from Flanders in the first century BC, were followed by the Romans (in AD 43), Saxons (fifth century), Danes (ninth century), Normans (1060s) and Flemish (fourteenth century). The latter opened dye-works alongside the River Lea, bringing to London new methods for working textiles. This set a pattern that exists to this day, whereby foreigners possessing skills undeveloped by Londoners arrive in the capital to rescue a stagnant local economy. In this way the Flemish were followed by Frankish calico-printers, French gardeners, Belgian brewers [...]

After the 1572 Massacre of St Bartholomew in France, a murderous attack on Protestants led by the king, Charles IX, many French silk workers fled to London. In France they had been known as *réformés* – they were members of the Reformed

Church John Calvin had set up in 1550 – but in England they became known as Huguenots, a word derived from the German *eidgenosse* or confederate.

When the authorities prevented the Huguenots settling in the City, citing their lack of support for the Church of England, the newcomers went east, colonizing the nearest available land, around the ruins of St Mary Spital, once a flourishing priory and hospital, which had become known as the Spital Fields. It was clearly defined territory. To the west was Bishopsgate, the Roman road leading from the City towards Hertfordshire. To the east lay a narrow track which led past the brick kilns (what is now Brick Lane). To the north were the fields of Shoreditch and Bethnal Green, and to the south archery and crossbow training ground which Henry VIII had granted to the Fraternity of the Artillery (now covered by Artillery Lane). […]

The Huguenot population soon divided itself into well-demarcated enclaves. The weaver, who comprised the majority of the local silk workers, lived in cramped cottages on what were then still semi-rural lanes – Fleur de Lys Street, Greenwood Alley, Sweet Apple Court. As the industry grew so the weavers' cottages spread further out, to Brick Lane and Bethnal Green.

The artisans lived in new houses on Elder Street and Wilkes Street, many of which survive, working at the top of the house in attics whose windows, known as 'long lights', occupied the entire length of the property. They filled these attics with looms and spinning-wheels that clanged and shook the room, and made the long scarlet drops of the fuchsias, which lined the window ledges in small pots, swing gently backwards and forwards. […] Spitalfields which lay beyond the powers of the City of London next door, was run as the Liberty of Norton Folgate. It had two charity schools, its own courthouse, almshouses, nightwatchmen and a daily rubbish collection. Its culture was the most sophisticated and advanced in Georgian London. The first gold medal winner at the Royal Academy of Arts, John Bacon Junior, was a Spitalfields resident. (The area has retained its link with art, in particular the avant-garde, being a recent home to Gilbert and George, Tracey Emin, Chris Ofili and Rachel Whiteread.) There were societies for music, recitation, history and horticulture. At well-attended mathematics lectures locals discussed exacting theorems. [...] The Huguenots formed mutual benefit societies to protect themselves in times of sickness. They worked and socialized together. The master weavers and artisans used the same churches, attended the same clubs, shopped for fruit and vegetables at Spitalfields market, and on Club Row traded the goldfinches, chaffinches and greenfinches they kept in small aviaries in the roofs of their cottages. They planted many flowers and introduced to the natives new dishes such as oxtail, which London butchers had previously thrown away. They also pioneered a taste of the hitherto unknown combination of fried fish with pieces of fried potato, reinvented in Manchester in the nineteenth century as 'fish and chips'.

Ed Gilnert, East *End Chronicles*

* * *

Meet Akeel. His family may be from Pakistan, but he's a Londoner born and bred, grabbing a takeaway coffee as he rushes for his train. Yet things aren't always easy for the second generation as they try to appease and fit in with two very different cultures.

Tuesday morning. Akeel runs up the stairs from Blackfriars tube to the overground, taking them two at a time, a pole vaulter leaping the horizontal. It is 8.29, if the 8.34 to Wimbledon arrives on time he has almost five minutes to pick up his double espresso, single caramel shot, and then grab a forward-facing seat on the left-hand side of the train. [...] Akeel is an east Londoner, born and bred. He discounts that half year in Pakistan when he was fourteen, it was not one of his best, his mother sick, his father preoccupied, Akeel sent off to an aunt and uncle and a raft of cousins who didn't want to share and didn't want an English boy living with them any more than he wanted to be there, not for the first few months at least. Then, just as he had become used to it, the land, the light, just when the cousins had accepted him and let him into the secrets of their world, he was sent home to Stratford in time for the clocks to go back and school finishing in the dark with a long bus journey home. And then there was more hassle at school, from the other Pakistani kids as well as the white ones, calling him country boy, village boy, the just-made yokel to their city-wise lads. Akeel remade himself very quickly that winter, upped the London in his school accent while keeping the elegance of his newly fluent Urdu for home, made himself the classic city rudeboy, two personas at least, both of them underpinned by the East London in his heart, that heart in his mouth, heart in his vowels.

Stella Duffy, *The Room of Lost Things*

✣ ✣ ✣

Brick Lane, the very heart of the immigrants' East End, is now firmly on the tourist trail with its wonderful Indian restaurants and the nearby trendy area of Spitalfields Market and the studios of smart young artists. The annual Curry Festival is now as regular a part of the London calendar as Trooping the Colour. Monica Ali's best-selling novel, Brick Lane *– together with the film based on it – has further raised the profile of the street.*

Nazneen walked a step behind her husband down Brick Lane. The bright green and red pendants that fluttered from the lamp-posts advertised the Bangla colours and basmati rice. In the restaurant windows were clippings from newspapers and magazines with the name of the restaurant highlighted in yellow or pink. There were smart places with starched white tablecloths and multitudes of shining silver cutlery. In these places the newspaper clippings were framed. The tables were far apart and there was an absence of decoration that Nazneen knew to be a style. In the other restaurants the greeters and waiters wore white, oil-marked shirts.

But in the smart ones they wore black. A very large potted fern or a blue and white mosaic at the entrance indicated ultra-smart.

'You see,' said Chanu. 'All this money, money everywhere. Ten years ago there was no money here.'

In between the Bangladeshi restaurants were little shops that sold clothes and bags and trinkets. Their customers were young men in sawn-off trousers and sandals and girls in T-shirts that strained across their chests and exposed their belly buttons. Chanu stopped and looked in a shop window. 'Seventy-five pounds for that little bag. You couldn't fit even one book in it.'

Outside a café he paused again. 'Two pounds ninety for large coffee with whipped cream.'

A girl at a wooden table on the pavement bent the screen of a laptop computer back and forth to angle it away from the sun. Nazneen thought of Chanu's computer, gathering dust. A spider's web shivered between keyboard and monitor.

They walked to a grocer's shop at the corner of one of the side streets. Nazneen waited outside. She walked a little way down the side street. Three-storey houses, old houses but the bricks had been newly cleaned and the woodwork painted. There were wooden shutters in dark creams, pale greys and dusty blues. The doors were large and important. The window boxes matched the shutters. Inside there were gleaming kitchens, rich dark walls, shelves lined with books, but never any people.

Monica Ali, *Brick Lane*

* * *

Rachel Lichtenstein's Jewish grandparents belonged to an earlier wave of immigration. On Brick Lane *is her investigation of the area's rich cultural history through her own family's past and the ever-changing face of this fascinating part of London.*

Brick Lane had been a mythical landscape for me as a child. I heard stories about it from my grandparents, who opened their first shop,

Gedaliah Lichtenstein's Watchmakers & Jewellers, at no. 67 in the 1930s. They were Polish Jewish refugees, hard-working people with a rich cultural and intellectual life. My grandmother told me about her friend, the great Yiddish poet Avram Stencl, who lived in Cheshire Street, just off the lane, in the heart of the sprawling Sunday market. Stencil called Brick Lane and the surrounding area of Whitechapel 'my *shtetl*, my holy acres, my Jerusalem in Britain'. The thriving Jewish community and the vigorous street life around him became the subject matter for most of his poetry. The first time I visited the street in the early 1990s as a young art student there were only the faintest traces left of that world.

Since then I must have walked up and down Brick Lane thousands of times, initially to search for signs of its Jewish past, checking doorposts for marks left by *mezuzahs* and rescuing books from the damp cupboards in abandoned synagogues. Standing outside the site of the former Russian Vapour Baths I devoured stories from the old Hasid who owned the shop there. Over the following decade I spent countless hours interviewing members of the elderly Jewish community, collecting stories of places and people, snapshots, fragments, whispers and hidden traces until I could mentally map the area as it had once been. [...] Many of these stories featured Brick Lane, the street itself, which had been at the heart of the Jewish East End from the late 1880s until the outbreak of the Second World War.

During that period Brick Lane and the surrounding area was known as the centre of the textile and clothing manufacturing industry in London. Rooms above shops and in the side streets off Brick Lane were filled with Jewish immigrants working long hours for poor pay in terrible conditions. On Saturdays, their only day off, the Orthodox men would dress in long black silk coats and wide brimmed fur hats before making their way towards the Machzike Hadath Synagogue. The younger ones would dress up in their best clothes and wander up and down Whitechapel High Street, in 'the monkeys' parade', looking for a date. This is how my grandfather met my grandmother.

When my grandparents lived in Brick Lane every shop in the street was occupied. There were printers, hairdressers, drapers, greengrocers and tobacconists. Milliners, leather manufactures, wine sellers and boot repairers among others. Most of the shop signs were written in Yiddish and English and the street was known as 'Little Jerusalem'. When war broke out in 1940 everything changed, the East End of London was badly bombed and many left for the safety of the countryside. [...]

Following trails left by my ancestors led me to the small synagogue in Princelet Street, a narrow turning just off Brick Lane, where my grandparents married. Inside I heard about a former resident called David Rodinsky, an Orthodox Jewish scholar who had lived in the attic rooms above the synagogue and mysteriously disappeared one day in the 1960s. Fascinated by this story I secured a residency in the building, which was undergoing restoration to become a museum of immigration. [...]

At the time I was working in the old synagogue I walked past the shops along Brick Lane selling sweetmeats, boxes of mangoes, brightly coloured saris and illuminated pictures of Mecca without ever entering them. Like most other tourists, the only Bengali-owned places I used to visit then were Indian restaurants for a cheap curry. In the early 1990s the Bhangra music spilling out of the shops, the call for prayer from the mosque and the chatter of voices speaking foreign languages were nothing more than an exotic soundscape for my wanderings. I had no real understanding of what was taking place in the Bangladeshi community around me. [...]

In 1999 I married a Muslim man whose father used to sell spices wholesale to the restaurants on Brick Lane in the early 1970s. Through him I found out more about the Muslim religion and culture and the Asian history of Brick Lane. Gradually, like learning a new language, I was able to read the street in a different way. [...]

It will never again be the first stop for the next new wave of migrants in London. The dockside, where many first arrived, is now accessible only to a privileged few who can afford apartments and private walkways and river views. Dilapidated properties in Spitalfields, once split into multiple rooms for cheap rents, have been restored and refurbished and are now worth millions. The Hasidic men in long dark coats with beards and sidelocks who occupied street corners, exchanging gossip and discussing business, were replaced by groups of Asian elders doing the same, wearing long white kaftans and open-toed sandals, their beards stained orange with henna. You still see these men shuffling quickly past the bars and clubs, trying to reach the mosque further down the road without attracting unwanted attention. Scuffles sometimes break out as racist abuse is hurled across the street as partygoers drink late into the night.

The latest arrivals in Brick Lane, the 'haircuts' (as some of the locals like to call them), are the ones buying up old warehouses and turning them into vintage-clothing stores or dot.com companies. The weekends also see thousands of other incomers descending on Brick Lane from across London to visit the many bars, clubs and restaurants. [...] The curry houses, originally established as cheap cafés selling food from Bangladeshi men stranded here without families and home-cooked meals, have become smart new restaurants, endorsed by Ken Livingstone and Prince Charles, an essential eating experience for every tourist visiting London. While documentaries and contemporary works of fiction discuss the 'fabulous architecture', 'waves of immigration' and 'unique ethnic mix' of Brick Lane, the people they celebrate are leaving the area. Young Bangladeshis can't afford to buy there and many want to escape the drug problems and poverty that exist in the streets behind the glitz of Banglatown.

Rachel Lichtenstein, *On Brick Lane*

* * *

Iqbal Ahmed extends the picture of this area.

There was a crowd outside what looked like a betting-shop. But it turned out to be a facility for sending money abroad, displaying exchange rates on bulletin boards. On the other side of the road, a dingy-looking shop sold haberdashery. There were also a few shops along this road selling synthetic fabrics. A radio blasted Hindi film songs from a record shop. A prevailing smell of curry emanated from the numerous restaurants on both sides of the street. The restaurants looked narrow with two rows of tables fitted in, but most of them were well-kept. These were the restaurants that had made Brick Lane well-known. A pile of empty tins of purified butter and cooking oils was lying on the pavement, to be collected by binmen. The pavement felt greasy around the lampposts. Brick Lane was getting ready for its annual curry festival: there were banners and posters everywhere announcing its date. [...]

We walked towards the north end of Brick Lane. The chimney of the old Truman Brewery, which had been given a new glass front, stood tall between the two ends of the road. Men in suits carrying portfolios were going in and out of the building. I was curious about their occupation. Anwar explained that the old brewery had been turned into a centre for fashion and information technology, and also that there was an artesian well beneath it. Across the road, I saw the art gallery, which had been brought to life a year ago by a certain professor through an exhibition of cadavers. As we passed the brewery, Brick Lane changed its character. The restaurants gave way to clothing shops run by artists and designers who specialised in street fashion. They sold combat trousers, hipster skirts and kimono tops in outrageous colours. The leather shops appeared again towards the end of the road. The black mannequins in the show-windows of the leather shops had collected a thick layer of dust. Notices affixed to their doors read 'Open to the Public'. [...]

I entered the Whitechapel Gallery for distraction, but I couldn't concentrate on the pictures there. It was the proximity of the City and its grand architecture to a slum which I found disconcerting. [...]

I saw a small group of Americans set out on a walking tour to witness the poverty in the area. The guide was explaining the meaning of the word 'ghetto' to them. He said that it was an Italian word, meaning foundry, and had been applied to the site of the first such place in Venice during Medieval times. The tourists stood outside 19 Princelet Street, which their guide told them was 'a museum of diversity'. Some of the Americans wanted to see it but the museum was rarely open to the public. Even though it was the only one of its kind in Britain, if not in Europe, the trustees needed funding to keep the doors of this museum open permanently. I learnt later that this place was exploring how London has always been shaped by new people from different countries and the museum was founded by the people whose ancestors had come to London as refugees.

It was here in Brick Lane that the distressing word 'refugee' had entered the English vocabulary, when French Protestants settled here after fleeing Catholic France towards the end of the seventeenth century. The Huguenots brought the silk weaving industry with them. The second wave of immigrants were Ashkenazi Jews, fleeing from Eastern and Central Europe during the 1880s to escape persecution. Many of them had arrived in London destitute, and found shelter in Brick Lane. They found work in tailoring workshops, which is why tailoring was considered by many people in London to be a Jewish trade. The third wave of immigrants came from Sylhet to escape poverty, only to live an abject life in Tower Hamlets. [...]

Brick Lane revealed itself in detail on my second visit. I noticed that many chartered accountants had offices above the shops. Perhaps these accountants balanced the books for the owners of the Indian restaurants. Pictures of the Mayor of London as a patron saint of Brick Lane, shaking hands with the restaurant owners, appeared in a number of shop windows. There were many travel agents in the side-streets, selling tickets for Aeroflot and Biman Airlines. The name 'Katz' was written on a door as a reminder of the past of Brick Lane. When I drifted towards Commercial Street, I discovered a purpose-built soup kitchen for the Jewish poor, erected in 1905. A Baroque church designed by Christopher Wren's apprentice looked outlandish in this setting. A listed building was being converted into lofts as a residence for professional couples. Property prices had already quadrupled around here in the last ten years. The houses in Princelet Street had become quaint.

Iqbal Ahmed, *Sorrows of the Moon*

✻ ✻ ✻

Rachel Lichtenstein recalls some of the great Jewish poets, artists and thinkers who frequented the Whitechapel Library – nicknamed 'the University of the Ghetto'.

He became a familiar face in Brick Lane, tipping his trilby hat to everyone he met, walking the streets in his shabby old coat, speaking in Yiddish to anyone left who would listen. He liked to write surrounded by the people of Whitechapel, the inspiration for much of his work, and he could often be seen scribbling away on an old notebook in the Lyons teashop on the Commercial Road or in the warmth and comfort of the Whitechapel Library, located on Whitechapel High Street near the south end of Brick Lane. Stencl was one of many immigrant Jews using the library then. From its opening to the outbreak of the Second World War the reading rooms were filled with the sound of schoolchildren discussing their homework, their parents and grandparents arguing in Yiddish, groups of intellectuals planning meetings and events, all of them escaping the confined spaces of their tenement homes to read, learn and meet friends at the free public library.

Bill Fisherman started using the library when he was about ten years old. 'The staff there were fantastic,' he said, 'you'd get all the help you needed. The building was known as the "University of the Ghetto". We all went. My father would read Yiddish newspapers, for us literature and history. The Whitechapel Arts group used to meet there in the reference library. Joseph Leftwich told me this, he was a survivor and met Jacob Epstein the sculptor there and Rosenberg the poet. The group started about 1905, a period of a lot of flourishing library circles in the East End. The library was a marvellous training ground for the young immigrants, they got a higher education there that most couldn't afford. The intellectual elite among the Jewish immigrants met in the library not in the synagogues: Rosenberg, Mark Gertler, Bomberg, the poet Rodker and Jack Bronowski the mathematician, scientist and writer, and of course Stencl, who'd write his poetry there and sometimes give readings.'

Rachel Lichtenstein, *On Brick Lane*

✳ ✳ ✳

Meanwhile, in another part of East London, a young
Chinese woman savours the pleasures of a traditional
café ...

custom *n* long-established activity or action; usual habit; regular use of a shop or business

The café is name greasy spoon, Seven Seas. All windows is foggy from the steam. You order tea as soon as you walk into. Noisy. Babies. Mothers. Couples. Lonely old man. You are opening the newspaper and start drink thick English Breakfast milky tea. And me being quiet.

I want talk to you. But you are reading paper. I have to respect your hobby.

'So where are you from?' I ask handsome waiter in white suit.

'Cyprus.' He smiles.

'Are these chefs also from Cyprus?'

'Yes.'

'So your Cyprus chefs cook English breakfast for English?'

'Yes, we Cypriots cook breakfast for the English because they can't cook.'

I see from open kitchen that sausages are sizzling on the pan. And mushrooms, and scrambled eggs, they are all waiting for being devoured.

I love these old oily cafés around Hackney. Because you can see the smokes and steams coming out from the coffee machine or kitchen all day long. That means life is being blessed.

In this café, there is a television set above everybody's head. The TV on but doesn't have any images, only can hear BBC news speaking scrambly from the white snow screen. It is a little disturbing for me, but it seem everybody in this place enjoy it. Nobody here suggest fix TV.

Suddenly white-snow-screen changes to green-snow-screen, the BBC voice continues. A man nearby eating some bacons with the *Daily Mirror* says to the chef:

'That's an improvement.'

'Yes, Sir,' replies the chef. 'Well, at least you don't have to eat your breakfast, read the paper and watch TV all at the same time.'

'That's true.' The man chew his bacons and concentrates on the page with picture of half naked blonde smiling.

I want to talk. I can't help stop talking. I have to stop you reading.

'You know what? I came this café before, sit here whole afternoon,' I say.

'Doing what?' you put down the paper, annoyed.

'I read a porn magazine called *Pet House* for three hours, because I studied English from those stories. Checking the dictionary really took lots of time.'

You are surprised. 'I don't think you should read porn mags in a café. People will be shocked.'

'I don't care.'

'But you can't do that. You'll make other people feel embarrassed.'

'Then why they sell these magazines in every little corner shop? Is also even sold in the big supermarket.'

I believe everything to do with the sexuality is not shameful in West. Do what you like.

The man next to us finished his bacons, half naked woman photo with huge breasts still being exposed.

'I think I go now buy another porn magazine,' I say, standing up.

'OK, you do whatever you want,' you say shaking head. 'This is Hackney after all. People will forgive you for not being *au fait* with the nuances of British customs.'

You dry up your cup of tea.

Xiaolu Guo, *A Concise Chinese-English Dictionary for Lovers*

❉ ❉ ❉

Patrick Wright fills in the Hackney picture …

Hackney was once a place of pastures and market gardens. Samuel Pepys practised archery here. Even today there is a public park in the borough known as London Fields. It is a place of modest attractions: some fine old plane trees, a new community centre, an open-air lido that, were it not for local objectors, the council would already have demolished. In the early morning, before the dogs come out, it is often full of seagulls.

Trains rattle by overhead. London Fields borders on the Cambridge line, and it's not a bad spot from which to observe passing academics. They stare back glumly, thanking their lucky stars for Grantchester Meadows and mistaking the figures on the ground for woebegone residents of the Victorian East End. It's easy to imagine them adding those contemporary asides that keep turning up in scholarly studies of Dickens, Doré, or life as it was in outcast London: 'Even today, one only has to take the train from Liverpool Street Station … '

London Fields certainly has its dismal aspect. There have been vicious assaults. Huge and unattended dogs run free. Young children from the nearby travellers' site invade the infants' playground in a terrifying and unbelievably foul-mouthed pack (not for them the clip on the ear with which Richard North once hoped to improve the area). As I walked out one Sunday afternoon I came across a Ford Cortina parked up against the railings: it was emitting grunts and rocking with copulation.

But despite the malevolence that sometimes drifts across it, London Fields also clings to an understated respectability. On most days of the year, it is an uneventful and slightly melancholy place. If it has a message for the world it is no longer the progressive Victorian one about the uplifting and civilizing effect of open spaces – green lungs as they used to be called – on the nation's most down-trodden souls. These days the park promises nothing so ambitious. It merely points out that people can be poor without always being beastly; that, no matter what writers like Tom Wolfe may suggest, the inhabitants of the inner city can get by without raping, mugging, and insulting each other at every encounter.

The park remains uncelebrated, but its name is too good to be true. 'London Fields … ' It doesn't take a master class in poetry to reveal the contemporary resonances of that archaic conjunction. In these ecological days 'London Fields' has come into its own as a prime piece of nomenclature, a movable asset that is far too good to be squandered on an obscure dog-patch in Hackney.

The estate agents were the first to act. Assisted by the usual clutch of lifestyle journalists, they went out one night in the early Eighties, levered the name up from that tired stretch of municipal ground, and humped it half a mile down the road. No longer confined to the park or the dishevelled part-industrial part-Bohemian zone around the railway arches on its east-side, 'London Fields' was now the new name for Mapledene – a pleasant and, as we know, relatively unbroken area of Victorian terraced housing that, through this act of renaming, was now being pulled away from the abysmal Holly Street Estate as its western edge. 'London Fields' was still a place of leafy respite, but it had become one that could be bought and sold: a rediscovered 'village' within walking distance of the City.

Patrick Wright, A Journey Through Ruins

✻ ✻ ✻

Most cities are characterized by marked contrasts and startling juxtapositions, but the proximity of the run-down streets of Hackney to the wealth of the City strikes Justin Cartwright with particular keenness.

We drove through a succession of run-down streets, bombed by plastic rubbish bags, past tracts of land overlooked by East European concrete apartment blocks. The concrete tells the inhabitants something about their relationship to the gentler world which the disordered old streets still manage to conjure up. It's a straightforward message, which they acknowledge with their garbage and graffiti.

From Hackney we suddenly found ourselves in the still streets of the City of London, where even the most ardent brokers and dealers had gone home. A pub coughed smoke and beer breath on to the road and two drunken girls stumbled out to catch the last bus, but the mausoleum stillness, the polished granite, the marble Doric columns, the window boxes of early narcissus, the clean streets, the bronze statues and monuments could have been a million miles from Hackney, rather than a few hundred yards. In Hackney they were sauntering off to the kebab houses and fried chicken huts; they were stealing cars and kicking empty beer cans along the streets; they were throwing up in pub toilets and rapping in church halls; they were waiting for minicabs, eating chilli tacos; they were gunning the motors of their little Ford XR 3s, pretending they were in *Miami Vice*; they were filing out of the urine-stained cinemas for a curry. Here in the City – St Petersburg – the money had gone calmly to bed. It was resting until morning in its marble and granite palaces. These buildings were solid, constructed of materials which were resistant to doubt. Why don't

116

they all rush in from Hackney and smash the place up? Posters in Hackney urged the workers to do just that. The Tory industrial military complex was keeping the workers down; multinational corporations must be confronted, and so on.

Unfortunately nobody was listening.

Justin Cartwright, *Look At It This Way*

✳ ✳ ✳

For all the East End's poverty and bad reputation, Daniel Farson rates highly the entertainment to be found there. And though, over the years, the acts may have changed, there are still plenty of talented performers giving locals and visitors a good night out.

Now I discovered the numerous East End pubs which pulsated with live entertainment in welcome contrast to the taped variety on television which had settled into a transatlantic rut.

Far from predictable, the entertainment ranged from modern jazz at Bermondsey (the south, and therefore the wrong side of the river), to stand-up comics and the female impersonators so beloved by the British.

I took Antony Armstrong-Jones and the actress Jacquie Chan to the Bridge House at Canning Town one Sunday lunchtime – Sundays were the festive exception – to join the crowd of dockers who cheered lustily a few minutes before closing time as the girl strippers removed every garment, and then staggered home to a late, traditional lunch. [...] With pubs featuring favourite turns, which attracted a following of regulars, it occurred to me that here was a form of music hall that had returned to its roots. There was the same challenge for the artist to establish himself immediately by sheer force of personality: also, a similar vulnerability, for though the pub performers had the armour of a microphone, they needed to rise above the clash and clatter of the crowd. Even more than with music hall, the audience was part of the fun. There was no courtesy towards an indifferent

117

performer who was drowned by noise, but if the customers took to an artist they listened attentively, though applause was sparse owing to the difficulty of clapping with a beer mug in one hand. [...] When an artist triumphed, the atmosphere was warm and the comments generous. Unlike the southern English who dared to be amused, the East Enders set out for the night determined to enjoy themselves, a quality they shared with the north. After all, what was the point of sinking to the occasion?

For me, the constant delight was the 'local talent': members of the audience who needed little prompting to get up on stage and perform, like the taxi-driver who impersonated the Al Jolson numbers whose sentimentality made them perennially popular. If the performers lacked refinement, they possessed a raw vitality which was more exciting than the images on television. By comparison, the West End nightlclubs looked stale.

Daniel Farson, *Limehouse Days*

✻ ✻ ✻

And back to Justin Cartwright for a glimpse of East London's latest development ...

On the way back from Billingsgate we drove through Docklands. [...] We turned a corner and the skies parted. The sun had not yet risen but it had done something more beautiful: it had leaked out behind the ribs of cloud, back-lighting them so that they acquired a mother-of-pearl sheen, the colour – well – the colour of mirror carp, the colour of tarnished silver by candlelight. In front of this luminous backdrop, the gantries of a hundred cranes rose into the sky and a railway carried a toy train high above the dock between the cranes and the middle distance. It was a scene from *Metropolis*, yet the sky behind was unmistakably by Turner as it melted into the glowing water of the dock.

'They're building the biggest new city in Europe here.'

Justin Cartwright, *Look At It This Way*

Up the West End

The West End is the beating heart of London, the centre of glamour, style and sophistication. It is a land of glitz and gold. Here are the bright lights and red lights of Soho, the romantic mews of Mayfair, the elegant but rigid streets of Marylebone, and the chic enclaves of Fitzrovia. Here is Oxford Street, London's most congested shopping stretch; here are the flashing neon signs of Piccadilly Circus, the most famous landmark in the world. Here is Regent Street, the ultimate in urban grandeur, and Old Compton Street, the epitome of hard-core hedonism. But it is also a place of loose morals, premeditated violence and necessary secrecy; the ulterior motive behind the gleaming smile. [...]

The West End is an easy place to locate. Controversy surrounding its borders is minimal compared to that which accompanies the East End, for instance. The West End consists of four constituent areas, each of which radiates away from Oxford Circus. Running clockwise from the north-west there are Marylebone, Fitzrovia, Soho and Mayfair. [...]

Despite lacking the visual architectural splendour of Amsterdam or Edinburgh, it is the sheer brazen scale of the West End that dwarfs all its rivals. [...]

Most of all the West End is a place built around enjoyment and entertainment – clubs, music venues, theatres, dance halls, comedy stores, brothels, cinemas, grand restaurants, cosy cafés, corner pubs, drinking dens. It has been home and host to the greatest of revellers and hedonists: Casanova, George IV, Oscar Wilde, Dylan Thomas, Nina Hamnett, Aleister Crowley, Henrietta Moraes, Tony Hancock, Syd Barrett, Francis Bacon ... a list that continues to grow. It is one of the few locales not just in London but in Britain where Bohemian behaviour is tolerated, expected even. [...]

This West End is a vast store of treasures, conspicuous in its confidence, found on and around some of the most famous streets in the world – Piccadilly Circus, Regent Street, Oxford Street, Savile Row, Carnaby Street, Fitzroy Square, Park Lane. Here the shops are bigger and the goods fancier, the food in the restaurants tastier, the drinks in the pubs smoother, the streets livelier, the nightclubs louder, the night out longer, the people happier, even the prostitutes – of either sex, sometimes both – better looking.

What other locale can match an area that contains the excitement of Soho, the refinement of Fitzrovia, the gentility of Marylebone and the class of Mayfair? Even Soho, long the sleaze capital of London, exudes a stylish sort of sleaze, style with rough edges – a potent mix. Shabby yet sophisticated, urban and urbane, Soho has long been *the* target for any self-respecting reveller, superior in every way to Camden Town, Brixton, Brick Lane, Notting Hill, Hampstead, or any other come-lately haven of hedonism. Its streets cater for everyone. While the discerning film goer sits in the Curzon Cinema on Shaftsbury Avenue, watching a rep classic directed by Michelangelo Antonioni, only a few hundred yards away on Winnett Street gullible northern football fans down for the weekend to watch the match are probably holed up in an illegal sex club, about to be stumped £295 each for consorting with a 'hostess' who a week previously was making a precarious journey from deepest Montenegro to London in the back of a lorry full of stolen cigarettes. [...]

Marylebone has become an elegant, urban twenty-first-century village. Credit for ridding London of the old dull

Marylebone of spiritless shops and sober Georgian town houses goes to the Howard de Walden estate, which owns the freehold for much of the area. [...]

They convinced Waitrose to open a branch. Never had the opening of a supermarket had so galvanizing an effect on an area. Soon there was a Conran shop and niche outlets. A fishmonger moved in, as did a French furniture company and Daunt's, the upmarket bookshop. Now Marylebone is one of the most thriving communities in London. Even the austere streets which Benjamin Disraeli compared to a 'large family of plain children' have a new sparkle.

Then there is Mayfair, the south-west section of the West End. Mayfair exudes an air of smug self-satisfaction. Its offices, home of prestige companies dealing in property, advertising, PR, wines, spirits and oil, were once the town houses of the aristocracy and the super wealthy who left for Kensington and Richmond in the 1950s and 1960s. Although there was a brief residential revival after the Arabs quadrupled the price of oil in 1974 and the sheikhs began moving into the area, Mayfair doesn't really need much of a population. Not when it has Savile Row, still the home of bespoke tailoring. Not when it has Cork Street, a few hundred yards to the west, lined with the country's most prestigious art galleries. And not when it has hotels like the Connaught, Claridge's and the Dorchester exuding an air of priceless panache.

Deep into Mayfair there is the elegant simplicity of Shepherd Market, where a villagey atmosphere prevails barely a quarter of a mile north-east of roaring Hyde Park corner. In the centre of the community the letters SHEPHERD MARKET can still be picked out in bold *sans serif* lettering on the parapet of one block. All around are low-rise, flat-faced brick houses, nestling everywhere they can find a space amongst the chaotic, romantic street pattern which appears to rearrange itself every time the visitor returns.

Ed Glinert, *West End Chronicles*

* * *

More has been written about Soho than about any
other part of the West End: it's a by-word for sex,
sleaze, Bohemianism ... and danger. A well-deserved
reputation, or not?

Now, about Soho, there's this, that although so much crap's written about the area, of all London quarters, I think it's still one of the most authentic. I mean, Mayfair is just top spivs stepping into the slippers of the former gentry, and Belgravia, like I've said, is all flats in houses built as palaces, and Chelsea – well! Just take a look yourself, next time you're there. But in Soho, all the things they say happen, do: I mean, the vice of every kink, and speakeasies and spielers and friends who carve each other up, and, on the other hand, dear old Italians and sweet old Viennese who've run their honest, unbent little businesses there since the days of George six, and five, and backward far beyond. And what's more, although the pavement's thick with tearaways, provided you don't meddle it's really a much safer area than the respectable suburban fringe. It's not in Soho a sex maniac leaps out of a hedge on to your back and violates you. It's in the dormitory sections.

Colin MacInnes, *Absolute Beginners*

* * *

There was more fun in five minutes in the Caves de France than an evening of sin in Soho. The district's reputation for villainy and vice was manufactured largely by imaginative journalists in bars far outside the district. 'The square mile of vice' was an easy label, used by two Sunday columnists in particular who delighted in giving Soho a bad name by presenting a scene of exaggerated violence with drug addicts, gambling dens, razor slashing, wide boys, and unspeakable sex. Their stories would start along these lines: 'As I walked along one of Soho's murky backstreets, a sinister figure stepped out of a doorway. It was Scarface, the nark. "'Ere," he said in a hoarse whisper ... '

Yet it was possible to walk through Soho at night and see nothing more shocking than the usual fight at closing time and the usual prostitutes. [...]

The girls in Soho were better natured than those in the neon-lit streets of Piccadilly and Leicester Square, who were so brazen that they once attacked the wife of an American officer because they resented her appearance on their 'beat'.

Kindness should not be examined too closely for the motive, but deserters from the armed forces told tales of the tarts' generosity and there seemed to be an innate loyalty to the pimps, as well as fear. [...] The turnover from one room amazed me, with men coming in and out with the regularity of a conveyer belt. And I was surprised to learn that one of the most successful girls was a lesbian, keeping a girl friend in her turn. You could find most of the vices in Soho if you looked hard enough and were ready to pay. I heard that there were pornographic films (legalised later in a membership cinema) and 'exhibitions'.

As for crime, Soho's reputation was worse than the reality. In the thirties there had been a series of unsolved murders which gave rise to the scare of a new Jack the Ripper: French Fifi was strangled in a Soho flat in 1935; Jeanette Cotton was strangled with a silk scarf in 1936; Constance Hind was battered with a flat iron, a thin wire around her neck; French Marie was strangled in a blazing flat in 1937. It was ironic that so many of the girls thought that a French prefix was as useful as a French letter.

Daniel Farson, *Soho in the Fifties*

* * *

A little vignette of Soho in the eighteenth century.
(Things were pretty hot then, too!)

Sex in the West End has long covered all manner of permutations, persuasions, proclivities and predilections: from the prospect of a knee-trembler with an underage Albanian asylum seeker in a grotty alleyway off Berwick Street Market to the possibility of upmarket fellatio with a duchess clad in pearls and soaked in expensive mid-European scent in an Upper Grosvenor Street town house. [...]

When Theresa Berkeley took over the White House, a Soho Square mansion with a painted chamber, grotto and skeleton room, in 1787, she installed a vast store of instruments of torture. These included a dozen tapering whip-thongs, cats-o'-nine-tails studded with needle points, supple switches, thin leather straps, curry combs, oxhide straps studded with nails and green nettles. She opened a brothel in 1828 at 28 Charlotte Street, Fitzrovia, which contained a machine for flogging gentlemen and where George IV was a regular visitor. Berkeley took her instruments of torture with her, and according to one Charlotte Street customer, 'they were more numerous than those of any other governess. Her supply of birch was extensive, and kept in water, so that it was always green and pliant. There were holly brushes, furze brushes and a prickly evergreen called butcher's bush.' Clients could be 'birched, whipped, fustigated, scourged, needle-pricked, half-hung, holly-brushed, furze-brushed, butcher-brushed, stinging-nettled, curry-combed, phlebotomized and tortured'. And if the urge for a more active role was irresistible there was a ready supply of willing girls who would be flogged in turn, namely Miss Ring, Hannah Jones, Sally Taylor, One-eyed Peg and the starkly monikered 'Bauld-cunted Poll'.

Ed Glinert, *West End Chronicles*

✻ ✻ ✻

And Soho in fiction with Keith Waterhouse's novel simply called Soho. *Meet Christine Yardley ...*

Except for the city itself, which after working hours is left to the caretakers and the cats and the odd penthouse millionaire, there is no London neighbourhood more resembling the restless downstream tide of the Thames than the ragged square mile of Soho.

Ask Christine. Christine Yardley is literally here today and gone tomorrow.

Here is here and now, but by this hour her five-inch heels are teetering on the threshold of a new day. It is dawn turning to watery sunlight as Christine latchkeys herself through a narrow doorway next to the darkened lobby of a marooned bed show, the last of its line in Soho, in Hog Court off Greek Street. The bank of illuminated doorbells is dimmed now, and all the other girls in the house are asleep. Not that Christine is of their number: she pays her own rent.

She kicks off her crippling shoes and climbs the four near-vertical flights to her room – roomette would be a better word – at the top of the house. She flops down on the unslept-in mattress on a wooden base that passes as a bed and throws back her pretty head to guzzle down the last dribble of Diet Coke from a sticky can on the cluttered bedside table doubling as a dressing-table. She lights a cigarette from a new packet of Benson and Hedges, a little present from an admirer.

She unzips her rubber dress from Zeitgeist in Peter Street and wriggles out of it. She adjusts her magnifying shaving mirror and removes her heavy makeup with Boots' No. 7, must remember to buy another jar. She takes off her ear-rings, her false eyelashes, and her long blue nail extensions, and pops them in the compartmentalised British Airways foodtray, breakfast size, which is where she keeps her trinkets.

She peels off her stockings and underwear. Perching her cigarette on the ashtray stolen from the ladies' at Soho House she levers herself into a corner shower cabinet the size of an upright coffin. The trickle of water is near freezing but she is careful to sponge away all traces of her heavy body perfume. She dries herself and sprays herself with Sport deodorant. She shaves.

She tosses her underwear in the sink to soak. She rolls up her stockings and suspender belt and drops them in a deep cardboard carton, her underwear drawer, in the curtained recess that serves as a wardrobe. From another cardboard box she retrieves St Michael underpants and socks and dons them, then takes a shirt from a wire coat-hanger. She hangs up the rubber dress and takes down a grey business suit.

Soon Christine Yardley is dressed again, but not as Christine Yardley. It is Christopher Yardley who descends the stairs and walks around the corner to the Bar Italia in Frith Street. After a frugal breakfast on a caffè latte and a roll, he strolls along Old Compton Street, across Cambridge Circus to Shaftesbury Avenue and then to Holborn and out of Soho.

It is quite a walk to Fenchurch Street where, a Sohoite no longer until this time next week, he toils on VAT returns and suchlike for a firm of accountants, but he has all the time in the world before he must be at his desk, and he needs this break to adjust from one body to the other. This evening he will go home to his divorced mum in Ruislip, who thinks he spends these weekly nights away working at the firm's south coast branch in Bournemouth.

Keith Waterhouse, *Soho*

❊ ❊ ❊

The West End isn't just sex: it's shopping, too. Oxford Street is one of the most famous shopping streets in the world. Though a little tattier, these days, than in the early years of the twentieth century, it's still recognisable from the description by the quintessential London writer, Virginia Woolf ... apart from the tortoises.

Down in the docks one sees things in their crudity, their bulk, their enormity. Here in Oxford Street they have been refined and transformed. The huge barrels of damp tobacco have been rolled into innumerable neat cigarettes laid in silver paper. The corpulent bales of wool have been spun into thin vests and soft stockings. The grease of sheep's thick wool has become scented cream for delicate skins. And those who buy and those who sell have suffered the same city change. Tripping, mincing, in black coats, in satin dresses, the human form has adapted itself no less than the animal product. Instead of hauling and heaving, it deftly opens drawers, rolls out silk on counters, measures and snips with yard sticks and scissors.

Oxford Street, it goes without saying, is not London's most distinguished thoroughfare. Moralists have been known to point the finger of scorn at those who buy there, and they have the support of the dandies. Fashion has secret crannies off Hanover Square, round about Bond Street, to which it withdraws discreetly to perform its more sublime rites. In Oxford Street there are too many bargains, too many sales, too many goods marked down to one and eleven three that only last week cost two and six. The buying and selling is too blatant and raucous. But as one saunters towards the sunset – and what with artificial light and mounds of silk and gleaming omnibuses, a perpetual sunset seems to brood over the Marble Arch – the garishness and gaudiness of the great rolling ribbon of Oxford Street has its fascination. It is like the pebbly bed of a river whose stones are for ever washed by a bright stream. Everything glitters and twinkles. The first spring day brings out barrows frilled with tulips, violets, daffodils in brilliant layers. The frail vessels eddy vaguely across the stream of the traffic. At one corner seedy magicians are making slips of coloured paper expand in magic tumblers into bristling forests of splendidly tinted flora – a subaqueous flower garden. At another, tortoises repose on litters of grass. The slowest and most contemplative of creatures display their mild activities on a foot or two of pavement, jealousy guarded from passing feet. One infers that the desire of man for the tortoise, like the desire of the moth for the star, is a constant element in human nature. Nevertheless, to see a woman stop and add a tortoise to her string of parcels is perhaps the rarest sight that human eyes can look upon.

Taking all this into account – the auctions, the barrows, the cheapness, the glitter – it cannot be said that the character of Oxford Street is refined. It is a breeding ground, a forcing house of sensation. The pavement seems to sprout horrid tragedies; the divorces of actresses, the suicides of millionaires occur here with a frequency that is unknown in the more austere pavements of the residential districts. News changes quicker than in any other part of London. The press of people passing seems to lick the ink off the placards and to consume more of them and to demand fresh supplies of later editions faster than elsewhere. The mind becomes a glutinous slab that takes impressions and Oxford Street rolls off upon it a perpetual ribbon of changing sights, sounds and movement. [...]

The places of Oxford Street ignore what seemed good to the Greeks, to the Elizabethan, to the eighteenth-century nobleman; they are overwhelmingly conscious that unless they can devise an architecture that shows off the dressing-case, the Paris frock, the cheap stockings, and the jar of bath salts to perfection, their palaces, their mansions and motor-cars and the little villas out at Croydon and Surbiton where their shop assistants live, not so badly after all, with a gramophone and wireless, and money to spend at the movies – all this will be swept to ruin. Hence they stretch stone fantastically; crush together in one wild confusion the styles of Greece, Egypt, Italy, America; and boldly attempt an air of lavishness, opulence, in the effort to persuade the multitude that here unending beauty, ever fresh, ever new, very cheap and within the reach of everybody, bubbles up every day of the week from an inexhaustible well. The mere thought of age, of solidity, of lasting for ever is abhorrent to Oxford Street.

Therefore if the moralist chooses to take his afternoon walk along this particular thoroughfare, he must tune his strain so that it receives into it some queer, incongruous voices. Above the racket of van and omnibus we can hear them crying. God knows, says the man who sells tortoises, that my arm aches; my chance of selling a tortoise is small; but courage! there may come along a buyer; my bed tonight depends on it; so on I must go, as slowly as the police allow, wheeling tortoises down Oxford Street from dawn till dusk. True, says the great merchant, I am not thinking of educating the mass to a higher standard of æsthetic sensibility. It taxes all my wits to think how I can display my goods with the minimum of waste and the maximum of effectiveness. Green dragons on the top of

Corinthian columns may help; let us try. I grant, says the middle-class woman, that I linger and look and barter and cheapen and turn over basket after basket of remnants hour by hour. My eyes glisten unseemlily I know, and I grab and pounce with disgusted greed. But my husband is a small clerk in a bank; I only have fifteen pounds a year to dress on; so here I come, to linger and loiter and look, if I can, as well dressed as my neighbours. I am a thief, says a woman of that persuasion, and a lady of easy virtue into the bargain. But it takes a good deal of pluck to snatch a bag from a counter when a customer is not looking; and it may contain only spectacles and old bus tickets after all. So here goes!

A thousand such voices are always crying aloud in Oxford Street. All are tense, all are real, all are urged out of their speakers by the pressure of making a living, finding a bed, somehow keeping afloat on the bounding, careless, remorseless tide of the street. And even a moralist, who is, one must suppose, since he can spend the afternoon dreaming, a man with a balance in the bank – even a moralist must allow that this gaudy, bustling, vulgar street reminds us that life is a struggle; that all building is perishable; that all display is vanity; from which we may conclude – but until some adroit shopkeeper has caught on to the idea and opened cells for solitary thinkers hung with green plush and provided with automatic glowworms and a sprinkling of genuine death's-head moths to include thought and reflection, it is vain to try to come to a conclusion in Oxford Street.

Virginia Woolf, *The London Scene*

✳ ✳ ✳

For those who want to lose themselves in crowds, London shops are perfect. In this short extract from a novel translated from French, a young girl recovering from a traumatic attack tests the progress of her slowly returning confidence with a trip to London.

Eva had just spent the afternoon in London.

That morning she had hurtled out of the station. Then she walked and walked, without direction, crossing streets, going up avenues, staring straight ahead. Then she slowed down and started to study faces. Not so much hostile as indifferent. Several times over she caught herself looking into shop windows, striving to recognise her face among so many others. She drowned in the anonymous crowds filling the big department stores. In the afternoon, she went and sat down in a deck chair on the banks of the Serpentine, then she went into the nearby art gallery, from which she rapidly exited, propelled outwards by the paintings she found hanging there. Craters filled with fire spilling out lava, enormous and distorted mouths coughing up giant toads, and menacing sorts of exploding vulvae from where serpents with red eyes emerged. They hit her in the face like a fist, rooting her to the spot for a moment, then she left, getting as far away as fast as she could. When she finally reached the outside gate she paused, for a long while.

Then she went back in, returning slowly past every single painting. On the way out she didn't dare take the tube, but jumped on a passing bus. The ill-tempered conductor muttered his disapproval. Eva escaped his wrath by jumping from the platform at the rear when it pulled up at a set of traffic lights.

She definitely preferred walking. Somewhere around the middle of the King's Road, she went and had a coffee at a French bistro. You could tell it would soon be summer. She would like to travel on, she told herself.

Alternating going on foot with taking the bus, she gradually found her way back to the station. She had waited there a while to hear her train announced, then she settled in to her compartment, a magazine open on her knees.

Some guy had come and sat down beside her. She would have preferred him to sit elsewhere, and she turned her head to avoid looking at him. However, when she focused on her reflection in the window with a slight feeling of apprehension, there was no avoiding him looking back at her. Or perhaps he was really just staring out at the platform: it was hard for her to read his gaze. The train pulled out of the station.

Renata Ada-Ruata, *Silence in the House*
translated by Amanda Hopkinson

* * *

Clarissa Dalloway thrills to every sight and sound of Bond Street. We follow her thoughts as she walks out to buy flowers on a glorious June morning.

She remembered once throwing a shilling into the Serpentine. But every one remembered; what she loved was this, here, now, in front of her; the fat lady in the cab. Did it matter then, she asked herself, walking towards Bond Street, did it matter that she must inevitably cease completely; all this must go on without her; did she resent it; or did it not become consoling to believe that death ended absolutely? but that somehow in the streets of London, on the ebb and flow of things, here, there, she survived, Peter survived, lived in each other, she being part, she was positive, of the trees at home; of the house there, ugly, rambling all to bits and pieces as it was; part of people she had never met; being laid out like a mist between the people she knew best. Who lifted her on their branches as she had seen the trees lift the mist, but it spread ever so far, her life, herself. But what was she dreaming as she looked into Hatchards' shop window? [...] Bond Street fascinated her; Bond Street early in the morning in the season; its flags flying; its shops; no splash; no glitter; one roll of tweed in the shop where her father had bought his suits for fifty years; a few pearls; salmon on an iceblock.

"That is all," she said, looking at the fishmonger's. "That is all," she repeated, pausing for a moment at the window of a glove shop where, before the War, you could buy almost perfect gloves. And her old Uncle William used to say a lady is known by her shoes and her gloves. He had turned on his bed one morning in the middle of the War. He had said, "I have had enough." Gloves and shoes; she had a passion for gloves; but her own

131

daughter, her Elizabeth, cared not a straw for either of them.

Not a straw, she thought, going up Bond Street to a shop where they kept flowers for her when she gave a party.

Virginia Woolf, *Mrs Dalloway*

❋ ❋ ❋

Virginia Woolf and her circle are always associated with Bloomsbury (the 'Soho of intellectuals', as German writer and academic Rüdiger Görner calls it). Not far from Oxford Street, though not strictly part of the West End, it contains the British Museum, modestly elegant squares, and a number of institutions of the University of London.

Bloomsbury's legendary status, that Soho of intellectuals, is due less to the British Library Reading Room in which Thomas Carlyle, Karl Marx, Lenin and George Bernard Shaw worked, but rather to the authors, artists and academics who were young in 1910, usually from solid Victorian homes and rebelling against their parents' narrow-minded morality. Amongst them were Virginia Stephen and her sister Vanessa, the two daughters of the great Victoria scholar Leslie Stephen, Lytton Strachey, avowed homosexual and starving essayist, Roger Fry who introduced French Post-Impressionism to England, but derided German artists such as Dürer, the artists Clive Bell and Duncan Grant as well as the great macro-economist John Maynard Keynes who valued freedom within relationships more than anything else, and later also Leonard Woolf, a colonial civil servant highly critical of British imperialism.

Living in Bloomsbury was an act of faith as it was considered a bit run-down in comparison to high Victorian upscale Kensington, where Virginia and Vanessa had grown up at Hyde Park Gate. According to the soon-to-be-deemed 'disreputable' young intellectuals, Bloomsbury was supposed to be a small Montmartre, a Quartier Latin *à l'anglaise*. Except it lacked the bistros, the strolling areas, the flair. But they affected the avant garde, encouraged scandal, and considered themselves superior to everything and everyone else. The centre point was formed by 46 Gordon Square where the Stephen daughters lived with their two brothers. After Vanessa's marriage to Clive Bell, who initially remained loyal to Gordon Square, Virginia and her brother Adrian moved to Fitzroy Square.

It would be misleading to imagine that Bloomsbury was the name for an internally homogenous group with a clearly defined sense of community. Nor was it an arena for unbridled passions. No, Bloomsbury represented a mostly Cambridge-educated individualism. Its hallmark was radical subjectivism as a collective experience. Thus whilst everyone spoke of free love, in reality most Bloomsberites were more faithful to their partners than many supposed Victorian paragons of virtue were to theirs.

Rüdiger Görner, *London Fragments*
translated by Debra Marmor and Herbert Danner

✳ ✳ ✳

And if you've had enough of Bloomsbury, a shortish walk will take you to Carnaby Street – worth a visit, though maybe not quite what it was in the Swinging Sixties.

Carnaby Street was named after a demolished local mansion, Karnaby House, and in the early nineteenth century was known for the Nag's Head pub, a hotbed of revolutionary political activity where the toast was 'May the last of the kings be strangled with the guts of the last of the priests'. The rag trade was long established around here. There were some seventy tailors on and around Golden Square by the First World War, although Carnaby Street itself had no connection with the industry until the 1950s when it was lined with small, blackened terraced houses, tobacconists and attic workshops that were cheap to rent.

In the mid 1950s photographer Bill Green opened a select clothes shop, Vince, at 15 Newburgh Street, one street along from Carnaby, selling imported Levi's (few people in Britain then owned jeans) and dandified clothes. Ready-to-wear stuff as opposed to Savile Row's tailored suits. Green's target customers were mostly homosexuals, as noted by George Melly who once explained how it was the only shop where 'they measured your inside leg each time you bought a tie'.

Vince's soon gained a reputation. Wolf Mankowitz celebrated the shop in his Soho beat novel *Expresso Bongo* in which 'sweating teenagers [wear] Vince Man's Shop jeans with heavy rollnecks, close-fitting Charing Cross Road teddy trousers and velvet-collared coats bought on hire purchase'. One of Vince's assistants, John Stephen, soon branched out and opened his own menswear shop, His Clothes, on nearby Beak Street. His Clothes specialized in scarves loosely knotted around the neck, velvet suits and cheap throwaway garments. When a fire damaged the premises in 1960 Stephen opened a new branch at 41 Carnaby Street. There he introduced new concepts into marketing clothes such as experimental window displays and racks on the pavement displaying goods. The clothes were Italian-styled – round-collared shirts, inch-wide ties, short jackets with side vents, five inches long – aimed at a young narcissistic crowd known as Mods. […]

By the mid 1960s John Stephen owned around a third of Carnaby shops, each sporting a variation of his name, such as Stephen John's Man's Shop. Carnaby Street, along with its Chelsea equivalent, King's Road, was now the shop window for youth fashion in England, and crowds flocked there at weekends. […]

Inevitably the publicity killed Carnaby Street, which soon began to attract chain stores. By the end of the decade it was filled with cash-in shops stuffed with inferior hipster jeans and second-rate Cuban heeled boots, patronized by what detractors denounced as 'weekend hippies'. The street enjoyed a brief revival at the end of the 1970s, when its stores latched on to punk, stocking tartan bum-flaps, knee-length lace-up boots and zip-festooned leather jackets, but by the late 1980s it had succumbed to nostalgia and overpriced tat.

Ed Glinert, *West End Chronicles*

* * *

A stroll down Carnaby Street towards Piccadilly will bring you out at Liberty's, one of 'the' great London department stores. The quirkiest and probably the most historically interesting of them all, it's as classy as ever ... though once inside, you may need a map.

One of London's most famous shops since it was opened by Arthur Liberty, a Buckinghamshire draper, in 1875, Liberty's was the ultimate in fashion between 1880 and 1920 and it has always been associated with the Arts and Crafts movement. The shop originally sold Japanese fans – Mr Liberty was one of the first to import oriental goods as well as silks and other fabrics in bulk.

Then in 1925, flushed with success, the company, which had by now acquired three adjacent shops, decided to rebuild. The result was the extraordinary mock Tudor building we see today, but this is only visible in Great Marlborough Street. On the side of the store that faces Regent Street, Liberty had to stick to the Portland stone from which the rest of Regent Street is built, but in Great Marlborough Street he could do what he liked. And in the great tradition of craftsmanship and individuality championed by William Morris (1834–1896), the man behind the Arts and Crafts movement, Liberty really let himself go in Great Marlborough Street.

Built around an interior courtyard, Liberty's conceals a remarkable and bizarre secret – it is made almost entirely from the magnificent oak timbers from two dismantled ships, HMS *Hindustan* and HMS *Impregnable*.

Not content with this, the owners of what was and still is one of London's most successful shops employed the best craftsmen – including several brought here specially from Italy – to install stained glass, magnificent staircases and superb carvings. Everything is handmade and unique.

What really ensured the success of Liberty's, however, was not the spectacular building, but the decision made much earlier by Gilbert and Sullivan to use Liberty fabrics for the costumes in their light opera *Patience* (1881).

Perhaps the most delightfully eccentric thing about Liberty's is that its staircases are built in such an odd way that at one time customers were always getting lost. All was resolved when, in the 1970s the then owners published a booklet which was available free to all regular customers entitled 'How Not To Get Lost In Liberty's'!

Tom Quinn, *London's Strangest Tales*

❊ ❊ ❊

If you want to go even further west, a few stops from Oxford Circus, on the Central Line, is Notting Hill Gate – the stop for Portobello Road and its famous market. Here is the area vividly described by Ruth Rendell at the start of her novel called simply Portobello.

It is called the Portobello Road because a very long time ago a sea captain called Robert Jenkins stood in front of a committee of the House of Commons and held up his amputated ear. Spanish coastguards, he said, had boarded his ship in the Caribbean, cut off his ear, pillaged the vessel and then set it adrift. Public opinion had already been aroused by other Spanish outrages and the Jenkins episode was the last straw to those elements in Parliament which opposed Walpole's government. They demanded British vengeance and so began the War of Jenkins's Ear.

In the following year, 1739, Admiral Vernon captured the city of Puerto Bello in the Caribbean. It was one of those successes that are very popular with patriotic Englishmen, though many hardly knew what the point of it was. In the words of another poet writing about another battle and another war: 'That I cannot tell, said he, but 'twas a famous victory.' Vernon's triumph put Puerto Bello on the map and gave rise to a number of commemorative names. Notting Hill and Kensal were open country then where sheep and cattle grazed, and one landowner called his fields Portobello Farm. In time the lane that led to it became Portobello Road. But for Jenkins's ear it would have been called something else.

Street markets abounded in the area, in Kenley Street, Sirdar Road, Norland Road, Crescent Street and Goldborne Road. The one to survive was the Portobello and from 1927 onwards a daily market was held there from eight in the morning to eight in the evening and 8 a.m. till 9 p.m. on Saturdays. It still is, and in a much reduced state, on Sundays too. The street is very long, like a centipede snaking up from Pembridge Road in the south to Kensal Town in the north, its legs splaying out all the way and almost reaching the Great Western main line and the Grand Union Canal. Shops line it and spill into the legs, which are its side streets. Stalls fill most of the centre, for though traffic crosses it and some cars crawl patiently along it among the people, few use it as a thoroughfare. The Portobello has a rich personality, vibrant, brilliant in colour, noisy, with graffiti that approach art, bizarre and splendid. An indefinable edge to it adds a spice of danger. There is nothing safe about the Portobello, nothing suburban. It is as far from an average shopping street as can be imagined. Those who love and those who barely know it have called it the world's finest street market.

You can buy anything there. Everything on earth is on sale: furniture, antiques, clothes, bedding, hardware, music, food and food and more food. Vegetables and fruit, meat and fish, and cheese and chocolate. The stalls sell jewellery, hats, masks, prints, postcards old and new, shawls and scarves, shoes and boots, pots and pans, flowers real and artificial, furs and fake furs, lamps and musical instruments. You can buy a harp there or a birdcage, a stuffed bear or a wedding dress, or the latest best-seller. If you want to eat your lunch in the street you can buy paella or pancakes, piping hot from a stall. But no live animals or birds are for sale.

Cheap books in excellent condition are on sale in the Oxfam shop. A little way up the road is the Spanish deli which sells, mysteriously, along with all its groceries, fine earthenware pots and bowls and dishes. There is a mini-market in most of the centipede's legs and at Portobello Green a covered market under a peaked tent like a poor man's Sydney Opera House. In Tavistock Road the house fronts are painted red and green and yellow and grey.

The moment you turn out of Pembridge Road or Westbourne Grove or Chepstow Villas and set foot in the market you feel a touch of excitement, an indrawing of breath, a pinch of the heart. And once you have been you have to go again. Thousands of visitors wander up and down it on Saturdays. It has caught them in the way a beauty spot can catch you and it pulls you back. Its thread attaches itself to you and a twitch on it summons you to return.

Ruth Rendell, *Portobello*

Londoners – old and new

Most Londoners are justifiably proud of their city's reputation as the most successful multi-racial city in the world, and one of the surest ways to catch the flavour of it is among the youngsters playing summer football in London's parks.

'Can we join your game?'

It's an action stopper every time. The game shudders to a halt as everybody sizes up the newcomers, two lads in Italy shirts with heavily accented English working their way around Regent's Park looking for a kickaround. 'Can we join your game?' Well, it's not as simple as that, mate. This might look like two dog-eared teams in mismatched shirts puffily chasing a flaccid ball over unmarked ground, but it's really an evenly tied humdinger, a finely poised 4–4. Pick the wrong Italian, and that satisfyingly tight and edgy tie could turn into a 10–4 romp. And who wants that?

139

Welcome to the world of summer football, when London's parks become a mass of under-athletic over-enthusiasm. Just after 8pm gangs of kids and grown-ups who should know better mob up at tube stations – Regent's Park, Hyde Park Corner, Clapham Common – and descend upon the nearby park to seek their pitch. Jumpers become goalposts, teams are picked and, after token warm-up, the game is on.

And what a game. Pitches are warped, with non-existent boundaries so that the keenest players will go haring off after the ball into the distance; fouls are rare, with every physical challenge followed by an apology; headers are met with open mouths and closed eyes; teams are mixed in race, sex, size and ability. Above all, though, people are playing not for points or prizes but for the hell of it. It's fun.

This changes when you're a couple of players short, the adolescent excuse of 'I forgot my kit' now replaced by the adult one, 'I've got to work late'. Anything less than eight is too few for a decent game among yourselves, so then you find yourself asking that pair of Italians to join in or, more thrillingly, challenging another group playing in the park.

Glances are stolen and whispered conferences abound: what about them, they look crap. Don't ask that lot, they're wearing shin pads. Check them out, they're all in Tottenham kits – they must be rubbish. Eventually the challenge is thrown down, considered, accepted, and the teams line up. At first it is tentative, nervy, almost polite, as you test each other out, softly sparring like virgin boxers. Then your opponents realize how crap you are, and thrash you 9–0.

In such cases, there are only two ways to lose: to some awesomely gifted foreign language students who score countless goals of great beauty and raise your spirits with their relentless exuberance; or to some ultra-competitive English accountants who celebrate each methodical goal with high fives and crush your spirit with their relentless commitment.

Indeed, it is almost terrifying how many cultural stereotypes are encountered; stocky, tricky southern Europeans who want to beat half-a-dozen players before scoring; willing but limited Scots; talented but slightly suspect east Europeans; willing but limited English; clueless Australians playing rugby. All are represented on this uneven playing field.

Here young and old, black and white, join together to bond in unexpected teams. And, most tellingly, here are the Asian footballers that we are told do not exist, playing huge, joyful, eager games and begging the question why no player from the subcontinent has yet broken through to play top professional football in this country. Well, they're out there, in the parks, having fun with us and wondering why their role models all play cricket.

Peter Watts, 'Rough Magic in the Park', *The Independent on Sunday*

❊ ❊ ❊

London has a long history of immigration.

London has always been a city of immigrants. It was once known as 'the city of nations', and in the mid-eighteenth century Addison remarked that 'when I consider this great city, in its several quarters, or divisions, I look upon it as an aggregate of various nations, distinguished from each other by their respective customs, manners, and interests'. The same observation could have been applied in any period over the last 250 years. It is remarked of eighteenth-century London in Peter Linebaugh's *The London Hanged* that 'here was a centre of worldwide experiences' with outcasts, refugees, travellers and merchants finding a 'place of refuge, of news and an arena for the struggle of life and death'. It was the city itself which seemed to have meaning. Its population has been likened to the eighteenth-century drink 'All Nations', made up of the remains at the bottoms of various bottles of spirit; but this is to do less than justice to the energy and enterprise of the various immigrant populations who arrived in the city. They

141

were not dregs or leftovers; in fact the animation and enterprise of London often seemed to invade them and, with one or two exceptions, these various groups rose and prospered. It is the continuing and never-ending story. It has often been remarked that, in other cities, many years must pass before a foreigner is accepted; in London, it takes as many months. It is true, too, that you can only be happy in London if you begin to consider yourself as a Londoner. It is the secret of successful assimilation.

Peter Ackroyd, *London: The Biography*

✳ ✳ ✳

So let's meet a few of the most recent 'new' Londoners.

THE POLISH MIGRANT

2 March: 11am, Warsaw bus terminal The Warsaw to London bus is about to leave. Every day, hundreds of Poles make the 26-hour bus journey to London in search of work. Since Poland joined the EU last May, 20,000 have arrived in the country. It's estimated there are 250,000 Poles living in London.

Wiola Andrzejewska (22), from Konin, three hours from Warsaw, boards the bus with her brother Slawek (20): 'This is the first time I have left Poland,' she says. 'I thought about coming to London about a year ago. I wanted to come for a sense of adventure. But also, the fact is, Polish people can legally work in Britain and bring money home. Compared to what we can make in Poland, it's good for us to come to Britain.

'We just booked our tickets a week ago and said to our family: "We are leaving." They think it's a good thing. It's a matter of being in this little town, Konin, and thinking, well, what can you do?

3 March: 3.30pm, Victoria coach station Wiola arrives in London with Slawek. 'I didn't sleep much on the coach. The most stressful thing has been arriving in London. We are very surprised because we didn't imagine London being so big. We don't have a map and we don't know where to go.

'Eventually, we decided to go to the Polish Cultural Centre in Hammersmith that we had heard about. There, my brother ended up meeting a guy, Jarek, and asked him if he knew where we could stay. Jarek said we could stay for the night at the rented house he shared with other Poles. We got a bus and got off a few stops before Heathrow airport. We stayed in our sleeping bags! I was so grateful for his kindness.'

4 March: 11am, the Wailing Wall, Hammersmith The *Sciana Placzu* ('Wailing Wall') is a little cornershop more famous in Poland than in Britain. The shop window is crammed with fliers, notes advertising job vacancies and accommodation, and notes to friends and relatives. Every kind of work is offered here, from catering and cleaning to pizza and newspaper delivery. Most make no mention of pay.

'Jarek suggested we go to the Wailing Wall to look for work,' says Wiola, 'but masses of people were crowded up against the window when we got there, so we decided to go back later. We have another lead for work, from when we were on the bus going to Jarek's house the night before. By chance, Jarek met an elderly Polish woman. She told him that she needed some girls to work in a place in Hammersmith and gave us the address. When we turned up, it was a dry-cleaner. It's run by Indians who don't speak English, but luckily there was a Polish woman working there who could translate, and she told us to come back again on Sunday morning.'

5 March: 8pm, Hotel Crimea, Ealing 'Last night we also found somewhere to stay. My brother bumped into some Poles on the street and they told him about this place, the Hotel Crimea. We don't have to pay a deposit. It's £65 per week. I share the room with my brother.'

At the end of her first year in London, Wiola had found decent accommodation as well as regular employment and babysitting work. She has decided to stay.

THE GHANAIAN DOCTOR

Kitted out in formal Victorian top hat and tails, Dr John Ferrel Easmon stares out from a black and white photo that shows his graduation from University College Hospital, Bloomsbury, in 1879. There is nothing unusual about this photo – apart from the fact Dr Easmon is black. 'We think he was probably the first black doctor at UCH,' says 45-year-old Charlie Easmon, Ferrel Easmon's great-grandson, and himself a doctor in Harley Street, where he set up his own practice in 2002.

Born in Sekondi in Ghana in 1961, Easmon now lives in Clapham with his Scottish wife and six-year-old son Byron. Although his efforts are concentrated on his Harley Street practice, Easmon is keen to retain his Ghanaian roots. 'We'd like Byron to be aware of both sides of his heritage. I'd like to take him to visit Ghana one day.'

THE AFGHAN WAITER

Nasser Abdul arrived in Britain in 1998, claiming asylum from war-torn Afghanistan with a fake passport he bought in Kabul for £6,000. 'I'm telling you all this, so you have an idea of what most Afghanis go through. To get a visa to Britain, you need power or money. Most Afghanis have neither. Once we are here, our asylum details can be properly processed,' says Abdul.

Abdul, 28, now works in an Afghani restaurant, Masa, in Harrow, but his story is typical of many of the 30,000 Afghans thought to live in London, most of whom fled the country after the Taliban came to power in 1996.

Abdul has great affection for his adopted city. 'I really like London. It's an old city, and makes you feel attached to it. I recently went on my first holiday in six years, but when I got there, I missed London so much I ended up changing my flight for an earlier ticket back.'

THE RUSSIAN INTERPRETER

In his neat grey suit, entrepreneur 39-year-old Sergei Kolushev is the consummate businessman. Kolushev is the managing director of Eventica, a Canary Wharf-based company that organises such business and cultural events as the Russian Economic Forum and the annual Russian Winter Festival. Splitting his time between Moscow and London, he perfectly represents the new batch of Russian entrepreneurs steadily making the capital their home.

Kolushev's wife, whom he met here, is also Russian: 'There's nothing wrong with American, French or English women, but, the Russian man needs to be spoiled by the Russian woman,' he says. He also wants his two-year-old son, Nikita Patrick, to be proud of his heritage. 'We speak Russian all the time to him and have a Russian nanny.'

THE AUSTRALIAN DANCER

Antipodeans have been hitting the backpacker trail to London since the 1960s, but 28-year-old dancer Mandy Liddell is part of a growing number of foreign professionals coming to work in London, staying and making it their home. While there are still plenty of backpackers paying their way by pulling pints in pubs across London, around 30 per cent of Aussies working here now are in banking, finance and other high-salaried professional jobs. These days it's Shepherd's Bush, or the more upmarket Fulham or Putney, where Liddell lives, that are hosting the new generation of Australians, rather than the seedy backpacker hotels of Earl's Court.

Her first few weeks in the capital read like the archetypal Aussie-in-London experience. 'I was staying in Bayswater in an awful house-share with a lot of my fellow countrymen. There were three rooms, with ten people in each room, and one bathroom. God, the dirt! The place was full of people working in pubs. We spent all our money on beer in theme pubs that I don't go to any more.'

Australians are also becoming a cultural force in London; there are antipodeans at the helm of the South Bank Centre and Sadler's Wells, as well as the Royal Ballet School and London Philharmonic Orchestra. And these days, fashion from down under doesn't just mean surf gear. Alannah Hill, Wayne Cooper and other top designers are stocked at Austique on the King's Road and have a strong following here.

'I don't have any desire to go back,' says Liddell. 'Sydney is amazing, but I don't miss it. Last Australia Day, I was in the Walkabout in Covent Garden. I ended up having an argument with another Australian. He was complaining about the weather and slagging off everything about Britain and I got so angry. OK it's cold, but go home if you don't like it.'

Rebecca Taylor, 'London Lives,' *Time Out*

* * *

Like all big cities, London has its share of residents who have 'sunk' beneath the difficulties of life. A brief passage in Robert Elms' novel In Search of the Crack *presents us with some of them ... and hints at the anonymity that can result from teeming city life.*

I jumped out of the cab at the corner of Oxford Street and Tottenham Court Road. The traffic was terrible round the one-way system, and I decided to walk into Soho. Crossing over into Charing Cross Road, I spotted that they were all there again. Junkies move even more slowly than tortoises and council workers. I know in the sixties they used to crowd round the toilets in Piccadilly Circus. Well, in twenty years, they've gone about 800 yards to their latest cosy little home, opposite Centre Point by the alley into Soho Square.

Almost every day I see them. Vacant lots, the south Bronx of humanity. You can tell when they started doing smack, because that's the last time they bought any clothes. Most of this lot dated to about 1974–6 and looked like they'd been standing out in the cold ever since. As I walked past and caught a couple of unseeing, empty eyes, I had little sympathy. But it's when you see them with their kids, hanging on to their decaying bodies, that it really hits home. They should have the dignity to go and die, but dignity is exactly what they haven't got left.

After turning round into Old Compton Street, I bought a paper off the stand. I buy a paper off that stand every day, and the man has never recognized me once.

Robert Elms, *In Search of the Crack*

* * *

Camden Town and its famous market is where to see 'innovative' ways of dressing. In London, pretty much anything goes: no-one (apart from the odd tourist) bats an eye-lid at startling punk hair-dos or mini-skirts that might as well be belts.

On our way home from Mornington Crescent we stopped to look at the old Camden Theatre which was renamed the Music Machine when it became a pop music centre about five years ago. Its old green dome and yellow pillars are unchanged but above and around the doors there are psychedelic lights and lettering, which make it look like an old lady, in stately hat and bodice, who has stepped into a young girl's glittering mini.

Said to M. as we walked on how glad I am that it has been opened for people's pleasure again after all those private years as a BBC studio.

Several punk girls came walking fast towards us, and it struck me again how like space fiction their get-up is; their make-up is inhuman too; some give the impression of *Grand Guignol*. The first we saw took long strides in long legs closely fitted with yellow stockings to the knee and tight black satin breeches to above the waist. A top of some bright colour, hair cropped and scraped with top knots sticking up. She had passed us in a flash, and as I looked back I had the impression that she was wearing a sword at her waist. It may have been a long cane, or an umbrella as tightly rolled as herself. Then a few yards behind her came the others straggling but with rapid steps like speckled glaring lights.

In spite of the bright clothes and the greens, yellows, scarlets of the hair in streaks, in patches or whole – sometimes a blotch of white on dark hair reminds me of a long-healed saddle sore on an old horse – in spite of the showy flash, there is a puritanical severity about the punk look, male and female. The skimpy scrimp of the boys' clothes – tight jeans often not long enough to cover their shins, jackets pinched at the armpits and chest with sleeves stopping short of the wrist – give them a poor and meagre look, especially if you compare them with the long-haired boys of a few years ago whose clothes were more amply cut. Then, since facial expressions can be designed and worn to fashion, the majority look as grim as any Wee Free Minister. It is startling to see such a look of severity, especially on the girls' faces in the evening outside a pleasure dome, but this I guess is fashion too.

David Thomson, *In Camden Town*

* * *

Who would have thought that Dostoyevsky – yes, author of those particularly heavy Russian novels – would have strolled down the Haymarket eyeing up the local talent …

In London the masses can be seen on a scale and in conditions not to be seen anywhere else in the world.

I have been told, for example, that on Saturday nights half a million working men and women and their children spread like the ocean all over town, clustering particularly in certain districts, and celebrate their Sabbath all night long until five o'clock in the morning, in other words guzzle and drink like beasts to make up for a whole week. They bring with them their weekly savings, all that was earned by hard work and with many a curse. Great jets of gas burn in meat and food shops, brightly lighting up the streets. It is as if a grand reception were being held for those white negroes. Crowds throng the open taverns and the streets. There they eat and drink. The beer houses are decorated like palaces. Everyone is drunk, but drunk joylessly, gloomily and heavily, and everyone is somehow strangely silent. Only curses and bloody brawls occasionally break that suspicious and oppressively sad silence ... Everyone is in a hurry to drink himself into insensibility ... wives in no way lag behind their husbands and all get drunk together, while children crawl and run about among them.

One such night – it was getting on for two o'clock in the morning – I lost my way and for a long time trudged the streets in the midst of a vast crowd of gloomy people, asking my way almost by gestures, because I do not know a word of English. I found my way, but the impression of what I had seen tormented me for three days afterwards. [...] I saw in London another and similar 'mass', such as you would never see on a like scale anywhere else. An unusual spectacle it certainly was. Anyone who has ever visited London must have been at least once in the Haymarket at night. It is a district in certain streets of which prostitutes swarm by night in their thousands. Streets are lit by jets of gas – something completely unknown in our own country. At every step you come across magnificent public houses, all mirrors and gilt. They serve as meeting places as well as shelters. It is a terrifying experience to find oneself in that crowd. And, what an odd amalgam it is. You will find old women there and beautiful women at the sight of whom you stop in amazement. There are no women in the world as beautiful as the English.

Fyodor Dostoyevsky, *Winter Notes on Summer Impressions*
translated by Kyril Fitzlyon

✻ ✻ ✻

London is famed for its theatres, but Jan Morris sees the whole city as a show, a performance in which all Londoners are players.

More than any other city in Europe, London is a show, living by bluff and display. People have always remarked upon its theatrical nature. In Victorian times it was Grand Guignol, and the smoky blackness of the city streets, the rat-infested reaches of the river, coupled with the lively squalor of the poor, that powerfully impressed susceptible visitors. In the blitz of the 1940s it was pure patriotic pageantry: the flames of war licking ineffectively around the mass of St Paul's, Churchill in his boiler-suit giving the V-sign from the steps of 10 Downing Street, Noël Coward singing 'London pride has been handed down to us' or 'A Nightingale Sang in Berkeley Square ... '

Today we are between the great civic performances that have punctuated London's history, but the greasepaint is always on, and the sensation of theatre is still endemic to the place. It is a city of actors always, as it has been since the days of Will Shakespeare and his troupers down at the Globe. You can hardly spend a day in London without seeing a face you recognize, and in this city, famous actors are not mere celebrities or glorified pop stars, but great men. They are figures of authority, honoured or ennobled. Laurence Olivier sits as a baron in the House of Lords. Sir Ralph Richardson lives like a grandee in his Regency house by the park. Sir Alec Guinness, Sir Michael Redgrave, Sir John Gielgud – these are the truest nobility of the capital: people who, like the admirals of an earlier English age, frequently sail abroad to do their country honour, fighting the Queen's battles in Rome or Hollywood, but who return always, full of glory, to this their natural estate.

The histrionic art is the London art *par excellence* – the ability to dazzle, mimic, deceive or stir. Look now, as you step from the restaurant after dinner, across the blackness of St James's towards Westminster. There is the floodlit Abbey, that recondite temple of Englishness; and there is the cluster of the Whitehall pinnacles; and there, the flash of the neons pin-points Piccadilly and intermittently illuminates Nelson on his pillar in Trafalgar Square; and riding above it all, high over the clockface of Big Ben in the Palace of Westminster, high in the night sky, a still small light, all alone, burns steadily above the city. It is the light that announces the House of Commons, the mother of all parliaments, to be in session below. There's theatre for you! There's showmanship!

Or pay a visit to the High Court in the morning, and see the performers of London law present their daily matinee. No professional actors ever played such unfathomable, judicial judges as the justices of Her Majesty's Bench, wrinkled like turtles beneath the layered carapaces of their wigs, scratching away at the notes on their high seats, or intervening sometimes with polysyllabical quips. No prime-time mimic could outdo the sharpest of the London barristers, who play their briefs like instruments, hold themselves whenever possible in profile and wrap their robes around them in the ecstasy of their accomplishment, like so many Brutuses assembling for the kill. Laughter in a London court is frequent and often heartless; there is a regular audience of hags and layabouts, and so infectious is the atmosphere of theatre that often the poor accused, momentarily hoisted into stardom, wanly smiles in appreciation.

With luck one may still see Cockneys in performance. The Cockney culture survives only precariously in the city of its origins, as the taxi-drivers, marketmen and newspaper vendors move out to the suburbs, are rehoused in high-rise apartments, or find their accents, their loyalties and their humour swamped in the sameness of the age. It is many years since officialdom cleared the flower sellers from Piccadilly Circus, and even the buskers of the London tradition, the escape artists who used to entertain the theatre queues, the pavement artists outside the National Gallery, are slowly being chivvied on to oblivion. But the culture *does* survive, and remains among the most truly exhibitionist of all traditions.

Sometimes at fêtes and functions, even today, you may see the pearly kings and queens, the hereditary folk monarchs of the Cockney vegetable-barrow trade, dressed in the curious livery, decked all over in thousands of mother-of-pearl buttons, which is their traditional prerogative. Better still, any Sunday morning, in the vast outdoor market of Petticoat Lane, among the shabby mesh of streets that lies to the north of the Tower, you may watch the Cockney salesmen exuberantly in action. Theirs is an art form straight from the music hall, or vice versa, perhaps; in their timing, in their sly wit, in their instinctive rebound from a failed joke, in their exhilarating air of grasping insouciance, the Cockney hustlers stand directly in the line of the gaslight comedians.

London is a stage! The big red buses of this city, moving with such ponderous geniality through the traffic, are like well-loved character actors. The beefeaters outside the Tower, holding halberds and dressed up like playing cards, are surely extras hired for the day.

Jan Morris, *A Writer's World*

* * *

Another writer to describe London as a theatrical performance is Joseph O'Neill, in his best-selling novel, Netherland.

Cardozo, from New York out of Parsippany, New Jersey, loves it here. He has a flat in Chelsea and a flat in Worcestershire who has forgiven him his exotic name. He wears pink shirts with pink silk cufflinks. He twirls a tightly furled brolly on sunny days. His pinstripes grow bolder and bolder. I wouldn't be amazed to see a signet ring turn up on his pinkie.

I understand something of what's going on with Cardozo, because when I arrived in London in my twenties I too felt like a performing extra. There was something marvellous about the thousands of men in dark suits daily swarming down Lombard Street – I even remember a bowler hat – and something decidedly romantic about the leftover twinkle of empire that went from Threadneedle Street to the Aldwych to Piccadilly and, like tardy starlight, perpetrated a deception of time. At Eaton Place, in drizzle, I half expected to run into Richard Bellamy, MP; and when I say that in Berkeley Square I once listened for a nightingale, I'm not joking.

But nobody here holds on to such notions for very long. The rain soon becomes emblematic. The double-deckers lose their elephants' charm. London is what it is. In spite of a fresh emphasis on architecture and an influx of can-do Polish plumbers, in spite, too, of the Manhattanish importance lately attached to coffee and sushi and farmers' markets, in spite even of the disturbance of 7/7 – a frightening but not disorienting experience – Londoners remain in the business of rowing their boats gently down the stream.

Joseph O'Neill, *Netherland*

In a troubled world, many new Londoners are escapees from war and persecution. Journalist James Fergusson helps Mir, the interpreter who guided him through the dangers of Afghanistan, when, with his life under threat, Mir has to flee his homeland.

I had told Mir in Islamabad that I would help him into the country but that once he was here he would be on his own, barring emergencies. That was our deal – and as far as I was concerned the sooner he started taking responsibility for his new life in the West, the better.

Even so, I grew anxious as the date of his flight drew nearer, because the question of where he would stay in London had not been resolved in advance. In truth I had no idea what I would do if he simply turned up and threw himself on my mercy. I might have been justified in holding him to the strict terms of the deal and turning him away, but we both knew I wouldn't do that, not now. I could end up having to put him up, and it wasn't hard to envisage a night on my sofa turning into two nights, three nights, weeks. After all, he had made a corner of the Live News offices in Islamabad his home for well over a month. I certainly didn't want that happening to me. My flat was simply too small.

He had told me that he would find somewhere all right. I had asked him about it several times but he always gave me the same vague answer, that he thought he knew some Afghans who would help him, no problem. So with two days to go I was relieved to hear via the Live News office telephone that he would be staying with Hamid, a family friend from his hometown of Mazar-i-Sharif who was already a resident here. What was more, he did not want me to meet him at the airport because Hamid would be collecting him himself. His plane would not be landing until midnight, he said, and since it was far from certain how long it would take him to clear immigration I should stay away because he did not want to inconvenience me. Although this was precisely the outcome I had connived at, I couldn't help feeling a little cheated. Mir's first landfall in the West would have been worth witnessing. I imagined him shambling though the sliding doors at the end of the customs and excise chicane, wide-eyed at the size of the place, the high-tech travelators, the carpeted hush, the adverts for booze, the lights and the clean steel lines and the unequivocal Western-ness of Heathrow Airport. His expression would have been something to see. But I made myself be glad instead that he had responded as intended to my arm's-length attitude, that he seemed after all to have understood the terms and spirit of our agreement. On the day of his flight therefore I merely made sure he had my telephone number and instructed him to ring immediately once he had arrived at Hamid's, whatever the time of night.

– *No problem*, he said, a little too cheerily for my liking.

– *And you know what to do? You're a tourist* until *they ask you for your passport.* Then *you ask for political asylum.*

– *Ask for passport – then say, 'political asylum'. I understand.*

I enunciated slowly, and not just because of the crackling of the line to Islamabad, nor even out of the consideration for his imperfect English. It was mainly nervousness at all the things that could still go wrong. There could be a spot check by immigration officials at Islamabad airport, for instance. Such things had happened before, and there was a serious risk that his story would not hold up under close interrogation. I thought again of my letter of sponsorship, carefully designed to persuade the British High Commission in Islamabad to grant him a tourist visa. This document had gone through many drafts, but thinking back it still struck me as clunkingly bogus.

Dear Mirwais. I am very much looking forward to seeing you again on your short holiday to London. I can't wait to show you Big Ben, Tower Bridge and the other sights you wanted to see. Our time will be short but I'm sure we will manage to fit them all in. Also, I have many journalist friends here who are anxious to meet you. Some of them could be very helpful to you in your career as a media worker when you return to Afghanistan ...

– *You will be unobtrusive, won't you?*

– *Unobwhat?*

– *Unobtrusive. Never mind. Just act natural – try to look like everyone else, OK?*

I had already told Mir to go straight to his seat when he boarded the plane, to talk to no one, to stay put throughout the flight. Now I told him again.

– *No problem, no problem*, he sang. [...]

I wished him a good trip and told him once again to call me when he arrived. He promised he would.

– *And, James?* he said finally.

– *Yes, Mir?*

– *I am werry excited.*

– *Good*, I said. *We'll talk when you get here.*

—*Insha'allah*, he replied. [...]

Two mornings later, a Saturday, I headed east by motorbike to the address Mir had given me, a house in Mafeking Avenue, London E6. According to my street directory this was the postcode for East Ham, in the borough of Newham. I had lived in west London all my life, and my knowledge of most districts east of the financial centre was uncertain, so my journey was punctuated by frequent stops for a look at the map. Mafeking Avenue is beyond the most easterly suburbs that even many Londoners had heard of. Almost everyone knows that West Ham has a football club. Some people know of Plaistow from the song by Ian Dury. But what is there to say about East Ham, or the communities of Plashet, Wallend or Manor Park? And these are still placed with 'proper' London postcodes. Out beyond the eastern arc of the North Circular ringroad the capital struggles on for another five miles at least, through Barking and Dagenham, barely thinning through Hornchurch and Upminster to the limits of the street directory. The immensity of the city was sobering. I had not expected my involvement with Mir to be broadening my horizons again so soon – certainly not this horizon, the eastern edge of my own home town. [...]

Outside the house in Mafeking Avenue a black man was sitting in an old white BMW, revving the engine to clean out the carburettor. The spluttering noise masked the sound of my bike's engine, but Mir was on the lookout and came onto the street the moment I arrived. It was several weeks since we had waved goodbye to each other through a taxi window in Islamabad. I hadn't forgotten the look on his face, hopeful and anxious at the same time, no doubt wondering if a foreigner would really deliver on a promise to help him. I could see it was no easy thing for him to relinquish the lifeline that I represented for him, even temporarily. He beamed, and fell on me with unaffected joy, hugging me and slapping my back.

– *I am here*, he said at last, as if he still couldn't quite believe it. *I am here*.

– *Welcome to London*, I replied, smiling – because in the end his presence here was improbable. I had stepped into this person's life and with a simple letter to the British High Commission in Islamabad had turned it upside down, altering its direction forever. It was an act of the purest existentialism, as though Mir and I had colluded outrageously to upset the natural order of things.

He looked the same: a little less chubby-cheeked than I remembered, maybe, but with the same shambling, flat-footed gait that made me laugh. He was wearing the same clothes I had last seen him in, a washed-out navy blue *shalwar qamiz*, the uniform of a zillion Pakistanis. I wondered what other colours he had, but quickly veered away from the thought and asked him how the trip had gone.

– *Hohh*, he said, his dark eyes wide with unironic amazement.

– *Go on – what was it like?*

– *It was … strange to start. The plane is werry big. And fast.*

He made a jet taking off with the flat of his hand and, leaning back, stared straight ahead in imitation of the unexpected G-force as he accelerated down the runway at Islamabad. I had forgotten that his previous flying experience was limited to military helicopters.

– *But after, it was nice*, he added equably. *Specially the food. And the women: hohh.*

I had insisted that Mir fly British Airways, reckoning on balance that a BA aircrew would be more sympathetic as well as better informed about the immigration rules in the event of some disaster en route. But I hadn't told him about the air hostesses he would meet on board, their dyed hair uncovered, their legs clearly on view beneath their uniforms. They may look unexceptional to Westerners, but to an untravelled Muslim they must have constituted a preview of paradise.

James Fergusson, *Kandahar Cockney*

* * *

In the post-war wave of immigration from the West Indies, new arrivals helped each other to survive the challenges of a new and sometimes hostile city – though Sam Selvon's Moses, from The Lonely Londoners, *wouldn't want to live anywhere else.*

One grim winter evening, when it had a kind of unrealness about London, with a fog sleeping restlessly over the city and the lights showing in the blue as if is not London at all but some strange place on another planet, Moses Aloetta hop on a number 46 bus at the corner of Chepstow Road and Westbourne Grove to go to Waterloo to meet a fellar who was coming from Trinidad on the boat-train.

When Moses sit down and pay his fare he take out a white handkerchief and blow his nose. The handkerchief turn black and Moses watch it and curse the fog. He wasn't in a good mood and the fog wasn't doing anything to help the situation. He had to get up from a nice warm bed and dress and come out in this nasty weather to go and meet a fellar that he didn't even know. That was the hurtful part of it – is not as if this fellar is his brother or cousin or even friend; he don't know the man from Adam. But he get a letter from a friend in Trinidad who say this fellar coming by the *SS Hildebrand*, and if he could please meet him at the station in London, and help him until he get settled. The fellar name Henry Oliver, but the friend tell Moses not to worry that he describe Moses to Henry, and all he have to do is to be in the station when the boat-train pull in and this fellar Henry would find him. So for old time sake Moses find himself on the bus going to Waterloo, vex with himself that his heart so soft that he always doing something for somebody and nobody ever doing anything for him.

Because it look to Moses that he hardly have time to settle in the old Brit'n before all sorts of fellars start coming straight to him room in the Water when they land up in London from the West Indies, saying that so and so tell them that Moses is a good fellar to contact, that he would help them get place to stay and work to do.

'Jesus Christ,' Moses tell Harris, a friend he have, 'I never see thing so. I don't know these people at all, yet they coming to me as if I is some liaison officer, and I catching my arse as it is, how I could help them out?'[...]

One day a set of fellars come.

'Who tell you my name and address?' Moses ask them.

'Oh we get it from a fellar name Jackson who was up here last year.'

'Jackson is a bitch,' Moses say, 'he know that I seeing hell myself.'

'We have money,' the fellars say, 'we only want you to help we to get a place to stay and tell we how to get work.'

'That harder than money,' Moses grunt, 'I don't know why the hell you come to me.' But all the same he went out with them, because he used to remember how desperate he was when he was in London for the first time and he didn't know anybody or anything.

Moses send the boys to different addresses. 'Too much spades in the Water now,' he tell them. 'Try down by Clapham. You don't know how to get there? They will tell you in the tube station. Also, three of you could go to King's Cross station and ask for a fellar name Samson who working in the luggage department. He will help you out.'

And so like a welfare officer Moses scattering the boys around London, for he don't want no concentrated area in the Water – as it is, things bad enough already. And one or two that he take a fancy to, he take them around by houses he know it would be all right to go to, for at this stage Moses know which part they will slam door in your face and which part they will take in spades.

And is the same soft heart that have him now on the bus going to Waterloo to meet a fellar name Henry Oliver. He don't know how he always getting in position like this, helping people out. He sigh; the damn bus crawling in the fog, and the evening so melancholy that he wish he was back in bed.

When he get to Waterloo he hop off and went in the station, and right away in that big station he had a feeling of homesickness that he never felt in the nine-ten years he in this country. For the old Waterloo is a place of arrival and departure, is a place where you see people crying goodbye and kissing welcome, and he hardly have time to sit down on a bench before this feeling of nostalgia hit him and he was surprise. It have some fellars who in Brit'n long, and yet they can't get away from the habit of going Waterloo whenever a boat-train coming in with passengers from the West Indies. They like to see the familiar faces, they like to watch their countrymen coming off the train, and sometimes they might spot somebody they know: 'Aye Watson! What the hell you

doing in Brit'n boy? Why you didn't write me you was coming?'
And they would start big oldtalk with the travellers, finding out
what happening in Trinidad, in Grenada, in Barbados, in Jamaica
and Antigua, what is the latest calypso number, is anybody dead,
and so on, and even asking strangers questions they can't answer,
like if they know Tanty Simmons who living Labasse in Port of
Spain, or a fellar name Harrison working in the Red House.

But Moses, he never in this sort of slackness: the thought
never occur to him to go to Waterloo just to see who coming up
from the West Indies. Still, the station is that sort of place where
you have a soft feeling. It was here that Moses did land when
he come to London, and he have no doubt that when time did
come, if it ever come, it would be here he would say goodbye to
the big city. Perhaps he was thinking is time to go back to the
tropics, that's why he feeling sort of lonely and miserable. […]

The changing of the seasons, the cold slicing winds, the
falling leaves, sunlight on green grass, snow on the land,
London particular. Oh what it is and where it is and why it is,
no one knows, but to have said: 'I walked on Waterloo Bridge,'
'I rendezvoused at Charing Cross,' 'Piccadilly Circus is my
playground,' to say these things, to have lived these things, to
have lived in the great city of London, centre of the world. To
one day lean against the wind walking up the Bayswater Road
(destination unknown), to see the leaves swirl and dance and
spin on the pavement (sight unseeing), to write a casual letter
home beginning: 'Last night, in Trafalgar Square … '

What it is that a city have, that any place in the world have,
that you get so much to like it you wouldn't leave it for anywhere
else? What it is that would keep men although by and large,
in truth and in fact, they catching their royal to make a living,
staying in a cramp-up room where you have to do everything
– sleep, eat, dress, wash, cook, live. Why it is, that although
they grumble about it all the time, curse the people, curse the
government, say all kind of thing about this and that, why it is,

that in the end, everyone cagey about saying outright that if the chance come they will go back to them green islands in the sun?

In the grimness of the winter, with your hand plying space like a blind man's stick in the yellow fog, with ice on the ground and a coldness defying all effort to keep warm, the boys coming and going, working, eating, sleeping, going about the vast metropolis like veteran Londoners.[...]

One night of any night, liming on the Embankment near to Chelsea, he stand up on the bank of the river, watching the lights of the buildings reflected in the water, thinking what he must do, if he should save up money and go back home, if he should try to make it by next year before changing his mind again.

The old Moses, standing on the bank of the Thames. Sometimes he think he see some sort of profound realisation in his life, as if all that happen to him was experience that make him a better man, as if now he could draw apart from any hustling and just sit down and watch other people fight to live. Under the kiff-kiff laughter, behind the ballad and the episode, the what-happening, the summer-is-hearts, he could see a great aimlessness, a great restless, swaying movement that leaving you standing in the same spot. As if a forlorn shadow of doom fall on all the spades of the country. As if he could see the black faces bobbing up and down in the millions of white, strained faces, everybody hustling along the Strand, the spades jostling in the crowd, bewildered, hopeless. As if, on the surface, things don't look so bad, but when you go down a little, you bounce up a kind of misery and pathos and a frightening – what? He don't know the right word, but he have the right feeling in his heart. As if the boys laughing, but they only laughing because they fraid to cry, they only laughing because to think so much about everything would be a big calamity – like how he here now, the thoughts so heavy he unable to move his body.

Still, it had a greatness and a vastness in the way he was feeling tonight, like it was something solid after feeling everything else give way, and though he ain't getting no happiness out of the cogitations he still pondering, for is the first time that he ever find himself thinking like that.

Daniel was telling him how over in France all kinds of fellars writing books what turning out to be best-sellers. Taxi-driver, porter, road-sweeper – it didn't matter. One day you sweating in the factory and the next day all the newspapers have your name and photo, saying how you are a new literary giant.

He watch a tugboat on the Thames, wondering if he could ever write a book like that, what everybody would buy.

Sam Selvon, *The Lonely Londoners*

* * *

London has not only been a city of refuge for the poor and anonymous: it has also had its share of 'celebrity refugees'.

Karl Marx's final refuge was the largest and wealthiest metropolis in the world. London had been the first city to reach a population of 1,000,000, a great wen that continued to swell without ever quite bursting. When the journalist Henry Mayhew went up in a hot-air balloon in hope of comprehending its entirety, he could not tell 'where the monster city began or ended, for the buildings stretched not only to the horizon either side, but far away into the distance … where the town seemed to blend into the sky'. Census figures show that 300,000 newcomers settled in the capital between 1841 and 1851 – including hundred of refugees who, like Marx, were lured by its reputation as a sanctuary for political outcasts.

But this 'super-city de luxe' was also the dark, dank monster that looms up from the opening paragraphs of *Bleak House*, written three years after Marx's arrival.

Francis Wheen, *Karl Marx*

* * *

Home-grown celebrities included, of course, Princess Diana. Richard Eyre's diary records Londoners' reaction to her untimely death – an outpouring of grief so

*'Mediterranean' that people wondered what had happened
to our reputation for being cool and undemonstrative.*

8th September I tried to get to Peter Eyre's flat last night on the
Embankment but couldn't get down Kensington High Street. Huge
crowds around Kensington Palace *and* round Harrods, which has
become an object of veneration. This is an outpouring of religious
feeling, but the old religion has been replaced by the new – it's
no less an endorsement of the monarchy, just a different sort. It's
revolt, or evolution – not revolution. John Mortimer was asked to
do a piece on Diana for the *Mail*. He went to Kensington Palace
and approached a mourner. 'Go away,' said the mourner, 'I don't
want to talk to the paparazzi.' Will Boyd thinks that the hysteria is
due to the myth of the fallen goddess – i.e. the goddess becoming
mortal, dying in the under(pass)world, but I think it's religious
passion: monarchy has *always* been the English religion, and the
faith has been in crisis recently. New belief is reaffirmed in the New
Religion, a better (and dead) Queen. I drove past Kensington and
Buckingham Palaces in the morning, early. Crowds of mourners
streaming towards the shrines – an Irish tricolour with the legend:
'WHEN IRISH EYES ARE CRYING'; a huge banner:
'DIANA OF LOVE'; a shield with the inscription 'DIANA,
FAIRY GODMOTHER OF THE NEEDY COLOMBIANS
IN MOURNING'.

Richard Eyre, National Service

❊ ❊ ❊

*London wouldn't function were it not for the energy
and dedication of its ordinary workers – people like
Ali, not living in the best of accommodation but doing
a good job in a large Bloomsbury bookshop.*

In the University area was an ornate corner building occupied by
a bookshop. For many years, I was curious about what it was
like inside. Then one evening, I got off halfway through Gower
Street on my bus journey home from work and went in.

163

The bookshop had a broad wooden staircase leading upwards to the first floor and downwards to the basement. The alcoves on the staircase landings featured busts of Hippocrates and Socrates. The staircase became very narrow at the upper floors. The bookshop was very busy. It was the beginning of the academic year, when commercial banks gave free book vouchers to freshers as a reward for opening an account with them. Some of the students looked shocked by the prices of their purchases. Evidently I was visiting the bookshop at the wrong time of year as it was too crowded for me to roam around, so I decided to leave without browsing.

I returned to the bookshop a few weeks later. The students were having their mid-term break, and the bookshop was very quiet. Shop assistants were busy filling the shelves with replacements for the books they had sold in the last couple of weeks. The new books arrived in plastic storage boxes from their warehouse. Three or four of these boxes were stacked up on wheels and then dragged through a corridor by a porter to different departments of the shop. A member of staff called Ali was being paged on the shop's public address system. I discovered second-hand and remainders sections on one of the floors and was browsing in the second-hand section when the porter arrived with new stock for the remainders section in the adjacent room. He had seen me examining the spine of a book in a set of volumes that interested me. The porter told me that there were new copies in the plastic boxes he was dragging, going on sale as remainders. He opened one of the boxes and picked up a set of books to show me. It was an American import. The price of the new set was one-third that of the second-hand set. In the meantime, the PA system announced the name 'Ali' again. The porter excused himself as he had to go to the office on the top floor. I was glad that he had saved me money by arriving there with the new books. After this, I visited the shop every now and again. […]

After frequenting the shop for many months, I bumped into Ali in Brunswick Square. He was surprised to see me drifting from the bookshop in another direction. Ali told me that he lived in the area in one of the flats above Brunswick Shopping Centre. I was always disorientated to see this concrete precinct amidst the brickwork of Bloomsbury. It was certainly a far cry from the Brunswick Square of E.M. Foster and John Maynard Keynes. There were many cantilevered flats built above the shopping centre. I was not sure whether the balconies of these flats, enclosed in glass and iron, were used as conservatories or storerooms by the residents. Many of the flats belonged to the council, but some of them were privately owned. The big shopping centre listed businesses which had disappeared long ago. In fact, I saw only a few shops open for trading. The rest of them were empty, displaying the names of previous owners on their windows. Among the shops that were still trading in this desolate shopping complex was a big charity shop where a few elderly residents were browsing through old clothes. Out of curiosity, I walked into another shop under the cantilevered flats that was open for business. It was a second-hand bookshop. The bookseller was working on a computer behind a big untidy counter. I complied with a notice at the door, asking customers to leave their bags at the counter. […]

The shopping centre included a cinema that showed art-house films. I assumed that the films were meant for those who visited Bloomsbury during the day, not those who lived in the flats above the cinema. The council tenants came from diverse backgrounds. I saw a few elderly Bengali men carrying shopping bags from a supermarket in the shopping centre. None of the shoppers looked as if they would have enjoyed art-house films. I left the Brunswick Centre from its eastern side, away from the entrance of the cinema. The concrete structure looked less painful from this side.

Iqbal Ahmed, *Sorrows of the Moon*

❋ ❋ ❋

Beer-swilling blokes in a well-known City pub fancy their chances with a young Chinese girl who's

unwittingly strayed into their lair: a recognisable kind
of Londoner? But maybe they're not so bad after all.

pub *n* building with a bar licensed to sell alcoholic drinks

Park my bicycle outside from Dirty Dick's, nearby Liverpool Street Station. Dirty Dick? That normal name for English pub? Anyway, it is first time I came into *building with a bar licensed to sell alcoholic drinks*. I hope you will take me into pub, but you went away somewhere unknown instead.

I sit in pub alone, trying to feel involving in the conversation. It seem place of middle-aged-mans culture. I smell a kind of dying, although it still struggling. While I sitting here, many singles, desperately mans coming up saying, 'Hello darling'. But I not your darling. Where your darling? 7 o'clock in the evening, your darling must be cooking baked bean in orange sauce for you at home ... Why not just go home spending time with your darling?

But mans here just keep buying pint of beer one after another. Some is drinking huge pint Lager, is like pee. Other buying glass of very dark liquid, looks like Chinese medicine. They watching football and shout together, without having food. In corner some tables with foods. Make me feel very hungry. See the food is biggest reason I am deciding go to pub. But everyone pretending food not there. Like is invisible or just for the good show. I take out my *Concise Chinese-English Dictionary*, start to study. I trying not thinking of the food too much.

In front of my table, five big mans all smoking cigarettes; this is the *fog* of London. After some times, mans come to my lonely table and ask something.

The way I am talking in English make everybody laugh. They must like me.

A young man buy me beer. He is the only good looking one.

I say: 'I feel so delightful drinking with you. Your face and words are very *noble*.'

The man surprised and happy. He stops his drinking.

'Noble, eh?'

'Yes,' I say, 'because when you start talk then you look very proud. I like the confidence. I don't have.'

The man holding his big pint listens careful but not sure about what I mean.

A while, he says: 'Love, you only think my words are noble because I can speak English properly' – oh *properly*, that word again! – 'but it *is* my mother tongue, you know. It's not that hard. But anyway, thank you for the compliment.'

'You deserving it.' I answer seriously.

But the man calls me 'Love'! Love is cheap object in London.

My eyes looking towards delicious feast on side table. Everything ready waiting but no action.

I think the man gets hint from me, so he introduces me to English food system in pub calling *Buffet*, is meaning same word for 'self service'.

'Why two words for same food system?' I ask him.

He laughs: 'Because one is the English word and one is the French word. The French word is more *noble*.'

All old mans laughing.

Buffet. Now I remember this noble word.

There are some white sticky stuffs on the plate. It looks like Tofu, but smells bad.

'What is this?' I ask bar man.

'That is goat's cheese, darling. Would you like to try some?'

In China we not have cheese. We not like drinking milk, until last ten years maybe. I feel very surprise. I thought goat is too skinny make cheese.

'No. Thanks. What that? That Blue stuff?'

'It's another cheese. Stilton.'

'Another stinking cheese with different names?' So many different cheeses! Like our Tofu system!

'Is this made by cow?' I ask.

'That's right, love,' the barman laughs loudly. 'Handmade by Communist cows.'

'What?' I am confused.

'Sorry to tease you, sweetheart. What you're trying to ask is "Is it made *from* cow's milk?" English is a bloody nightmare, isn't it?'

Xiaolu Guo, *A Concise Chinese-English Dictionary for Lovers*

✷ ✷ ✷

And some slightly different City men (but continuing the 'cheese' theme) – this time in a famous old pub on Fleet Street.

The Old Cheshire Cheese is on Fleet Street, halfway from the High Court to Ludgate Hill. It is possible that Shakespeare frequented the old pub (it was rebuilt in 1667, following the setback of the previous year), a possibility somewhat oversold on the sign outside. It was, however, Dr Johnson's local, and Dickens knew its dark, creaking, wooden interior and cramped stairs. More recently, from the end of the nineteenth century and for most of the twentieth – until they decamped to less dear offices where the docks used to be – it was usually full of journalists. (So full that when Polly the pub parrot died in 1926 obituaries appeared in over two hundred publications worldwide.) Now the only newsmen are from Reuters, over the road; the others have been supplanted by investment bankers from Goldman Sachs, and lawyers from the Middle Temple, and tourists – lots of tourists – and salesmen.

Entering the narrow brick passageway where the pub's entrance is – under a huge old lantern with 'Ye Olde Cheshire Cheese' in Gothic letters on its milky glass – Paul remembers, with some nostalgia, how he and Eddy Jaw used to work together in offices nearby, the offices of Northwood Publishing, and themselves spend long afternoons in the Chesh. That was some years ago, and it came to a sudden end when the contract they were working on was withdrawn. Which was a shame, because things had been very prosperous – 'fucking dial-a-deal' in the argot of the salesmen – and pushing open the pub's broad door, Paul smells again, in the distinctive woody scent of the interior – similar to that of a Wren church – the spectacular success that the withdrawal of the contract had interrupted.

He remembers where they used to sit, in the square, skylit room – himself, Eddy, the Pig, Murray and the others. This part of the pub, he is disappointed to see, has been divided into smaller spaces, now full of people, so he makes his way to where the wooden stairs go down, and steadying himself with a hand on the low ceiling, descends to the vaulted rooms below – the former cellars – and down yet more stairs, stone this time, into the loud, high-ceilinged basement bar. It is half past five and every part of the pub is packed. Eddy is not there, so Paul goes back upstairs to his favourite place, the snug on the other side of the panelled entrance hall from the Chop Room restaurant (which does not seem to have changed much since the late eighteenth century, except that the waiting staff are now mostly Antipodean), where there is a fireplace with orange coals in a black grate, and a muddy painting of a man wearing a wig, and a window of thick, imperfect glass – he used to while away whole afternoons under that window – and wealthy American bankers talking shop. He decides that he should settle somewhere, or he and Eddy will spend the whole evening wandering through the pub, saying 'Sorry, excuse me, sorry', without ever seeing each other, so he goes back downstairs to a sort of mezzanine between the two subterranean levels, where a few small tables are squeezed into the painted brick alcoves formed by the ceiling vaults. One of these tables is vacant, and there he sips his pint of Ayingerbrau, lights a cigarette, and looks over the laminated menu, as if it were something utterly mysterious.

David Szalay, *London and the South-East*

* * *

> *In a piece he is writing for the New York press, the protagonist of Justin Cartwright's novel,* Look At It This Way, *paints a rather too honest picture of contemporary, fast-food-fed Londoners, as well as those obsessed with their 'body image'.*

The sky is the colour of a mullet's skin, grey with flecks of minerals. Outside my windows, the park is subdued. It's been trying to rain all day, as they say around here.

I am faxing a message to New York:

Bums. Arses. Fannies. Tushies. Sit-upons. Derrières. Khyber Passes. Botties.

I believe you can chart a nation's social history by the shape of the nation's bottom. In Victorian times there was a theory that the criminal classes could easily be identified by the science of phrenology. Their eyes were set too close together; their occipital lobes were constricted; their rational impulses were squeezed out by poor development of the skull. It was scientific. In this spirit I launch my enquiry into the disappearance of the small and wiry Londoner. The jockey-shaped Cockney, he of the fast fingers and the pipe-cleaner limbs, is an endangered species. Bottoms, and breasts (bristols, boobs, knockers, etc.) are growing unchecked. Londoners are eating McDonald's, Burger King and Kentucky Fried Chicken. They live entirely on these protein-packed foods with the consequence that they are becoming bulky. The little pickpockets, purse snatchers, chimney sweeps, and sneak thieves have vanished in one generation. Like much of London, they will only be a memory soon.

Boys tower over their traditionally formed parents and grandparents. They have muscles and bellies where their parents were held together with bits of string. And the girls! They are ballooning into fantastic shapes. The fattest of them have huge pear-shaped butts, which they none the less compress into stone-washed jeans or short black skirts. Even the least stout have ducks' bottoms waggling beneath them as their legs struggle to carry the additional weight. They seldom run, but when they do the whole construction totters dangerously. And they are always eating. If they are not actually sitting to eat, they are snacking on bags of cheese-and-onion-flavoured potato chips, or 'crisps' as they call them. Even children on the way to school carry these little bags of poison.

In the more expensive parts of town, women are working their bodies. In these areas they eat sensibly – fish, salad, pasta with fresh tomato sauce – and they have their hair done frequently. Hairdressers in high-rent Chelsea specialize in the glossy look. The women with the tight, under-control bottoms also have gleaming, under-control hair. In the other, and more numerous, neighbourhoods – dreadful places like Peckham, Kilburn and Holloway – perhaps despairing of their unmanageable bottoms, women are tormenting their hair. They want to look (like Annie Lennox of the Eurythmics) interesting and independent. But they forget *la loi du canard*: short hair emphasizes the burgeoning backside. No matter: they shave the area above their ears, they tickle the front up into little spikes, they wear crew cuts, brush cuts and table cuts. Out in the suburbs, the encircling darkness, they still tease their hair into ringlets so that it flaps all over their heads like a poodle's on retrieval duty.

The City is changing too. The streets are a bedlam of building works and excavation. 'Cladding' is all the rage. Brutal sixties office blocks of leprous concrete with blue panels of a plastic compound called 'quartzite', once fashionable, are being 're-clad'. This requires a glamorous new glass skin and a pediment on top of the building to hide the lift shaft and services. On ground level the building must now 'interact' with the passers-by. The theory of noted London architect, Richard Rogers, that essential services should not be denied but exhibited – like breast-feeding in public – finds no favour with the corporate mind. The corporate person is still in the ascendancy. He is in league with the real world; he uses the expensive seats on airplanes; he eats at restaurants which set a lot of store by 'presentation'. This presentation involves fancy work with ingredients, forced marriages between fruit and flesh, the pressing into service of obscure berries and arson with expensive liqueurs.

Other, older buildings are becoming penthouses, lofts, work-spaces, drawing stations. The emphasis here is on brightly coloured beams and exposed brickwork. (I have a former hay-loft myself.) Wonder of wonders: after all these years of neglect it has been discovered that London has thousands of acres of derelict warehouses, chapels, smokehouses, rope factories, chandlers, pulley makers and grain stores. Professional people are moving into these spaces – 'space' is a big word – previously occupied by barometer makers, brewers, unitarians, sea captains, fishmongers, watchmakers, shipbuilders, lascars, rice merchants, spice traders ('the smell of cinnamon pervades the place'), coopers and a myriad more, all forgotten. The river is making a comeback. Colourful galleries (aka *'galleria'*), harbours, marinas and wharves are appearing everywhere. Little waterbuses skim up and dow n the Thames from Docklands to Chelsea. There are regattas of ancient barges and steam vessels. Old things are in, but they must be fully restored. 'Restoration' is a big word too. It is surprising, therefore, that the mania for restoring the body has not taken more of a hold. The body is enjoying the benefit of affluence all too clearly.

Justin Cartwright, Look At It This Way

London Transport

First, the bad news: for Alice Thomas Ellis there's not much to choose between the various hells of bus, cab, tube or your own car when it comes to getting about the capital – especially in the rain.

I may have remarked before that I seldom venture out of Camden Town. I now realise that this is because it is hardly possible to venture out of Camden Town. One could take the tube to the wider world, I suppose, but I'm not going to. Beryl had to go on the Northern Line the other morning because she couldn't get a cab and she said it was *hell*. One day, again due to the absence of cabs, she had to come home on a Hoppa and she didn't like that either. There are too many other people going back and forth by these means. Some of them are robbers and some are mad, and they're all in too great a hurry to mind whether they walk on your feet or push you off the platform or under the bus.

Last week I was invited to lunch at the Gay Hussar, not a million miles away from here. That'll make a pleasant change, I thought, accepting with alacrity. While we're at it, I said to myself, we may as well deliver some books to a venue in Central London where they were required. I informed Janet of this plan and said she could drive me, thus saving cab fares. It was pissing down with rain and she said dubiously that the roads would be congested but if we set off in good time we should make it eventually. Some hours later we realised that I might, with my luck, arrive at the Gay Hussar in time for tea, or possibly just hit the cocktail hour. Then as the skies grew ever darker and we sat amidst the stationary cars, lorries and buses we decided to sod the whole thing and go home. I had a dryish cheese roll for a late lunch instead of whatever they were having at the Gay Hussar and after that I watched the end of *Gaslight* on telly, occasionally glancing out of the window at the increasing gale bending what remains of the trees in the neighbours' gardens and reflecting that it was perhaps just as well some of these trees had fallen over and squashed some of the parked cars because one or two more vehicles on the roads would have brought the metropolis to a total standstill.

When we were stuck just outside Trafalgar Square Janet whiled away the time by describing some of the landmarks. I've never liked London so I've never learned much about it. I've been to Trafalgar Square before and to Buckingham Palace, and I've looked at the Houses of Parliament and I knew Downing Street was out there somewhere – and Scotland Yard – but I couldn't have taken you to any of these famous sites or told you where they were in relation to each other. I still couldn't, but I am now at least aware that the top of Big Ben is visible from wherever we were – the end of the Strand I think. There was a church in the middle of the road. Janet says it's one of Wren's, but even she isn't absolutely certain.

This extraordinary ignorance of the city one lives in is surely unusual. Parisians can direct the stranger to the *Deux Magots* with no trouble at all. Florentines know their Florence and when I lived in Liverpool I could have quartered the place blindfold. London is perhaps too big, and poorly signposted. I used to know Chelsea quite well but I recently got off the 31 bus on to which I had climbed in a fit of bravado, found myself at the World's End and walked round in a huge circle before arriving at my intended destination – about two minutes' walk from the World's End if one had only been concentrating and the street signs had been clearer. Some of this lack of interest in one's surroundings is due to the hopeless feeling that faceless and ruthless powers are in control – local councils for the most part – ripping up the paving stones at random, closing down the little shops and authorising the erection of nightmarish mega-stores. There was a criminal lunatic around at one time who proposed to drive a motorway smack through the Old Piano Factory, but happily he ran out of funds. I seem to remember he had a beard, and this intended motorway was his most passionately favourite thing in life. The disappearance of the few landmarks one does recognise under building sites, tower blocks and roads makes it even more difficult to find one's way home. I went into a pub by one door the other evening, came out by a different one and thought I'd fallen into something by Kafka. The ABC building has disappeared, Camden Road is unrecognisable and I could have been in Outer Mongolia for all I knew. Plotting a course by the stars and guided by the smell of rotting vegetable matter I made my way to the familiar market and so to bed. They intend to abolish the street market, and if they do I'll be utterly lost.

Janet suggests putting curtains in the car and installing a coffee machine and some bookshelves since she spends so much time just sitting in it. Then it won't matter if we get lost. Our address will be Stationary Vehicle somewhere in the Strand on the way to the Gay Hussar.

Alice Thomas Ellis, *Home Life: Book Three*

❋ ❋ ❋

On the other hand, Mrs Hawkins, in Muriel Spark's delightful novel A Far Cry from Kensington, *seems quite happy to spend her days on the top of a double-decker bus.*

I spent my days taking long rides on the top of buses all over London, to the furthest outskirts and termini. Stanmore, Edgware, Bushey, Chingford, Romford, Harrow, Wanstead, Dagenham, Barking. There were few streets intact although the war had been over ten years. Victorian houses, shops, churches, were separated by large areas of bomb-gap. The rubble had been cleared away, but strange grasses and wild herbs had sprung up where the war-demolished houses had been. While it was still light I rode past the docks and the railway sidings, and the dark pubs not yet open, until it was time to go home again. London was still sooty from coal fires in those days. Wembley, Hackney, Islington, Southall, Acton, Ealing. And sometimes I walked round the City, soon to be reconstructed with eloquent, rich high-rises. Sometimes I went to Richmond, to Greenwich, to Dulwich, Hampton and Kew where I walked in the vast lonely parks on dry days and was solicited at times by men in raincoats whom I thoroughly scared off. Surbiton, Ewell, Croydon and as far as Orpington. So I spent my days after days on the top of the buses staring out of the window and watching with discreet eyes my fellow passengers, most of them shabby, and, if they were not alone, listening with half an ear to their talk, mostly about their families and friends, their shopping and their jobs; and not once in all those long rides did I hear a snatch of conversation about a general topic.

At time I felt faces looming over me. The conductor, the passengers as they passed to get on or off, shrill schoolchildren and burly mothers who had been unable to find a seat on the lower deck. I felt like Lucy Snowe in *Villette*, who walked, solitary in Brussels on a summer night, among the festival crowds; the faces pressing round her, of people made hilarious by the occasion, were made even more grotesque by her state of hallucination induced by laudanum.

There was no such hectic celebration in sober London but I experienced a throb and a choking of hysteria in the London voices around me and in the bland and pasty, the long and dour, the pretty and painted faces of the people. Barnet, Loughton, Hendon, Northolt, Willesden, Camberwell, Plumstead, Kingston, Bromley. I had lunches in noisy pubs, leaving half on my plate, to the consternation of many barmaids whose eyes seemed to me too wild, their lips too red to be real. I had tea and half a bun in tea-shops where no waitress cared what I didn't eat.

Muriel Spark, *A Far Cry from Kensington*

* * *

But whatever has happened to the famous British bus queue? Though recording Thatcherite Britain, Patrick Wright's observations are just as true today.

For as long as I can remember, conservatively inclined commentators have been lamenting the decline of the London bus queue. Indeed, it is said that this venerable British institution doesn't really exist any more: its ordered and generally accepted civilities having been replaced by a brutish stampede in which the pushiest get through first, while the frail and well mannered are left standing, if they are lucky, in the gutter.

For these prophets of doom, the line at the London bus stop symbolizes the very spine of the nation, and the ominous blurring that can be seen at its edges is a sign of fatal degeneration. In reality, however, the London bus queue isn't always so bad. Things have certainly reached a sorry state in the West End, especially in the summer when no trick is too low for natives forced to dodge through swarms of back-packed visitors. Down on the corner of Tottenham Court Road and Oxford Street, the bus queue is a sordid scrum, but take a ride from there to a residential part of the inner city and the situation improves considerably.

Dalston Junction is not on any tourist's itinerary, and the crowd that gathers at the bus stop here is as mixed as could be found anywhere in the country. Its members come from all four corners of the earth, and they certainly don't look like a group of people who have been raised to the same set of rules.

The queue here exists in a state of constant disintegration. A few sticklers may stand resolutely in line at the point where the sign urges them to 'Form Queue This Side', but the overall impression is of people milling about: pacing up and down, shuffling from one foot to the other, wandering out into the road to stare down it in impatient anticipation, or leaning back against the wall ready to close in when a bus finally comes into view. Some who gather at this bus stop aren't going anywhere at all. There's one disorientated woman who turns up sporadically and hangs about for hours, muttering to herself as the buses come and go. While others set off on their journeys, she treats the queue as a refuge, moving into it as if it were an asylum, a cardboard box, or the latest cut-rate experiment in community care.

The crowd may be densely packed, but it's also full of distance, and not just of the artificially created Sony Walkman variety. A fair amount of inter-racial examination goes on over distances far wider than the proximities of the street would suggest. People stand a few inches apart, and check each other out over the great chasms that centuries have placed between them. Tiny misrecognitions can suddenly flare.

Sometimes a speaker steps out to address the queue. The last one I heard was vehemently egalitarian and anti-Thatcherite, but beyond this it was hard to place him more precisely even on Dalston Lane's richly differentiated political spectrum. His sign read 'The government knows how the brain works. And it proves we all have equal intelligence. Mrs Thatcher doesn't want anyone to know.' He stood there calling out 'Enough is enough', and occasionally venturing out into clipped and speedily recited elaborations: 'Languages are easy – I could teach you German in one minute' or 'This is the wealthiest planet in the universe. We should all be living like Kings.'

Conversations break out too. A wide range of topics is available to the seasoned bus-stop philosopher, most of which can be gathered under the single heading of 'Helpless Speculation'. Whatever your origins or standing in the wider world, to be waiting at a bus stop at Dalston Junction is to have joined the ranks of the underdog, and that is enough for a tentative opening. The initial exchange is likely to concern the invariably inadequate doings of 'they' who run the bus services so badly: stacking up the buses so that none come for half an hour and then five rush through all at once, or chopping the bus route into smaller and smaller sections so that nobody can be sure that the bus, when it finally does arrive, will take them more than half-way to their destination.

Some quite unique flights of fancy become possible once this theme is properly established: 'they' become the council, the government, the gentrifiers, the social workers, the police, or anybody else who gets you down, and temporary agreements of the most unlikely kind are struck. I've heard an affluent City type find common ground with a destitute pensioner on the subject of Margaret Thatcher's unpatriotic meanness. I've heard an amicable conversation about immigration between a West Indian for whom 'they' were the immigration authorities and a sullen white native who started out with something very different in mind.

People swap stories about the time when the first deregulated buses showed up, bringing a further touch of visual anarchy to the increasingly chaotic London street scene. The cream-and-purple vehicles of 'Kentish Buses' came thick and fast on the first day; they still reeked of plastic glue and the drivers didn't always know where they were going. There are hilarious stories about passengers guiding them along the route, or covertly hijacking them and leading them through dismal housing estates, right up to their own front door.

When the bus finally arrives, everything changes. Conversations break off as people prepare to board through a whole series of time-sanctioned manoeuvres. Knowing how the odds are stacked against them, elderly ladies turn themselves into missiles: heads down, elbows out, tongues sharpened to a lacerating point. Just as classic is the spiv's route to the top. This one is for the boys and young men, and it surely descends from the days of old rear-entry tram: step smartly round the side, let a few people off, and the push in, your passage eased by the unstated excuse that you're only going upstairs for a smoke.

There is a white supremacist way of barging in and another associated with black defiance. There are liberal and feminist manoeuvres, too. I recently saw a young woman muscling in as brazenly as anyone and then, when she had made it to the front, pausing with a magnanimous display of sisterhood to allow two or three of the thirty or so people she had displaced into the bus before her. Finally, there is the slow advance of the disgruntled rump: the elderly and infirm, the mild-mannered, people who just don't feel up to it that day. They get to watch these deft performances from close up. They also board the bus last.

Nobody could mistake what happens when the bus arrives at Dalston Junction for an entirely orderly queue. But neither is it just the advance of a mob following the law of the jungle. Each time a bus pulls up the crowd negotiates a messy but still intricately structured settlement between the ideal of the orderly queue and the chaotic stampede. This result is far from perfect. It may occasionally trigger a fierce trading of insults, racist outburst, and even an exchange of blows. But it is still governed by an etiquette that dictates how far the disintegration can be allowed to go.

The biggest threat to the inner-London bus queue doesn't come from cultural degeneration at all. Instead, it's known as OPO – the abbreviation by which the people at London Regional Transport like to refer to their new One-Person Operated buses. The great thing about the old Route Master buses is that they allow a certain latitude. Some of the conductors may behave like tin-pot dictators and try to impose discipline, but the majority know that they are on the rear platform to defuse conflicts, pick up stragglers, and even to entertain. Compared with this, OPO has a brutalizing effect: it scorns the artful compromises of the traditional London bus queue, insisting instead upon a sullen and slow moving line in which latent conflicts are far more likely to explode.

Patrick Wright, *A Journey Through Ruins*

* * *

But let's go for a ride on the top of the number 16 bus
with brilliant London blogger 'Diamond Geezer' – who
also notes the collapse of the traditional British queue.

Our capital's first coherent system of bus route numbering was
introduced on Monday 2nd November 1908. Only one London
bus still plies the same route it did 100 years ago, and that's the
16. Its route has been stretched and tweaked and contracted
over the years, but the current journey from central London
to the suburbs is identical (one-way-systems excepted) to the
Edwardian omnibus original. I've been for a centenary ride on
its modern double decker equivalent, just to see if anything else
about the journey is still the same. Destination Cricklewood.

Nobody queues for buses any more. Not in the street outside
Victoria anyway. The 16's not allowed in the shiny bus station,
there's no room, so each service kicks off in gridlocked Wilton
Road beneath a picture of a musical witch. Passengers attempt
to guess precisely where the driver will stop, then charge willy
nilly for the door in an attempt to grab the least worst seat
for the journey ahead. I wanted upper deck front left – alas
no longer an open-topped pleasure, but at least now glassed
in to protect me from passing branches. And off through the
one-way streets of Belgravia, peering down through autumnal
leaves into the Queen's back garden [...].

I'd been fortunate to catch a bus running a few minutes behind
the previous service, so we sailed past most of the early bus
stops without pausing. My top deck solitude was only broken
as we started up the Edgware Road. Most of the pensioners and
pushchairs and veiled ladies stayed downstairs, but one gentleman
ascended to claim the other front seat where he proceeded to read
his exotic newspaper. It's a bit of Arabian bazaar up this stretch
of road, full of shisha cafés and Maroush restaurants, and even
1908 travellers would have noted Middle Eastern migrants settled

in the area. They'd probably not have recognised the casino or the multi-storey drum-like primary school, however, and they'd have been surprised at the scale of the Waitrose supermarket preparing to open here later in the month.

More passengers. A young boy scampered up the stairs, closely followed by his dad, and noted with visible disappointment that both of the front seats were taken. The pair of them tucked into the seat immediately behind me, and I felt warm breath on my ear as the youngster leaned forward to peer out of the front window. Fat mum squeezed in beside me shortly afterwards, chewing relentlessly beneath her pink headscarf and keeping firm hold on a plump leather clutch bag. I tried hard to cut out the chatter, knowing full well that all three of them wished I wasn't here. And at the next stop they were gone. [...]

On past a variety of Kilburn stations and the odd theatre, to ascend Shoot Up Hill. I was joined on the top deck by Gary Salisbury and his wife, easily identified from the name, address and telephone number written for all to see on a luggage tag hanging from his rucksack. If you ever meet Gary do try hard not to giggle at his fedora. The happy couple were heading for Cricklewood Broadway, a long shopping parade which would have been new when the first route 16 passed this way. It's now showing its age. Here cheap furniture shops sell piled-up sofas to cost-cutting landlords, and the Quick Clean Coin Operated Laundry still boasts of its featured Frigidaire Washers. The Crown Hotel maintains a certain Victorian grandeur, if you like giant pubs with Irish hospitality and don't mind the ultra-modern extension attached next door. Not for me thanks. By the time we reached Cricklewood Lane, two stops from the end of the ride, I was the only passenger left aboard. [...]

100 years on, route 16's changed out of all recognition. The buses have a roof and talk to you. The streets are full of competing private transport. Shops sell barely imagined goods at vastly-inflated prices. Children ride alone and shout rude words from the back seat. But there's still only one sensible

way to get from central London to Cricklewood, and that's straight up Watling Street. The 16 follows in Roman footsteps, and its long history continues with every journey.

Blogger Diamond Geezer, 'Bus 16: Victoria – Cricklewood'

✳ ✳ ✳

Enough of the buses. The Tube next ... with words of warning from Rüdiger Görner.

The Londoner refers to this infernal object of his enduring love-hate relationship as 'The Tube'. A few statistics. The Tube totals 280 kilometres of track, of which one-third is subterranean. The first subterranean line (between Paddington and Farringdon Street) was opened in 1863, and that all-important north-south connection in London, the Northern Line, in 1890. By 1900 London had the most modern, electrified Underground network; it has now become the most outdated, inefficient and expensive in the so-called civilised world. On average, two despairing people throw themselves in front of trains pulling into stations each week. It is also statistically proven that slipping on *green* grapes is the most frequent cause of accidents on the platforms and passageways of the Underground. More frequent even, and this may be surprising, than carelessly discarded banana skins; because rubbish bins are to be sought in vain on the platforms: they were removed because of the threat of the IRA hiding bombs in them, a threat that has continued from newer sources.

There can be no doubt that the Tube is a cultural centre, a social studies subject of the first rank, an experience, an emotive word, a political issue in view of its proverbially poor service. Depending on your taste, you may count on the positive side of the ledger that the Tube offers its own world of advertising. It brings forth poetry and comforts those who are combating shortage of breath and panic attacks with individually mounted poems arranged at the level of the handrail. The Tube served as an air raid shelter in the Second World War; buskers are now allowed to perform on colourful platforms, sponsored by a major brewery.

The Tube is no place for claustrophobes; any more than it is for talkative types. One can practice instantaneous assessment of people without ever exchanging a word. In the overcrowded carriage, where you come into quite close physical contact with others, not a word is ever spoken. Should the train come to an unscheduled halt in the middle of a tunnel for any length of time, you might hear an appropriately distorted voice whispering some sort of explanation over the tannoy into the sauna-like atmosphere. Anyone tempted to let loose some verbal expression of displeasure amongst these passengers, all pressed together like sardines in a tin, unmistakably reveals himself as a person of limited self-control caused by a deficient upbringing – a foreigner, in other words. [...] Everybody reads on the train, and the various reading techniques people develop on the Tube are amazing. They bury their glances in printer's ink, turn the pages skilfully, while the rattling and shaking of the train often requires acrobatic adjustments of balance in order to counter the centrifugal force. Often a page is reread several times because despite all efforts or insufficient balancing skills, it is impossible to turn the page. One's glance remains glued to this single page in order to avoid any possible eye-contact with fellow passengers. A one-centimetre gap to the next person must be preserved in all circumstances. Physical contact – even if only back-to-back – suggests something immoral. On one occasion last summer I observed (I am following my irregular diary notes here) the following incident. An innocent, overly ripe, voluptuous young London girl, with a breathtaking neckline that exposed subtly tattooed breasts for general pleasure, indignantly pulled her arm away from the man seated on her right. This visibly shy, gaunt, bespectacled grey-suiter, probably an accountant (London has the greatest density of accountants of all major cities) must have touched her with his arm. A withered anorexic-woman sat on the girl's left reading D H Lawrence's *Women in Love.*

Rüdiger Görner, *London Fragments*
translated by Debra Marmor and Herbert Danner

✻ ✻ ✻

On the other hand, novelist and philosopher Iris Murdoch was an enthusiastic 'Undergrounder'.

After leaving the office I would travel either to Sloane Square or to Liverpool Street to have a drink in the station buffet. In the whole extension of the Underground system those two stations are, as far as I've been able to discover, the only ones which have bars actually upon the platform. The concept of the tube station platform bar excited me. In fact the whole Underground region moved me, I felt as if it were in some sense my natural home. These two bars were not just a cosy after-the-office treat, they were the source of a dark excitement, places of profound communication with London, with the sources of life, with the caverns of resignation to grief and to mortality. Drinking there between six and seven in the shifting crowds of rush-hour travellers, one could feel on one's shoulder as a curiously soothing yoke the weariness of toiling London, that blank released tiredness after work which can somehow console even the bored, even the frenzied. The coming and departing rattle of the trains, the drifting movement of the travellers, their arrival, their waiting, their vanishing forever presented a mesmeric and indeed symbolic fresco: so many little moments of decision, so many little finalities, the constant wrenching of texture, the constant destruction of cells which shifts and ages the lives of men and of universes. The uncertainty of the order of the trains. The dangerousness of the platforms. (Trains as lethal weapons.) The resolution of a given moment (but which?) to lay down your glass and mount the next train. (But why? There will be another in two minutes.) *Ah qu'ils sont beaux les trains manqués!* as I especially had cause to know. Then once upon the train that sense of its thrusting life, its intent and purposive turning which conveys

185

itself so subtly to the traveller's body, its leanings and veerings to points of irrevocable change and partings of the ways. The train of consciousness, the present moment, the little lighted tube moving in the long dark tunnel. The inevitability of it all and yet its endless variety: the awful daylight glimpses, the blessed plunges back into the dark; the stations, each unique, the sinister brightness of Charing Cross, the mysterious gloom of Regent's Park, the dereliction of Mornington Crescent, the futuristic melancholy of Moorgate, the monumental ironwork of Liverpool Street, the twining *art nouveau* of Gloucester Road, the Barbican sunk in a baroque hole, fit subject for Piranesi. And in summer, like an excursion into the country, the flowering banks of the Westbound District Line. I preferred the dark however. Emergence was like a worm pulled from its hole. I loved the Inner Circle best. Twenty-seven stations for fivepence. Indeed, for fivepence as many stations as you cared to achieve. Sometimes I rode the whole Circle (just under an hour) before deciding whether to have my evening drink at Liverpool Street or Sloane Square. I was not the only Circle rider. There were others, especially in winter. Homeless people, lonely people, alcoholics, people on drugs, people in despair. We recognized each other. It was a fit place for me, I was indeed an Undergrounder.

Iris Murdoch, *A Word Child*

❋ ❋ ❋

Could the Underground be a likely place for romance
to blossom? Henry James imagines it could be.

The accident had been as natural as anything in London ever is: Kate had one afternoon found herself opposite Mr Densher on the Underground Railway. She had entered the train at Sloane Square to go to Queen's Road, and the carriage in which she had found a place was all but full. Densher was already in it – on the other bench and at the furthest angle; she was sure of him before they had again started. The day and the hour were darkness, there were six other persons, and she had been busy placing herself; but her consciousness had gone to him as straight as if they had come together in some bright level of the desert. They had on neither part a second's hesitation; they looked across the choked compartment exactly as if she had known he would be there and he had expected her to come in; so that, though in the conditions they could only exchange the greeting of movements, smiles, silence, it would have been quite in the key of those passages that they should have alighted for ease at the very next station. Kate was in fact sure that the very next station was the young man's true goal – which made it clear that he was going on only from the wish to speak to her. He had to go on, for this purpose, to High Street, Kensington, as it was not till then that the exit of a passenger gave him his chance.

His chance put him, however, in quick possession of the seat facing her, the alertness of his capture of which seemed to show her his impatience. It helped them, moreover, with strangers on either side, little to talk; though this very restriction perhaps made such a mark for them as nothing else could have done. If the fact that their opportunity had again come round for them could be so intensely expressed between them without a word, they might very well feel on the spot that it had not come round for nothing. The extraordinary part of the matter was that they were not in the least meeting where they had left off, but ever so much further on, and that these added links added still another between High Street and Notting Hill Gate, and then between the latter station and Queen's Road an extension really inordinate. At Notting Hill Gate, Kate's right-hand neighbour descended, whereupon Densher popped straight into that seat; only there was not much gained when a lady, the next instant, popped into Densher's. He could say almost nothing to her – she scarce knew, at least, what he said; she was so occupied with a certainty that one of the persons opposite, a young-ish man with a single eyeglass, which he kept constantly in position, had made her out from the first as visibly, as strangely affected. If such a person made her out, what then did Densher do? – a question in truth sufficiently answered when, on their reaching her station, he instantly followed her out of the train.

Henry James, *The Wings of the Dove*

✳ ✳ ✳

If you ever get lost in London, you can always grab a cab and say, 'Take me to … ', like Walshingham in H. G. Wells' Kipps, who teaches his less experienced friend not to be afraid of jumping into a hansom cab.

London was Kipps' third world. There were, no doubt, other worlds, but Kipps knew only these three; firstly, New Romney and the Emporium, constituting his primary world, his world of origin, which also contained Ann; secondly, the world of culture and refinement, the world of which Coote was chaperon, and into which Kipps was presently to marry, a world, it was fast becoming evident, absolutely incompatible with the first; and thirdly, a world still to a large extent unexplored, London. London presented itself as a place of great grey spaces and incredible multitudes of people, centering about Charing Cross station and the Royal Grand Hotel, and containing at unexpected arbitrary points shops of the most amazing sort, statuary, squares, restaurants – where it was possible for clever people like Walshingham to order a lunch item by item to the waiters' evident respect and sympathy – exhibitions of incredible things – the Walshinghams had taken him to the Arts and Crafts and to a Picture Gallery – and theatres. London, moreover, is rendered habitable by hansom cabs. Young Walshingham was a natural cab-taker; he was an all-round, large-minded young man, and he had in the course of their two days' stay taken Kipps into no less than nine, so that Kipps was singularly not afraid of these vehicles. He knew that wherever you were, so soon as you were thoroughly lost, you said 'Hi!' to a cab, and then 'Royal Grand Hotel'. Day and night these trusty conveyances are returning the strayed Londoner back to his point of departure, and were it not for their activity, in a little while the whole population, so vast and incomprehensible is the intricate complexity of this great city, would be hopelessly lost for ever. At any rate, that is how the thing presented itself to Kipps, and I have heard much the same from visitors from America.

H. G. Wells, *Kipps*

＊ ＊ ＊

But maybe it's better to know exactly where you're going, or things could turn a little nasty ...

He got off the train at St Pancras, a lone man without luggage, the same suit, a new white T-shirt beneath. Pale winter sun leaked in through the grey glass vault overhead and made him feel both depressed and determined. He moved swiftly through the crowd and went out of the station to the open air where the black cabs waited. He got into the first one and said, 'Dickens Hotel, Park Lane.' [...] The driver started the meter and the cab chugged into life. The driver was not a talker and Mick was glad of that. He looked at the adverts lining the inside of the cab, one for a laptop computer, one for a plastic surgery clinic. Then he looked out of the cab window at the thick traffic, the motorbikes weaving in and out, at the blurred air, the people hurrying along the pavements, late for something. He hated everything he saw, and he allowed an expression of condescending disgust to settle on his face. London. [...] At last the cab driver spoke. He said 'What hotel did you say, mate?'

'The Dickens,' Mick replied.

The driver scratched the rolls of flesh at the back of his neck. 'I don't know that one.'

'I thought you London taxi drivers knew everything.'

The driver seemed undecided whether or not to take offence, but simply said, 'I know Park Lane but I don't know any Dickens Hotel.'

'Is that right?' Mick said, unhelpfully.

'OK,' the driver said, 'we'll find it when we get there.'

They got there and Mick was quietly impressed. This looked much better. This was more of a pleasant version of London. There was still too much traffic but at least there was a park and the hotels looked moneyed and comfortable. He looked at their names, and they all seemed vaguely familiar, places heard about on television or read about in the papers: the Dorchester, the Inn on the Park, the Hilton, but there was no Dickens. The driver stopped the cab before the road dragged him into the current of traffic swirling round Hyde Park Corner.

'I didn't like to say anything,' he said, 'but I didn't think there was a Dickens Hotel here.'

Mick sat impassively.

'I don't suppose you know what number Park Lane?' the driver asked.

As a matter of fact Mick did. He had a business card from the hotel. He took it out of his breast pocket and without saying a word handed it to the driver who looked at it for less than a second and then shook his head in mocking, disbelieving sympathy.

'You from out of town?' he asked.

'So?'

'You want bloody Park Lane, Hackney.'

'Do I?' said Mick. 'Take me there then.'

'I'm not going to bloody Hackney.'

'What's wrong with Hackney?'

'When you find someone to take you there, you'll find out. That's a tenner you owe me. Now on your way.'

'You're taking me there,' Mick said.

'No, I'm not, pal.'

Mick sat still and imperious. He wasn't going to lose his first argument in the big city.

'Out,' said the driver and he stepped from his cab. He opened the rear door and Mick could see he was carrying a baseball bat. That amused him.

'I said out. Or else.'

190

Mick, unruffled, said, 'You'll need more than a baseball bat,' and he exploded into violence. He grabbed the bat from the driver's hands, swirled it round and hit him across the nose twice. He leapt out of the cab, knocked the driver aside and went to the front where he kicked in both headlights. He was thinking of smashing the windows with the bat, puncturing the radiator, thinking of giving the driver a proper going over, when a sudden change came over him, as though a fatherly restraining hand had been put on his shoulder, sanity returning. He threw the bat aside and began to walk slowly away. 'I hate this town,' he said, and he broke into a run, dashing into the streets behind the big hotels before the driver could find any allies.

Geoff Nicholson, *Bleeding London*

❉ ❉ ❉

The most unforgettable London cabby in fiction just has to be Will Self's Dave Rudman.

Outside in the Mile End Road, Dave unlocked the cab and stood for a moment looking west to where the buildings of the City stacked up. There were new blocks at Aldgate and down towards the Tower of London; a thicket of cranes sprouted over the old Broad Street Station, and above it all reared the black, glassy stack of the NatWest Tower. Another course of London was being laid on top of the last, millions of tons of steel, concrete, brick and stone, weighing down on the present, pressing it into the past.

While here, in the East End, magenta buddleia spears and coils of fluffy rosebay willowherb sprang from between the sheets of corrugated iron that fences off the bombsite behind the pub. Benny had once told Dave that during the war sand had been gouged from the top of Hampstead Heath and poured into bags that were then piled in front of the hospitals and government ministries. When the ack-ack ceased and the barrage balloons were winched down, the pulverized terraces of the East End were swept up, loaded on to trucks, and dumped in the hollows and dips where the sand had been dug. Round and round it went, London's auto-cannibalism. It made Dave feel queasy to be standing suspended over such deep time, on the taut cable of a summer evening. He lowered himself into the cab and, starting the engine, felt better immediately, and better still when within seconds his Faredar peeped and he netted a commuter heading for Fenchurch Street. [...]

Dave was renting Chitty Chitty Bang Bang on the full-flat. The open-top, straight-six Bentley was a *pig to handle*, and the wings were mostly useless in Central London. The flying car grunted and squealed at the rank under the heavy steel joists of St Pancras. A fare came flapping out of the greenish aviary of the station, a tall stick of a man, his white beard and black robe giving him a vulturine appearance. 'Where to, guv?' Dave asked him, and the fare replied stiffly, 'Parl-men-till.'

The fare was a *tedious old fucker*, who couldn't forbear from lecturing Dave on London's architecture. Dave hated birds – especially old human ones; he hated their alien stare, their hollow bones, their greasy feathers, their hard, pointed lips. The fare's thesis was simple: the city had ceased to evolve after the Great Fire. The last three hundred and fifty years were only a series of recapitulations, the erection of new-old buildings, tricked out in the styles of lost civilizations. He pointed out the neo-Gothic station frontage, its triplets of lancet windows complete with quatrefoils, its angled and flying buttresses, its iron pinnacles and gabled niches. Despite himself Dave craned to look up and piloted Chitty Chitty Bang Bang into the gulch being excavated for the Channel Tunnel Terminal. Luckily, its wings spontaneously unfurled, the huge car swooped back up on to the roadway. The fare was unfazed. He discoursed on the wooden, barrel-vaulted roof of King's Cross, then directed his attention to the neoclassicism of the terraced houses lining Royal College Street – their snub façades alluding to the possibility of stately porticos, their anorexic pilasters referencing temples long since crumbled. 'Vares nuffing nú unnersun, mì sun.' The fare spoke the broadest of cockney, vowels crushed to death by rumbling lorries on the Mile End Road. 'Doan ask wy ve öl daze wuz bé-er van vese, coz U aynt gó ve nous fer í. Lemme tellya, no geezer az a fukkin clú abaht iz oan tyme, yeah? Ees juss lyke a fukkin sparer –'

'The sparrows are nearly all gone in London,' Dave put in

'Eggzackerly!' In the rearview mirror Dave saw the old man's bony digit waggle. 'Eggzackerly, lyke a fukkin sparer aw a bitta bá-erred cod.'

'They're going inall.'

'Rì agen, gawn, cort inna eevul fukkin net, mayt, an eevul fukkin net vat juss cum aht uv ve fukkin sky.'

Coming up Highgate Road, Dave used the steep slope after the railway bridge to take off, and Chitty Chitty Bang Bang unfurled its wings once more, and soared up over the redbrick, 1930s blocks of Lissenden Gardens. He banked the flying car and came in on a flat approach to the summit of Parliament Hill, touching down on the path with hardly a bump. They rolled to a halt, and the fare got out. Dave searched the dash for a meter but couldn't find one. There was hardly any point in trying, for when he looked again he saw that the old man had done a runner, pelting off down the hill towards the Highgate Ponds, his long black robe streaming behind him. 'I s'pose I'll just have to wipe my mouth on that one,' Dave muttered to himself.

Dawn was silvering the mirrored buildings of the City – further to the east the bridge at Dartford floated above the riverine mist. The streetlights were still on, phosphorescent trails in the oily swell of streets and buildings. Dave felt an aqueous queasiness when he saw the long line of the North Downs to the far south – they were distant islands, uninhabited and uninhabitable. At his back he sensed the ridges of Barnet and then the Chilterns rising up, wooded shores against which London lapped. [...]

At night Dave worked the mainline stations – Victoria and Paddington mostly. The west of London felt warmer in the winter, better lit, less susceptible to the chill of deep time. The fares were frowsy under the sodium lamps. In the back of the cab they slumped against their luggage, and Dave drove them home to Wembley, Twickenham and Muswell Hill. Or else they were tourists bound for the Bonnington, the Inn on the Park or the Lancaster – gaunt people-barns, where maids flitted through the lobbies, cardboard coffins of dying blooms cradled in their arms. In the wee-wee hours he parked up at an all-night café in Bayswater and sat reading the next day's news, while solider citizens lay abed waiting for it to happen. His fellow night people were exiguous – they wore the faces of forgotten comedians, unfunny and unloved.

Dave took junkies to score in the All Saints Road, tarts to fuck in Mayfair, punters to bet in the Gloucester Road, surgeons to cut in Bloomsbury, sous chefs to chop in Soho. He noticed nothing, retained nothing – glad only to be driving, moving through the whispering streets, feeling the surface beneath his wheels change from smooth to rough to rougher to rutted. In the blank dawns, when Hyde Park seethed with mist, he would find himself rattling through Belgravia, a bony fag stuck in his skull, and seeing the queues of visa applicants – already at this early hour lined up outside the consulates – it occurred to him that *these are the people I dropped off a few hours ago … They can't fucking stand it here any more than I can … They want out right away …*

Will Self, *The Book of Dave*

* * *

Ranging from the charming, discreet and helpful (most of them) to the unnervingly sullen, from the one-man political soap-box (a dying breed) and the obsessive oral autobiographer (their lives are clearly more interesting than yours and only a freak of circumstances has kept them out of the House of Lords), London cabbies are a breed apart. Here's a final trip with one who knows where he's going … But don't let it put you off: there aren't that many around like him.

In the middle of the road came a taxi, indicator yellow and welcome. I raised one arm, trying to look rich, generous and anxious to go wherever the taxi-driver wanted instead of pursuing some selfish plan of my own. The last occasion on which I boarded a taxi, the driver told me he was "going home" and could only take me to Fulham. I explained I didn't want to go to Fulham. I was by this time sitting in the back of the cab. "Listen," said the taxi-driver, "I'm going to Fulham. You can come if you like. If you don't like – hop out." In the end he agreed to take me somewhere where he thought I might get another cab. We reached Shepherd's Bush. Not a cab in sight. He peered round hopefully and said, pointing to an old Wolseley abandoned on the Hammersmith Road, "There's one!" "That," I said, "is a private car." He relapsed into silence, and hunched up over the wheel, potato-faced with sorrow at the situation. "This has become a battle of wills, hasn't it?" I said. "Yes," he said, sadly. After a half-hour wait he took me to Paddington, and left me at the taxi rank, by which time an uneasy mutual respect had developed between us. Taxi travel is, after all, not a game for softies.

So I put my whole soul into the hailing gesture, and as the taxi swerved into the side of the road, I stepped out, extended a seigniorial hand towards the cab-door and put sweetness, firmness and money into the way I said:

"Archway please."

Greatly to my surprise, the man nodded and allowed me in. An eccentric obviously.

Nigel Williams, *My Life Closed Twice*

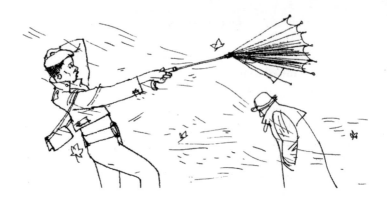

Whatever the weather

What?! No fog?!! ... Pea-soupers were real enough before Parliament passed the Clean Air Act in 1956, but much of London's reputation as a city of constant fog and rain is a literary throw-back. Tourists who get their ideas of London from reading Dickens and other nineteenth-century novelists are in for a big surprise.

fog *n* mass of condensed water vapour in the lower air, often greatly reducing visibility

'London is the Capital of fog.' It saying in middle school textbook. We studying chapter from Charles Dickens's novel *Foggy City Orphan*. Everybody know Oliver Twist living in city with bad fog. Is very popular novel in China.

As soon as I arriving London, I look around the sky but no any fogs. 'Excuse me, where I seeing the fogs?' I ask policeman in street.

'Sorry?' he says.

'I waiting two days already, but no fogs,' I say.

He just look at me, he must no understanding of my English.

When I return Nuttington House from my tourism visiting, reception lady tell me: 'Very cold today, isn't it?' But why she tell me? I know this information, and now is too late, because I finish my tourism visiting, and I wet and freezing.

Xiaolu Guo, *A Concise Chinese – English Dictionary for Lovers*

* * *

So we'll get the old 'literary' weather out of the way first. It has the advantage of creating the right atmosphere for dark and dastardly deeds.

It was by this time about nine in the morning, and the first fog of the season. A great chocolate-coloured pall lowered over heaven, but the wind was continually charging and routing these embattled vapours; so that as the cab crawled from street to street, Mr Utterson beheld a marvellous number of degrees and hues of twilight; for here it would be dark like the back-end of evening; and there would be a glow of a rich, lurid brown, like the light of some strange conflagration; and here, for a moment, the fog would be quite broken up, and a haggard shaft of daylight would glance in between the swirling wreaths. The dismal quarter of Soho seen under these changing glimpses, with its muddy ways, and slatternly passengers, and its lamps, which had never been extinguished or had been kindled afresh to combat this mournful reinvasion of darkness, seemed, in the lawyer's eyes, like a district of some city in a nightmare. The thoughts of his mind, besides, were of the gloomiest dye; and when he glanced at the companion of his drive, he was conscious of some touch of that terror of the law and the law's officers which may at times assail the most honest.

As the cab drew up before the address indicated, the fog lifted a little and showed him a dingy street, a gin palace, a low French eating-house, a shop for the retail of penny numbers and two-penny salads, many ragged children huddled in the doorways, and many women of many different nationalities passing out, key in hand, to have a morning glass; and the next moment the fog settled down again upon that part, as brown as umber, and cut him off from his blackguardly surroundings.

This was the home of Henry Jekyll's favourite; of a man who was heir to a quarter of a million sterling.

Robert Louis Stevenson, *The Strange Case of Dr Jekyll and Mr Hyde*

✳ ✳ ✳

London had the advantage of one of the most gloomy atmospheres in the world. During this opening spring weather, no light and scarcely any warmth can penetrate the dull, yellowish-grey mist, which incessantly hangs over the city. Sometimes at noon we have for an hour or two a sickly gleam of sunshine, but it is soon swallowed up by the smoke and drizzling fog. The people carry umbrellas at all times, for the rain seems to drop spontaneously out of the very air, without waiting for the usual preparation of a gathering cloud … A few days ago we had a real fog – a specimen of November weather, as the people said. If November wears such a mantle, London, during that sober month, must furnish a good idea of the gloom of Hades. The streets were wrapped in a veil of dense mist, a dirty yellow colour, as if the air had suddenly grown thick and mouldy. The houses on the opposite sides of the street were invisible, and the gas-lamps, lighted in the shops, burned with a white and ghastly flame. Carriages ran together in the streets, and I was kept constantly on the look-out, lest someone should come suddenly out of the cloud around me, and we should meet with a shock like that of the two knights at a tournament. As I stood in the centre of Trafalgar Square, with every object invisible around me, it reminded me, (hoping the comparison will not be accepted in every particular) of Satan resting in the middle of Chaos. The weather sometimes continues thus for whole days together.

Bayard Taylor, *Views Afoot*

✳ ✳ ✳

The famously murky opening of Bleak House *represents a moral fog as well as a meteorological one.*

London, Michaelmas Term lately over, and the Lord Chancellor sitting in Lincoln's Inn Hall. Implacable November weather. As much mud in the streets, as if the waters had but newly retired from the face of the earth, and it would not be wonderful to meet a Megalosaurus, forty feet long or so, waddling like an elephantine lizard up Holborn Hill. Smoke lowering from the chimney-pots, making a soft black drizzle with flakes of soot in it as big as full-grown snowflakes – gone into mourning, one might imagine, for the death of the sun. Dogs, undistinguishable in mire. Horses, scarcely better; splashed to their very blinkers. Foot passengers, jostling one another's umbrellas, in a general infection of ill temper, and losing their foot-hold at street-corners, where tens of thousands of other foot passengers have been slipping and sliding since the day broke (if this day ever broke), adding new deposits to the crust upon crust of mud, sticking at those points tenaciously to the pavement, and accumulating compound interest.

Fog everywhere. Fog up the river, where it flows among green aits and meadows; fog down the river, where it rolls defiled among the tiers of shipping, and the waterside pollutions of a great (and dirty) city. Fog on the Essex marshes, fog on the Kentish heights. Fog creeping into the cabooses of collier-brigs; fog lying out on the yards, and hovering in the rigging of great ships; fog drooping on the gunwales of barges and small boats. Fog in the eyes and throats of ancient Greenwich pensioners, wheezing by the firesides of their wards; fog in the stem and bowl of the afternoon pipe of the wrathful skipper, down in his close cabin; fog cruelly pinching the toes and fingers of his shivering little 'prentice boy on deck. Chance people on the bridges peeping over the parapets into a nether sky of fog, with fog all around them, as if they were up in a balloon, and hanging in the misty clouds.

Gas looming through the fog in divers places in the streets, much as the sun may, from the spongey fields, be seen to loom by husbandman and ploughboy. Most of the shops lighted two hours before their time – as the gas seems to know, for it has a haggard and unwilling look.

The raw afternoon is rawest, and the dense fog is densest, and the muddy streets are muddiest, near that leaden-headed old obstruction, appropriate ornament for the threshold of a leaden-headed old corporation: Temple Bar. And hard by Temple Bar, in Lincoln's Inn Hall, at the very heart of the fog, sits the Lord High Chancellor in his High Court of Chancery.

Never can there come a fog too thick, never can there come mud and mire too deep, to assort with the groping and floundering condition which this High Court of Chancery, most pestilent of hoary sinners, holds, this day, in the sight of heaven and earth.

On such an afternoon, if ever, the Lord High Chancellor ought to be sitting here – as he is – with a foggy glory round his head, softly fenced in with crimson cloth and curtains, addressed by a large advocate with great whiskers, a little voice, and an interminable brief, and outwardly directing his contemplation to the lantern in the roof, where he can see nothing but fog.

Charles Dickens, *Bleak House*

❋ ❋ ❋

A bit more bad weather – a stormy night this time.
Sherlock Holmes and Doctor Watson's quiet evening
at home in Baker Street is not set to last …

It was a wild, tempestuous night towards the close of November. Holmes and I sat together in silence all the evening, he engaged with a powerful lens deciphering the remains of the original inscription upon a palimpsest, I deep in a recent treatise upon surgery. Outside the wind howled down Baker Street, while the rain beat fiercely against the windows. It was strange there in the very depths of the town, with ten miles of man's handiwork on every side of us, to feel the iron grip of Nature, and to be conscious that to the huge elemental forces all London was no more than the molehills that dot the fields. I walked to the window and looked out on the deserted street. The occasional lamps gleamed on the expanse of muddy road and shining pavement. A single cab was splashing its way from the Oxford Street end.

'Well, Watson, it's as well we have not to turn out tonight,' said Holmes, laying aside his lens and rolling up the palimpsest. 'I've done enough for one sitting. It is trying work for the eyes. So far as I can make out, it is nothing more exciting than an Abbey's accounts dating from the second half of the fifteenth century. Halloa! halloa! halloa! What's this?'

Amid the droning of the wind there had come the stamping of a horse's hoofs and the long grind of a wheel as it rasped against the kerb. The cab which I had seen had pulled up at our door.

'What can he want?' I ejaculated, as a man stepped out of it.

'Want! He wants us. And we, my poor Watson, want overcoats and cravats and galoshes, and every aid that man ever invented to fight the weather. Wait a bit, though! There's the cab off again! There's hope yet. He'd have kept it if he had wanted us to come. Run down, my dear fellow, and open the door, for all virtuous folk have been long in bed.'

Arthur Conan Doyle, 'The Adventure of the Golden Pince-Nez'
in *The Return of Sherlock Holmes*

❊ ❊ ❊

The Great Frost of 1684 was an historical fact, here beautifully described in the imaginative world of Virginia Woolf's Orlando.

The Great Frost was, historians tell us, the most severe that has ever visited these islands. Birds froze in mid-air and fell like stones to the ground. At Norwich a young countrywoman started to cross the road in her usual robust health and was seen by the onlookers to turn visibly to powder and be blown in a puff of gust over the roofs as the icy blast struck her at the street corner. The mortality among sheep and cattle was enormous. Corpses froze and could not be drawn from the sheets. It was no uncommon sight to come upon a whole herd of swine frozen immovable upon the road. The fields were full of shepherds, ploughmen, teams of horses, and little bird-scaring boys all struck stark in the act of the moment, one with his hand to his nose, another with the bottle to his lips, a third with a stone raised to throw at the raven who sat, as if stuffed, upon the hedge within a yard of him. The severity of the frost was so extraordinary that a kind of petrifaction sometimes ensued; and it was commonly supposed that the great increase of rock in some parts of Derbyshire was due to no eruption, for there was none, but to the solidification of unfortunate wayfarers who had been turned literally to stone where they stood. The Church could give little help in the matter, and though some landowners had these relics blessed, the most part preferred to use them either as landmarks, scratching-posts for sheep, or, when the form of the stone allowed, drinking troughs for cattle, which purposes they serve, admirably for the most part, to this day.

But while the country people suffered the extremity of want, and the trade of the country was at a standstill, London enjoyed a carnival of the utmost brilliancy. The Court was at Greenwich, and the new King seized the opportunity that his coronation gave him to curry favour with the citizens. He directed that the river, which was frozen to a depth of twenty feet and more for six or seven miles on either side, should be swept, decorated and given all the semblance of a park or pleasure ground, with arbours, mazes, alleys, drinking booths, etc., at his expense. For himself and the courtiers, he reserved a certain space immediately opposite the Palace gates; which, railed off from the public only by a silken rope, became at once the centre of the most brilliant society in England. Great statesmen, in their beards and ruffs, despatched affairs of state under the crimson awning of the Royal Pagoda. Soldiers planned the conquest of the Moor and the downfall of the Turk in striped arbours surmounted by plumes of ostrich feathers. Admirals strode up and down the narrow pathways, glass in hand, sweeping the horizon and telling stories of the north-west passage and the Spanish Armada. Lovers dallied upon divans spread with sables. Frozen roses fell in showers when the Queen and her ladies walked abroad. Coloured balloons hovered motionless in the hair. Here and there burnt vast bonfires of cedar and oak wood, lavishly salted, so that the flames were of green, orange, and purple fire. But however fiercely they burnt, the heat was not enough to melt the ice which, though of singular transparency, was yet of the hardness of steel. So clear indeed was it that there could be seen, congealed at a depth of several feet, here a porpoise, there a flounder. Shoals of eels lay motionless in a trance, but whether their state was one of death or merely of suspended animation which the warmth would revive puzzled the philosophers. Near London Bridge, where the river had frozen to a depth of some twenty fathoms, a wrecked wherry boat was plainly visible, lying on the bed of the river where it had sunk last autumn, overladen with apples. The old bumboat woman, who was carrying her fruit to market on the Surrey side, sat there in her plaids and farthingales with her lap full of apples, for all the world as if she were about to serve a customer, though a certain blueness about the lips hinted the truth. 'Twas a sight King James specially liked to look upon, and he would bring a troupe of courtiers to gaze with him. In short, nothing could exceed the brilliancy and gaiety of the scene by day. But it was at night that the carnival was at its merriest. For the frost continued unbroken; the nights were of perfect stillness; the moon and stars blazed with the hard fixity of diamonds, and to the fine music of flute and trumpet the courtiers danced.

Virginia Woolf, Orlando

❊ ❊ ❊

The same phenomenon was described by the famous diarist, John Evelyn, with a greater focus on the difficult realties.

Sunday, 1 January 1684

The weather continuing intolerably severe, streetes of booths were set upon the Thames; the air was so very cold and thick, as of many yeares there had not been the like. The small pox was very mortal …

9th. I went across the Thames on the ice, now become so thick as to beare not onely streetes of boothes, in which they roasted meate, and had divers shops of wares, quite acrosse as in a towne, but coaches, carts and horses, passed over. So I went from Westminster Stayres to Lambeth, and din'd with the Archbishop …

16th. The Thames was fill'd with people and tents, selling all sorts of wares as in the Citty.

24th. The frost continuing more and more severe, the Thames before London was still planted with boothes in formal streetes, all sortes of trades and shops furnish'd and full of commodities, even to a printing presse, where the people and ladyes tooke a fancy to have their names printed, and the day and yeare set down when printed on the Thames: this humour tooke so universally, that 'twas estimated the printer gain'd £5 a day, for printing a line onely, at sixpence a name, besides what he got by ballads, &c. Coaches plied from Westminster to the Temple, and from several other staires to and fro, as in the streetes, sleds, sliding with skeetes, a bull-baiting, horse and coach races, puppet plays and interludes, cookes, tipling, and other lewd places, so that it seem'd to be a bacchanalian triumph or carnival on the water, whilst it was a severe judgement on the land, the trees not onely splitting as if lightning-struck, but men and cattle perishing in divers places, and the very seas lock'd up with ice, that no vessels could stir out or come in. The fowles, fish, and birds, and all our exotiq plants and greenes universally perishing. Many parkes of deer were destroied, and all sorts of fuell so deare that there were great contribution to preserve the poore alive. Nor was this severe weather much less intense in most parts of Europe, even as far as Spaine and the most southern tracts. London, by reason of the excessive coldnesse of the aire hindering the ascent of the smoke, was so filled with the fuliginous steame of the sea-coale, that hardly could one see crosse the streets, and this filling the lungs with its grosse particles, exceedingly obstructed the breast, so as one could hardly breath. Here was no water to be had from the pompes and engines, nor could the brewers and divers other tradesmen worke, and every moment was full of disastrous accidents.

4 February

I went to Says Court to see how the frost had dealt with my garden, where I found many of the greenes and rare plantes utterly destroied. The oranges and mirtalls very sick, the rosemary and laurels dead to all appearance, but ye cypress likely to endure it.

5th. It began to thaw, but froze againe. My coach crossed from Lambeth to the Horseferry at Millbank, Westminster. The booths were almost all taken downe, but there was first a map or landskip cut in copper representing all the manner of the camp, and the several actions, sports, and pastimes thereon, in memory of so signal a frost ...

8th. The weather was set in to an absolute thaw and raine, but ye Thames still frozen.

John Evelyn, *Diary*

❊ ❊ ❊

But with the climate changing, we're unlikely to see such extremes. Real London winters tend to be just rather damp and soggy, as described by a very young resident, eleven-year-old Jemma Leech, in her prize-winning entry for a London writing competition.

In London the winters were warm and wet. No snow or ice, just rainy gumboot-puddled walks in Brockwell Park, while the summer-packed paddling pool filled of its own accord with rainwater, autumn leaves and rainbows of crisp bags. We disappeared into the secret garden underneath palisades of sleeping creeping clematis and wisteria, swapping the dry dark with the wet light as we trailed the paving maze to the fishpond at its heart. Blackbirds waded in patches of newly dug earth, taking worms from the mud as an avocet might from a turning-tide bare beach. A robin called to me from the crumbling wall, saying 'spring will be here soon, believe me'. [...] From the top of the hill in the park we had watched fireworks break out all across the city that Fifth of November, as if in domino from common to common. But on that Christmas Day the mist had come down, the park was an island and we were cut off from the mass of humanity beyond the mist. It was just me, my brother and sister and our weary parents inhaling the fog like perfume on a cloud of silage steam, 'grateful' for the relief it brought from the stench of London. That mist-bound land was our kingdom that day and I was its princess, adorned with a crown of diamond drips and drops, soon dried by the warmth of our terraced palace on Hawarden Grove.

Jemma Leech, 'A Hawarden Grove Christmas'

✳ ✳ ✳

Moving on to April and the joy of a London spring.

I opened my window to an April night and, looking down into the London square, saw that new leaves were silver-white in the lamplight. Into my room came an earthy smell and the freshness of new grass. The top boughs of the trees were etched against the saffron stain of a London sky, but their boles descended into a pool of darkness, silent and remote as the primeval forest. The fretful traffic sped left and right against the railings, and beyond lay that patch of stealthy vitality older than London. What an amazing thing is the coming of spring to London. The very pavements seem ready to crack and lift under the denied earth, in the air is a consciousness of life which tells you that if traffic stopped for a fortnight grass would grow again in Piccadilly and corn would spring in pavement cracks where a horse had spilt his 'feed'. And the squares of London, so dingy and black since the first October gale, fill week by week with the rising tide of life, just as the sea, running up the creeks and pushing itself forward inch by inch towards the land, comes at last to each remote rock pool.

The squares of London, those sacred little patches of the country-side preserved, perhaps, by the Anglo-Saxon instinct of grass and trees, hold in their restricted glades some part of the magic of spring. I suppose many a man has stood at his window above a London square in April hearing a message from the lanes of England.

H.V. Morton, *In Search of England*

✻ ✻ ✻

A windy April day in Kensington Gardens sets off a
relationship between an old man and a young woman
in A. N. Wilson's novel The Sweets of Pimlico.

Each morning, since it was a harsh April, she stayed indoors and read books from the Public Library about Natural History. In the afternoon, however fierce the weather, she walked in Kensington Gardens and repeated to herself the names of at least half a dozen of the species that she had been studying in the morning. [...]

The wind blew in icy gusts, so strong and cold that one caught one's breath and felt unable to move without pain; like the weather on lacrosse afternoons. And then the wind would suddenly subside, leaving one gasping. [...]

She was the only person at the Round Pond. The harshness of the wind had driven away even the most hardened of nannies, pushing prams, or Spring Visitors looking for undesirable companionship. The trees were noisy and frenzied. Early blossoms flew about like confetti. Evelyn pulled her woollen hat more firmly on to her head and breathed hard into her mittens.

But it was as she turned back, down the path to the left of the Round Pond, that she realised that she was not alone in braving the weather. First, she saw some white envelopes scurrying down the path in front of her. And then, from behind, she heard a very foreign voice calling out, "Please! The letters! Please! If you would be so kind!"

Homo sapiens, male, aged, was her automatic reflection.

A stout old man, with a puce complexion and a white beard, ran along shouting. He waved a walking-stick in the air. But it looked more like a piece of decoration than something which he needed to help him get along.

Evelyn was naturally athletic. She ran after the letters and soon picked them up. [...]

"Too kind," he said, collapsing on to a conveniently placed bench, which he tapped gently with his finger-tips, indicating that the girl was to sit beside him. She did so, telling herself that he was clearly a person with whom it was eminently safe to sit on a park bench in Kensington, and wondering at the same time if she believed it.

When she was close to him, she could see that there were very small veins all over his face; that what had looked like an even red from a distance was actually composed of many little rivers of blue and pink flowing beneath the surface of his cheeks. One of his eyes was rather bloodshot. He had a good head of hair, a thick white profusion, with no traces of baldness.

Puffing, a little exaggeratedly, he put a brown hat on his head and rubbed his cheeks with the palms of his hands. Evelyn was aware of the smell of moth-balls which appeared to be emanating from his expansive tweed trousers, whose creases hung loosely over highly-polished brown shoes like curtains sweeping a parquet floor.

She began to wonder if the old gentleman was going to have a heart attack; and, if people had heart attacks, what one did.

The occasional bird, pigeon or sparrow or starling – sometimes the first of the swifts and swallows – flew, or was blown past. Sometimes a Boeing 707, or an aeroplane so high in the clouds as to be unidentifiable, sent down its melancholy sigh through the winds.

"My hat!" the old gentleman suddenly exclaimed.

He had been unwise to put it on his head without holding it there. At first, Evelyn took his exclamation as metaphorical, but when she saw what had happened, she sprang to her feet and ran after it. Every time she stopped to pick it up, the wind tossed it a little further out of her reach, on to the lawn, up the slope, down the slope, until it found a resting place in a flower-bed. *Kerria japonica* and *prunus tenella* were almost in flower at the back of the border shading irises and narcissi and late crocuses at the front. The hat was perched on the twiggy entrails of a thick, only slightly flowering forsythia bush. She grabbed it and triumphantly laughed. [...]

"Here you are," she said, extending the hat out to him, faintly with the tone of "and mind you look after it better in future."

"What a decrepit old fool I am; a worn-out old wind-bag," her companion protested. "Your excellent young legs, with the speed of Apollo, did what my worn-out stumps could never have done." There was an air of drama, combined with a hint of lechery, very faint, injected into his entire manner as he spoke – if *spoke*, is not too mild a word to describe the way in which he seemed to declaim his words – which confirmed Evelyn's inkling that he was an actor. But his face had a vaguely spiritual quality – something about the way in which the lips appeared to be constantly tasting something, and the eyes forever staring into the distance – which was powerfully alluring.

"Why should you run around parks in search of an Old Age Pensioner's belongings?"

"It was nothing, really." He half embarrassed, and half delighted her.

"My dear, you have a social conscience. You have retrieved an Old Age Pensioner's hat." This seemed to amuse him considerably. "I have fought against your country in a world war. But still they pay me a pension, and you retrieve my hat. You have rendered me an inestimable service. How to repay it?

Perhaps you would permit me to repay you with tea, perhaps, and perhaps, some cakes?"

This was an excellent idea, and it was pronounced in accents a good deal less foreign than those in which he had addressed her at first.

"I live in Pimlico," he said, as they turned for the Palace Gate. "It is too far, or I would invite you there. The hotel yonder does a very tolerable brew." He took evident pleasure in this idiomatic turn of phrase. They crossed Kensington Road, and, as they dodged the traffic, he took her arm.

The showy portals of the Earl of Oxford Hotel did not look very promising to Evelyn, who had very developed notions about what constituted "a good cup of tea". But, as they swung through the circular doors, it was suddenly warm and quiet. The carpet beneath her feet felt very soft. The old gentleman lead the way – he was clearly familiar with the place – to a large "lounge" where they sat down in a corner in an expansive leather sofa. After the noises of wind and traffic, there was an almost eerie silence.

A. N. Wilson, *The Sweets of Pimlico*

✳ ✳ ✳

But there's nothing like summer in the city: it's when London really comes into its own. Journalist Eduardo Reyes enjoys the democratising effect of the long hot days and the odd juxtapositions they can throw up ... like the sounds of rapper P Diddy meeting the William Morris-inspired architecture of Charles Voysey.

On a good summer day in London, its people are aware of one another – and inhabit common space – as at no other time in the year. And as the good days tend to cluster together between the storms and periods of cool, drizzling disappointment, that sense of what makes up your community gains momentum.

It's there in the centre of London where, with the exception of the Tube and the buses, a hot day has the effect of improving everyone's mood and democratising the city. So pleased is everyone by the light and by the warmth the baked turf, the brick and the pavements feed back into the air that they will happily stand, sit or crouch in the cramped outside spaces around the city's bars from early evening till last orders – as close as if they were on a crowded commuter train, but consenting and content. Thin white wine, lager and love are in the air – even for the couple who have taken their puzzled, but pleased, toddler to the nearest bar after the child's customary pre-bed bath.

And from the centre to the suburbs, high up in the limpid evening light, first swifts, and later bats, turn and speed on the currents of warm air.

In London's yellow- and red-brick Victorian suburbs – from Kennington to Tooting, Kentish Town to Colindale, Mile End to Stoke Newington, and Fulham to Ealing – the long streets, and the shorter cross-roads that link them, are lined with a mix of whole houses (bought for a song twenty years ago, or on a City bonus in the last five years), council properties, and the rented and bought flats of professionals. With the rickety sashes raised (and often propped), the music and conversation, parties and secrets of each spill into the common space. Cramped parties and barbeques and dinners *à deux* continue later than was intended on the patios and gardens to the rear, and different accents of class, region and country mingle as they otherwise would not.

Cars with loud music pounding from open windows stop to drop off and pick up, and teenagers with a little swagger talk on street corners later than they usually would. Here in London the loud Rap with its backdrop of box hedges, wheely bins and casement windows, is the only place on earth where P Diddy and Voysey might collide on a street corner.

The parks and the commons are also heavily used in summer, and the wearers of shell suits and items from the Boden catalogue do not, or cannot, give each other the same wide berth as at other times of the year – if you have a bull dog or a labrador, a 'fun' tank top or a Dolce and Gabanna belt, the need to occupy the same spaces laid out by *rus-in-urbe* visionaries is shared, for you'll find every kind of Londoner on the common or at an urban lido.

They planned well, the capital's visionaries and architects of the past – though they could not have foreseen how we would live, nor the use we would make of their ideals and architectural pattern books. But in the ozone-heavy air above the red-tiled roofs, above the parks, plane trees, cars, barbeques and sashes, the swifts and the bats those visionaries would have seen are still playing in the warm city evenings.

Summer, as no other time of the year, reminds us why we choose to live in London.

Eduardo Reyes, 'Voysey and P Diddy: London in Summer'

And the rest is history ...

A few jewels from the formidable treasure chest of writing on London's history, starting with the theatre of Shakespeare's time, recreated by Sam Wannamaker's new Globe Theatre on London's South Bank, next to Tate Modern.

The theatre of Shakespeare's day was part of London's vast entertainment industry, and the playhouses stood amid other venues of leisure and pleasure – baiting-rings and cock-pits, bowling-alleys and dicing-houses, taverns and brothels. These places were typically found in the old 'liberties' of the city, beyond the writ of the civic authorities. The Liberty of the Clink in Southwark, where the Globe stood, was a brothel quarter from time immemorial; the prostitutes were called 'Winchester geese', as the liberty was administered by the Bishop of Winchester.

A stone's throw from the Globe stood the celebrated brothel called Holland's Leaguer, run by Elizabeth Holland. A seventeenth-century woodcut shows a formidable, moated little fortress on the riverbank. A wooden jetty leads to a tall studded gate, beside which stands a bouncer armed with a tall pike; a small square hatch in the gate permits the vetting of visitors. This hatch was a common feature of brothels: it is probably the origin of Pickt-hatch ('pickt' = spiked), a zone of the red-light district in Clerkenwell of which Wilkins's Cow Cross Street establishment was part. Another architectural feature of the brothel is the latticed window, which is both a security arrangement and a form of excitement – the girls half glimpsed within, in provocative states of undress: 'those milk-paps/That through the window-bars bore at men's eyes' (*Timon*, 4.3.117–18).

If the moralizers are to be believed, the theatre itself was little more than an annex to the brothel, and sexual assignations were as much part of the entertainment as the play itself. In that 'chappel of Satan, I meane the Theatre', says Anthony Munday, you will see 'harlots utterlie past all shame, who press to the forefront of the scaffolde ... to be as an object to all mens eies'. According to Thomas Dekker, prostitutes were so frequently in the theatre that they knew the plays word for word – 'every punck and her squire, like the interpreter and his puppet, can rand [rant] out by heart' the speeches they have heard. A generation later, in the 1630s, William Prynne notes the proximity of theatres and brothels – 'the Cock-pit and Drury Lane, Blackfriars play-house and Duke Humfries, the Red Bull and Turnball Street; the Globe and Bankside brothel houses'. Hence 'common strumpets and adulteresses, after our stage-plays ended, are often-times prostituted near our playhouses, if not in them (as they may easily be, since many players, if reports be true, are common pandars)'.

Trulls, trots, molls, punks, queans, drabs, stales, nuns, hackneys, vaulters, wagtails – in a word, whores – were everywhere, but professional prostitution was only part of it. According to the same writers the theatres were a general free-for-all of assignations, pick-ups and uninhibited flirtations, a place where 'light & lewd disposed persons' congregated for 'actes and bargains of incontinencie'.

Charles Nicholl, *The Lodger: Shakespeare on Silver Street*

❖ ❖ ❖

The Great Plague that decimated London in 1665–66 ended with the Great Fire of London. Both are

witnessed by Thomas, a character in Neil Hanson's
The Dreadful Judgement.

The tolling of bells counting the dead had stilled at the approach of night, and the iron-studded gates shut behind him with a crash that echoed in the abrupt silence. He glanced up at the sky and a shiver of fear ran through him as he saw how quickly the light was fading. He hurried away through the eerie, echoing streets. They had been so little used these past months that clumps of grass were growing from them.

No prentice boys called in customers or shouted their masters' wares – the shops were all shuttered and barred. There were no hawkers or strolling gallants, no coaches or sedan chairs, no horses clattering over the cobbles, no drays or wagons labouring up the steep streets from the waterfront. It was so quiet that the sound of the river rushing through the arches of the bridge on the flood tide could be heard throughout the city.

There was not even a dog or cat to be seen. They had been hunted down and slaughtered, skewered by halberds or poisoned with ratbane. Gathered by the rakers, the corpses were piled in their thousands on the laystalls just outside the city walls along with the street sweepings and the contents of emptied middens and houses of office. Hundreds more were cast into the stinking Fleet Ditch, where foraging hogs gorged themselves on the bounty.

Even the Thames, the great highway of London, was deserted. No lighters or wherries plied the waters, and the wharves, once lined with merchantmen jostling for space to unload, stood empty. Captains unable to take their cargoes to other, safer ports tied up only long enough to empty their holds with fevered haste, then fled for the safety of the open sea, praying that the pestilence had not sailed with them. […]

In every street he saw houses marked by a crude red cross with the message – part warning, part entreaty – 'Lord have mercy upon us' daubed on the door. In the meaner lanes, courts and alleys, almost every house bore the stigma. On some the crosses had been faded by the sun to the colour of dried blood. Others were crimson, fresh-painted. Their doors and ground-floor shutters were locked and bolted from the outside and a guard with a halberd stood watch.

From behind the shutters and from the dark interiors of the upper floors came sounds that chilled the blood: the ravings of madmen deep in the grip of fever, the cries of babies and children that no voice sought to soothe, and the screams that spoke of pain and torment beyond endurance.

The plague nurtured in the festering tenements of the liberties and out-parishes during the early part of the year had spilled over the walls to invade the heart of the city itself. Most of the sufferers were poor. The tradesmen, merchants and people of quality had long since fled to the sanctuary of the countryside. Their houses were locked and bolted, the shuttered windows blind to the suffering of those servants turned onto the streets to survive as best they could.

Amid the exodus of terrified citizens, only those, like Thomas, whose business forced them to stay, or those too poor to flee, remained. Now it was too late. The gates were closed against London's own citizens, but even if they were thrown wide open, one hundred thousand souls could never leave. They lay beneath the swollen earth of the parish churchyards or tumbled in heaps into the plague pits dug beyond the city walls. […]

Thomas saw at last the familiar tower of St Margaret's, rising out of the warehouses and mean housing jostling around its skirts. He turned into Fish Street Hill, past the Star Inn. It had been much used by stagecoaches, but now its door was locked and the great wooden gates in the archway leading to the stable yard were closed.

As he approached the plain church, 'a proper church, but monuments has it none', he kept his nosegay clamped to his face to ward off both the miasma of the plague and the stench that assailed his nostrils. It was neither the familiar stink from the shambles in Little Eastcheap – where in any event few of the butchers and poulterers remained – nor the dank mud-smell drifting up from the river. The foul odour emanated from the churchyard, where the newly dead clustered outside the walls outnumbered the living praying for salvation inside.

Black rats, ravens and carrion crows quarrelled and clawed at the surface of the freshly turned earth in the cramped churchyard; in the space of a single summer, it had been raised several feet above its previous level. As the daylight faded, the rats grew bolder, scuttling along the foot of the walls and foraging among the heaps of filth in the kennels. They seemed no more sinister than the other denizens of the night: the robbers spilling from criminal sanctuaries that even the watchmen dared not penetrate, to pillage the empty houses of those who had fled the city, or plunder the corpses of those trinkets that the plague nurses and drivers of the dead-carts had not already looted. […]

It was eight o'clock. As Thomas pushed away his plate he heard the bell of St Margaret's begin to toll. He would have recognized it anywhere, its peal as distinctive to him as the voices of his children among the noise of the city streets. The sound swelled at once, echoed by the bells of St Magnus at the foot of the hill, St George in Botolph Lane, St Michael in Crooked Lane and St Leonard in Eastcheap, spreading out across the city, tolling from a hundred church towers, with the great baritone peal of St Paul's rising above them all.

As the echoes faded and died, Thomas saw wisps of smoke curling around the open casement and moments later there was the crackle of flames. He ran to the door. Smoke was swirling from a blaze at the head of the lane. Figures ran to and fro, briefly outlined against the flames, and the reflected firelight glittered from the gilded star hanging over the passage leading to the inn. Lower down the hill, by the church entry, the glow of another blaze made the shadows dance on the walls, and a wall of flame and dense, choking clouds of smoke barred the lane by King's Head Alley.

Shouting to their daughters to follow, Thomas and Elizabeth ran from the house and up the lane. The fires were well ablaze now, and the air was heavy with smoke and the smell of burning pitch. The searing heat scorched his cheeks as they ducked down the church entry.

As they emerged onto Fish Street, they stopped, stupefied at the sight. Fires blazed all the way down the hill and burned the length of the bridge. Flames even rose from ships moored in midstream on the river and speckled the darkness on the Southwark bank.

He turned to look west and saw the sky, full dark now, lit by a glow that stretched from one end of the city to the other. The ramparts of the city walls were capped with fire and gouts of flame flared from every street, casting a baleful glare on the stone towers and spires of the churches, tall as great oaks, that rose above the huddled houses.

Above them all stood the mighty bulk of St Paul's, its towering walls and squat, square tower ringed by a circle of fire. Great blazes burned at every angle of the walls, the flames licking at the crumbling stonework.

The smoke from a thousand fires rose even higher into the still, humid air, obscuring the moon and staining it ochre. It disappeared from sight as the smoke merged with the black clouds gathering in the night sky. A dark pall hung motionless over the city and the stench of burning pitch and brimstone smelled like the gates of hell.

Neil Hanson, *The Dreadful Judgment*

✽ ✽ ✽

A more positive scene: shopping in the rebuilt London of 1700.

At six o'clock in the morning in summer or sunrise in winter, the London housewife or her servant was summoned by the market bell six days a week to shop for food. There were a couple of hours of brisk trading in which City regulations ensured she had priority before tradesmen, hawkers and the suburban shopkeepers moved in to buy their stocks. There were no fixed prices and she had to bargain hard, judging the quality and weight of the goods herself. She paid in cash. Her purchases would be handed over unwrapped and she carried them home without help. She was lucky in at least one respect. London was a city of plenty. Not only was there a rich variety of foodstuffs from the provinces, but London was a great port which imported more exotic goods than could be produced at home. 'For pleasure, or luxury, London is a magazine, where all is at hand, and scarce any thing wanting that money can purchase. Here is to be had, not only what Europe affords, but what is fetched by navigation from the remotest parts of the habitable world.'

Since the Great Fire the old haphazard arrangement of congested street markets had been superseded by four new sets of buildings, where pattern and order replaced the free-for-all mixtures of goods. Leadenhall in the street of that name was the grandest of these new markets, consisting of myriad stalls in four spacious open courtyards. This was a major market for meat. Sheep and cattle were brought into London on the hoof, sold to the butchers at Smithfield and slaughtered behind their premises and in back yards in the City itself and just outside the walls. In lieu of refrigeration, slaughtering was necessarily a regular occurrence. The blood and offal posed a constant problem in waste disposal. The stink was particularly odious for those in the vicinity, not least the churchgoers passing Butcher Hall Lane on the way to St Paul's on Sunday morning.

At Leadenhall beef was sold on 100 stalls, leaving 140 stalls for mutton, veal and poultry. Turkey had become popular and they were walked from Norfolk in droves of up to 1,000. Poultry was fattened up in London storehouses before being taken to market. Country wives brought in chickens and rabbits to sell. There were rows for fish, rows for butter, rows for cheese. Wholesalers could go to Queenhythe market for corn and to Billingsgate for fish – both conveniently situated along the north bank of the Thames where the cargoes were unloaded – and to the Stocks (named after the gillyflowers on sale there) in Poultry for fruit and vegetables. The Swiss visitor César de Saussure was impressed:

> Nowhere can you see finer markets than in London, especially those of Leadenhall, of Stocks Market, and several others; they are vast, covered, and shut in, and in them you can find every kind of butcher's meat, the finest in all the world, and kept with the greatest cleanliness. England is celebrated, and justly so, for her excellent meats, especially beef and veal, mutton being rather coarse, often tasting of tallow, but full of juice. In these markets an abundance of every kind of salt and fresh water fish is to be found; also vegetables and poultry of every description.

For the housekeeper who did not feel up to the market, help was at hand. César de Saussure explains: 'Besides these public markets, quantities of small vendors go through the streets, especially in the morning, calling out their wares for sale; thus, if you prefer it, you need not leave your house to buy your provisions.' Against the constant thunder of iron-wheeled coaches and carts on cobbled paving, the streets rang to the hawkers' cries: 'Four for sixpence, mackerel!', 'Twelve pence a peck, oysters!', 'Cherries ripe-ripe-ripe!' and 'Pippins fine? Pippins fine?' Hawkers and itinerant pedlars were greatly resented by the shopkeepers who paid rates and rent for their premises.

The milkmaid carrying a pair of churns on a shoulder yoke was a daily visitor. 'Milk maids below!' Asses, whose milk was much sought after for young children and those with digestive problems, were led from door to door and milked straight into the customers' jugs. Cows for milking were kept in London and César de Saussure felt particularly at home when he visited the nearby village of Islington which was famous for its cow pastures and dairies.

Maureen Waller, *1700: Scenes from London Life*

* * *

The history of a city is largely the history of its progress in practical matters like sewage systems, adequate running water and rubbish collection and disposal. London was a pretty smelly place until the Great Stink of 1858 finally forced the government to act. Through the eyes (and nose) of Tom, in Clare Clark's The Great Stink, *we get more than a whiff of what London was like in the nineteenth century.*

The stinks came in layers, each one thick and sticky as the river sludge on the soles of your boots. If you only used your nose you could pick them out neat as fleas.

At the bottom of the stink was the river. It stretched a good few streets back from the banks, in fact there weren't many places in the city you couldn't catch a whiff of it on a warm day, but in Thames-street it was certain as the ground you stood on. You couldn't see so much as the surface of the water through a fog like this one, not even if you hung right over the river wall, but you couldn't miss knowing it was there. The smell was solid and brown as the river itself. The water didn't know nothing of any modesty or shame. It wasn't going to hide its filth among the narrow alleys and rookeries in the lower parts of town like them in the Government might wish to do. It grinned its great brown grin and kept on going, brazen as you like, a great open stream of shit through the very centre of the capital, the knobbles and lumps of rich and poor jostling and rubbing along together, faces turned up to the sky. The rich ladies could close their doors and muffle their noises all they wanted; theirs stank same as anyone else's and out here was the proof, their private doings as clear to see as if they was on display at the Crystal Palace. There were times, morning and evening in particular, when there was twenty steamers at least churning their great wheels below London Bridge, when the water was so dense and brown it seemed that it should bear a man's weight, so as he could walk clean across it without so much as wetting his feet. On a hot day the stink could knock you flat. Through the windows of hansoms on London Bridge Tom had seen ladies swoon dead away and white-faced gentlemen cover their mouths with handkerchiefs. But on a November afternoon the salt-water tang of the sea ran in silvery threads through its thick brown stink, at least up as far as Southwark. Sometimes, when Tom came out on to the river bank at night down Greenwich way, he swore he could see the salt rising from the river, glinting and dancing above its muddy plough like clouds of silver midges.

The next smell you got, when you was done with the river smell, was the sour soot-smudged stink of the fog. London's fogs came in all sorts and each one smelled only of itself. This one was a slimy yellow-brown gruel that sank and crawled along the streets, skulking into courts and cellars, looping itself around pillars and lampposts. You tasted it more than smelled it. It greased itself over the linings of your nostrils and choked your chest, distilling in fat droplets in your eyebrows and whiskers. When Tom breathed through his mouth it coated his tongue with the taste of rancid lard, faintly powdered with the black flour of coal dust. It had mouldered over the city for close to a week, rusting iron and smearing soot over all it touched. Through its gloom the buildings looked like grease stains on a tablecloth.

South of the river, of course, the fog got itself mixed up with the smoke. There were parts of Bermondsey where the sky looked like it was held up by nothing but chimneys and the same again in Southwark. Each smoke had its own particular flavour, so as you could always tell where you were. The smoke from the glue manufacturers had a nagging acid smell that caught in the back of your skull and made you dizzy, while the soap-boilers, their stink had the sickly flavour of boiling fat. The match factories' chimneys pissed a kind of yellow smoke that reeked bad as the alley behind a public house. Then there was the particular drugging smell of hops from the breweries, which didn't smell nothing like the reek of leather and dog shit from the tanneries. South of the river you could smell the change in the neighbourhood when you crossed the street.

Here in Thames-street the smell was all of its own. In a fog like this one the market was no more than a dirty smudge looming out of its moat of mud, the everlasting clamour of the hucksters muffled even thirty yards off. But the reek of fish, stale and fresh, that was stately and self-important as a church. As its base, for foundations, was the seashore smell of seaweed and salt water, and upon these smells were built, layer by layer, reek by reek, the pungent stinks of smelt, of bloater, of sole, herring, whiting, mussel, oyster, sprat, cod, lobster, turbot, crab, brill, haddock, eel, shrimp, skate and a hundred others. The porters that hustled between the boats and the stalls carried them from shore to shop and back again, every inch of them given over to the intoxicating brew of stinks. The stallholders swung their knives in it and sent it splattering across their bloodied wooden boards. Their leather hats and aprons were dark and stiff with the contents of a thousand fish stomachs. Streaks of blood striped the fish-women's arms, their faces, the hems of their quilted petticoats, Fish scales caught in the mud on their boots and glinted like scraps of silver. Melting ice slid from their tables, shiny and thick with fish slime. Beside them wooden crates packed with straw leaked salt and fish fluids into ditches and gullies. Even if you was only in Billingsgate an hour or less the stench caught in the pelt of your greatcoat so that you carried a whisper of it with you the remainder of the day.

Tom stood aside as a fish fag bullied her way through the crowd, a dripping basket of flounder on her head. When the stalls finally were shut for the day and the fish-women went home, the flattened mess of their bonnets and caps and hair would be lush with the stink. In Thames-street the everyday every-place smells of London, smells so common you had to remind yourself to smell them at all, crept into the nostrils for no more than a moment before being straight-ways knocked out again. Tobacco, the rotting straw and dung of a cab-stand, hot bread, the pungent gush from an uncovered sewer, the occasional surge of roasted beef and spilled porter from an ale-house door, the hot red heart of a lit brazier, none of them were any match for the fish. Not even the sharp sour odour of unwashed clothes and bodies and breath, a smell that had occupied Tom's nostrils without pause for all the decades of his life so that he no longer took any account of it at all, not even that could make more than the faintest scratch on the proud edifice of stink that was Billingsgate Market.

Clare Clark, The Great Stink

✣ ✣ ✣

Something a little more pleasing: dawn at the old Covent Garden fruit and vegetable market, before its transformation into a tourist attraction of dinky shops and street entertainers.

As the dawn was just breaking he found himself close to Covent Garden. The darkness lifted, and, flushed with faint fires, the sky hollowed itself into a perfect pearl. Huge carts filled with nodding lilies rumbled slowly down the polished empty street. The air was heavy with the perfume of the flowers, and their beauty seemed to bring him an anodyne for his pain. He followed into the market, and watched the men unloading their wagons. A white-smocked carter offered him some cherries. He thanked him, and wondered why he refused to accept any money for them, and began to eat them listlessly. They had been plucked at midnight, and the coldness of the moon had entered into them. A long line of boys carrying crates of striped tulips, and of yellow and red roses, defiled in front of him, threading their way through the huge jade-green piles of vegetables. Under the portico, with its grey sun-bleached pillars, loitered a troop of draggled bare-headed girls, waiting for the auction to be over. Others crowded round the swinging doors of the coffee-house in the Plazza. The heavy cart-horses slipped and stamped upon the rough stones, shaking their bells and trappings. Some of the drivers were lying asleep on a pile of sacks. Iris-necked, and pink-footed, the pigeons ran about picking up seeds.

After a little while, he hailed a hansom, and drove home. For a few moments he loitered upon the door-step, looking round at the silent Square with its blank, close-shuttered windows, and its staring blinds. The sky was pure opal now, and the roofs of the houses glistened like silver against it. From some chimney opposite a thin wreath of smoke was rising. It curled, a violet riband, through the nacre-coloured air.

Oscar Wilde, *The Picture of Dorian Gray*

✳ ✳ ✳

In her memoirs, veteran romantic novelist Barbara Cartland recalls upper-class London in the early 1920s … and seeing the Charleston danced in an unexpected location.

London in 1919–20 was structurally unchanged from the Edwardian days. Gas-light was still common in the private houses. Piccadilly was a line of dignified mansions and clubs; the great houses, such as Devonshire, Grosvenor, Dorchester, Lansdowne and Londonderry, were all inhabited by their owners.

Devonshire House had magnificent wrought-iron gates tipped in gold facing into Piccadilly. […]

I wasn't interested in people who were dead or too old for me to meet them, but it always seemed to me that the gates of Devonshire House and the great high walls had a special magical quality for stimulating the imagination.

Behind its garden there was Lansdowne House – of perfect Adam design – facing into Berkeley Square, and dividing these two princely mansions was a narrow passage, which was a private right of way. One day every year Lord Lansdowne sent his men to lock and bolt the doors at each end of the passage, but for the other 364 days it was available as a short cut between Curzon Street and Berkeley Street.

Many crimes had taken place in Lansdowne Passage, with its high, sightless walls; but it was not the stabbings, the robberies or the vile assignations that I thought about when I walked through Lansdowne Passage, or the beautiful, passionate Devonshires, but of the ghost which is reputed to haunt it. […] Londonderry House was the centre of the political world. Great receptions were held there on the eve of Parliament. Political hostesses were said still to exert a considerable influence over leading Ministers.

Lady Londonderry, who always looked like Boadicea in her chariot, carried the fabulous Londonderry diamond tiara as if it was a crown. In fact, it looked not unlike one. I remember being very overawed by her and the glittery, bejewelled and bedecorated company as I climbed from the marble hall up the great winding staircase to where at the top she and Lord Londonderry received their guests.

There was the stentorian announcement of names, the chatter of educated voices, the rustle of silks, the heat of people crowded together, moving very slowly step by step, the fragrance of scent and flowers, and an occasionable whiff of mothballs. […] In Park Lane Sir Ernest Cassel's mansion was a monument to Edwardian taste and a financier's money. He had bought eight tons of Tuscany marble, and even the kitchens were lined with it. His dining room, with its antique oak panelling and great arched ceiling, could seat more than 100 guests. […]

The Charleston arrived in London from the United States in the summer of 1925, and was received in state by sixty dancing instructors assembled by the *Dancing Times* at the Carnival Club in Dean Street. Then it swept the country, but not without a great deal of criticism and opposition. It was banned by hotels and in public halls as 'a Negro dance'.

'I set my face absolutely against the Charleston,' Mrs. Wilfred Ashley said. 'I think acrobatics in the ballroom are in the worst of taste.'

This was followed by my own remarks, which sound now very pompous, and I can't think why I ever made them.

'It is only the very objectional Oxford-trousered, tight-waisted kind of young man,' I said, 'who is to be seen doing the Charleston, and the girls who dance it will wear ultra-short frocks, ultra tight, and use make-up to excess. It is all hideously vulgar.'

Naturally nobody paid any attention, any more than they listened to the Vicar of St. Adrian's, Bristol, who declared:

> 'Any lover of the beautiful would die rather than be associated with the Charleston. It is neurotic! It is rotten! It stinks! Phew! Open the windows!'

But the fact that the Prince of Wales was seen doing it extremely well in every night-club naturally took the sting out of such opposition.

Santos Casani, a well-known dance instructor, demonstrated the steps of the Charleston on the roof of a taxi moving down Regent Street. He and his staff gave as many as 280 lessons a day.

Barbara Cartland, *We Danced All Night*

* * *

> *Once an integral part of London's social life, Lyons tea-shops have disappeared into the realms of 'history'. Penelope Fitzgerald resurrects one for her novel* At Freddie's.

Hannah suggested – because she knew they always closed at seven – a Lyons teashop. […]

Lyons teashops might almost have been particularly designed for the resolution of such awkward situations, and perhaps when, fifteen years later, the teashops were discontinued as uneconomic the situations disappeared with them. In a Lyons, as Hannah had reflected, the limits of communication had to be reached by seven o'clock, while at the same time it was necessary to share a table or at all events to sit very close to other customers, so that although everyone restricted their elbows, their bodies and their newspapers and by a long established convention showed no signs of understanding what they overheard, they provided all the same a certain check on human intimacy. The rosy-tinted looking-glasses on every wall also acted as a restraint on the undemanding clientèle who would rather keep their eyes on their plates than be caught looking at their own reflexions.

At Lyons, the females, if escorted, sat at a table and 'kept the place' while the males queued for what was needed and carried it back, as their remote forebears had done, with difficulty. During this process the tea overflowed into the saucers. Later the sugar, which was only put out on every fourth table, had to be borrowed and exchanged. There was always a good deal of apologising at Lyons.

Penelope Fitzgerald, *At Freddie's*

* * *

Now that London is such an established multi-racial city, it's hard to remember how difficult life could be for West Indians answering the post-war invitation to work in Britain – forced to live in the poorest areas and regularly faced with blatant and unchallenged racism.

Outside a thick mist wrapped itself around the street. Leila bit her bottom lip and trembled like a needle on a gauge. She took the long curve and walked with head bent, shoulders sloping, towards the bus stop. She clung to a small cluster of bright flowers. As she passed by, the children stopped playing, seemingly more out of habit than curiosity. She remembered that this was a school holiday and they had nothing else to do while their parents were at work. At the end of the street she joined a short queue of six or seven people, all of them West

Indians, and waited for the bus. Across the road a lorry hurtled by, throwing up bits of rubbish and paper high in the air.

She sat in the front seat on the top deck of the bus, looking down at the people and the life in the street below. She noticed that in some areas there were many coloured people and in other areas there were very few. She noticed that coloured people did not drive big cars or wear suits or carry briefcases, that they seemed to look sad and cold. She noticed that the eyes of white people on the posters never left her no matter how quickly she glanced at them. The rivers that the bus lurched over were like dirty brown lines, full of empty bottles and cigarette ends, cardboard boxes and greying suds of pollution. Leila knew that this was normal. She would have to try harder to get used to such things if she was going to make anything of her life here.

The bus turned another corner and Leila stared out of the window. She worried about her mother, whom she was going to visit. She looked at the snaking, endless streets which were full of people carrying umbrellas, weaving in and out of one another's paths, so hurried, private English faces with newspapers and rubbish curled around their feet like dead vines. Then the bus splashed to a halt at a new set of traffic lights, and Leila noticed that the lettering got smaller and more hurried, as if the artist was running out of paint and time.

'IF YOU WANT A NIGGER NEIGHBOUR VOTE LABOUR.'

They turned right into a road where the children played happily among broken bottles and bricks. Between the identical houses she could see not even the smallest fraction of an inch. Then the bus stopped to wait for a lorry to pull out and Leila looked down a side street. Two little girls, their faces blackened with grime and filth, bounced merrily upon an old mattress. For a moment they forgot their other friends and lost themselves in simple pleasure.

On the street corner a middle-aged woman, painted to appear as if young, modelled with a lamp-post. She looked dirty. Leila thought she probably smelled even worse. A child, a coloured boy, who needed a good bath and a meal, stared at the bus and wiped his nose across the back of his sleeve. This is not yet winter, thought Leila, and the boy has a cold. The bus moved off and passed another of the women, this one leaning up against a parked car and filing her nails, happy to leave the lamp-posts vacant. Leila looked away and began to try and calculate the number of times she had made this journey to the hospital.

Caryl Phillips, *The Final Passage*

✱ ✱ ✱

Moving on from the fifties to the time when London began to 'swing': it seemed to be the most happening place in the world, and anyone who lived through it is probably marked for life. Travel writer Rory MacLean takes us back.

London moves me like a great artist, forever surprising me, reinventing herself, seducing me in ways both fresh and familiar. A bold new sculpture of sweeping lines and mirror glass. A canvas of raw colour and laughter beside the Thames. A hot Soho play about her long, fiery past. She's contrary, complex and creative, an anarchist of a thousand faces, tender and bleak, ambitious and callous. She panders to the market of course, too often putting profit above principle, and her greatest work remains herself. Yet she inspires such zest for life: dancing all night, awakening at dawn to enthuse about fashion and money and the newest inde sounds.

At one pivotal moment of her inventive life – perhaps the years with the greatest hold on the popular imagination – she wore skinny ribbed sweaters and mini-skirts, cut her hair at alarming angles and changed the way we see the world. Alongside New York and San Francisco, she was the herald and harbinger of the Sixties, the place and time where the women's movement, gay lib, the environment and pop music became mainstream. Forty years on from the Summer of Love, I spent a day seeking out her enduring Sixties creations, swaying to the beat of those years' soaring optimism and cultural innovation.

Where did her ingenious decade begin? Perhaps in Soho at the short-lived Blue Gardenia Club when The Beatles – minus George Harrison and with Pete Best on drums – made their first, impromptu London appearance in 1961? Or on the platform of Dartford station when LSE student Mick Jagger bumped into his old school friend Keith Richards? Jagger was carrying some blues records, Richards his guitar. Or perhaps at Better Books on Charing Cross Road? It's here that the first imported copy of *On the Road*, by Beat author Jack Kerouac, kick-started a generation's journey, with his soul 'stripped naked', his body 'hungry for release', his heart 'mad to live, mad to talk, mad to be saved, desirous of everything at the same time.'

To begin I chose the world's most famous zebra crossing. Even at ten in the morning, a universe of fans queued to be photographed crossing Abbey Road, penning lyrics and love notes on the wall of a white-fronted Georgian mansion. Here the Beatles successfully auditioned for George Martin and created most of their music, even naming their last album after the EMI studio. When George Harrison died the staff stood massive speakers on its forecourt and blasted 'All Things Must Pass' onto the assembled mourners. There wasn't a dry eye in St. John's Wood. Now followers come in such numbers to the pop shrine that the wall and its flowing graffiti must be painted over every month.

'Bazaar was a banner, a battle cry, a symbol of the new sophistication,' the late veteran jazz singer George Melly once trumpeted. 'For good or ill, the embryonic concept of "Swinging London" was conceived in that small, disorganised shop in the King's Road.' In the absence of a yellow submarine or Magic Bus, I crossed London by tube (changing at Warren Street near to where the Brook Clinic supplied the first birth control pills to unmarried women in 1964). At her shop Bazaar, Mary Quant created the 'Chelsea Look' and the mini-skirt, wrestling fashion away from the privileged few and giving it to the young. Since then Bazaar's premises have morphed into the West Cornwall Pasty Company, by way of rag shops and a Häagen-Dazs ice cream parlour. 'I don't think this branch will be open for much longer,' said the Pole in the faux-Sassoon bob serving me from behind the counter. 'How can I sell enough pasties to pay £175,000 annual rent?'

A Frisbee-toss across Kensington the other iconic Sixties boutique has also vanished. Biba stood feathered hat-and-shoulders above the competition (Granny Takes a Trip, Carnaby Street and Kensington Market where Freddie Mercury sold shoes for a time). Despite opening in two undistinguished rooms off Ken High Street, Barbara Hulanicki – its founder and designer – sold her entire stock in the first hour of trading. Girls from as far away as Manchester and Liverpool queued outside their jam-packed venue of desire. Every few hours Hulanicki wiped their nose marks off the windows with a damp cloth. Her exotic, must-have clothes, Lurex and beads were also incredibly cheap. In 1966, for £15, the price of a Mary Quant party dress, a woman could walk out of Biba in a new coat, frock, shoes and hat. Fashion, together with pop music, declared Britain to be the most inventive country in the world. […]

'Rock stars. Is there anything they don't know?' asked Homer Simpson, the enduring defender of subversive counterculture ideals. I needed lunch and on the heels of rock stars aplenty made my way to Picasso, the plain and popular King's Road café which hasn't changed its décor in half a century.

'A lot of famous people have been through here but I don't remember their names,' admits the discreet and jovial Modesto Barani, manager since 1961. His bubbly waitress Tanja Combe is happier to drop names. Bob Geldof, who always orders the special stracciatella soup, is such a regular customer that letters can be left for him behind the till. Robbie Williams drinks white coffee. Gordon Ramsay treats his children to egg on toast. Geri Halliwell, aka Ginger Spice, never leaves without kissing Modesto.

In the Sixties Michael Caine and Terence Stamp used to hang

out at Picasso picking up birds. When Michelangelo Antonioni started filming *Blow-Up* around the corner, the lead actor David Hemmings regularly came here to fortify himself with tumblers of neat vodka. That definitive Sixties film used London – Chelsea, the unfinished Economist Building and Maryon Park – to create the perfect period piece. As I walked down to 100 Cheyne Walk, where the movie's legendary three-day party scene was shot, I reflected on Antonioni's conscious focus on style over substance. He knew well that 'Swinging London' was a copywriter's invention, a synthetic label dreamed up in the New York offices of *Time* magazine. Like *Blow-Up*, 'Swinging London' became an instant media myth.

'My first trip to Eel Pie Island was with my boyfriend an hour after he'd dealt with my virginity,' Judy Astley revealed beside the Thames. The sun was shining and our thoughts were on hedonistic histories. 'Once over that little footbridge it was other-worldly; tatty hippie magic to a nice middle-class schoolgirl with an essay on Chaucer to get back to. Pink Floyd (with Syd) were playing, complete with bubble light-show and we smoked Morning Glory seeds on the river bank in a hopeless attempt to get stoned.' Astley, author of 14 best-selling novels, now lives with her music-business husband in a Twickenham house (bought from Pete Townshend) which overlooks the tiny Thames island of boat-houses and picket-fenced gardens. In the Sixties she frequented – in spite of a parental ban – the crumbling Eel Pie Island Hotel, venue for young artists like Jagger, Eric Clapton, Jeff Beck and Long John Baldry. George Melly often played at the hotel, and remembers seeing sex 'rising from the island like steam from a kettle'. He was not alone in finding it very difficult not to get laid on Eel Pie. The hotel burned down in the Seventies and was replaced by a housing development. In a hall over a boatyard one resident tried to put on a gig featuring a local band a few years ago. His neighbours complained about the noise.

Across town in Chalk Farm, the Roundhouse has been more successful in keeping music live. In October 1966 the former locomotive maintenance depot hosted the decade's greatest fancy dress, the 'International Times First All-Night Rave Pop Op Costume Masque Drag Ball' (ten shillings at the door). Paul McCartney arrived dressed as a sheikh. Marianne Faithful won the prize for the skimpiest costume (an innovative variant on a nun's habit). Antonioni brought Monica Vitti and Pink Floyd's van backed into the giant jelly. In later years the Doors played here, Peter Brook staged his celebrated production of *The Tempest* and recently Van Morrison and Pink Martini performed in its boldly rejuvenated performance space.

The Sixties generation set out to change the world by changing itself. On the Aldermaston CND marches and at the Grosvenor Square demonstrations (which inspired Jagger to write Street Fighting Man), protestors believed their actions would help ban the bomb and get the troops out of Vietnam. In early 1969 the governors of the LSE, unnerved by the événements in Paris and homegrown radicals, erected iron gates and grilles around the campus to lock out striking students. In response the protestors decamped to the University of London Union, notoriously invading the Malet Street swimming pool. I plunged in myself for an afternoon swim, thinking of the anarchists who'd jumped in before me, stripped to the buff, and the more modest Marxist bathers who had retained their underwear. […]

My day ended as did so many Sixties nights, in a Wardour Street cellar. The Marquee Club was the place to hear new pop music – as The Troubadour was for folk – giving the Stones, The Who, the Yardbirds (featuring their new guitarist Eric Clapton), Rod Stewart and Bowie some of their first gigs, jogging forward to embrace punk and new wave bands like the Clash and the Pretenders until closing in 1988. Today its glazed tile entrance leads up to private Soho Lofts, but live music plays on in its basement, now the glamorous, Conran-designed Cuban restaurant. The wide circular staircase sweeps down into a dark, sprawling Hispanic beats bar where from time to time – as a bartender would have me believe – Clapton secretly returns to sip daquiris.

We live in an age of spin and cynicism, with our lives ordered, our music packaged and our creativity often impinged upon by profit margins. Yet in the matter of personal relationships, emotional honesty and individual choice, London – and her Sixties' artistry – has bequeathed us an enduring, potent legacy.

Rory MacLean, 'Revisiting Swinging Sixties London', *The Sunday Telegraph*

✳ ✳ ✳

Some things change for the better, some for the worse. Some just change. And some – like a London Saturday football match – stay pretty much the same. Here's protagonist Tony in Robert Elms' novel In Search of the Crack, *thinking about it all.*

The journey across town in a train wasn't really hard. The tangle of tourists and day trippers, shoppers and shop-lifters, girls who work and boys who rarely do was actually entertaining. Everybody seemed to be wearing bright colours and carrying Benetton bags, which is strangely disconcerting when you are off to see Fulham play at Craven Cottage. I saw many people who didn't look like my memories.

I saw nothing, though, of marauding terrace terrors in search of an off. This was a little disappointing, but little else had changed about Saturday, especially the way I felt. I still understood why I got excited. It is nice to know that the thing you thought was so important for all those years really is.

Coming out of the underworld, I laughed.

There were a couple of kiddy casuals, seriously dressed in this season's vogue, slipping small amounts of silver into the hand of the man when I went to hand in my ticket. Those elemental things, of course, never change.

But Fulham has gone. The area around Hammersmith Station remains reassuringly wrecked. But once you escape the flyover, you're into a ghetto. Monotonous, homogeneous rows of hatchbacked houses, where City drones and sons of Sloanes hold barbecues and talk in philistine tones. Gone are the children who scraped their knees and the families who waited in the rain for buses to take them to relatives in Paddington and Shepherd's Bush. Gone even are most of the criminals, to Surrey or somewhere. The river isn't grubby any more; it's lined with estate agents' lights.

I don't know if that old Fulham was worth fighting for. The one where my Uncle Jack, who knew Johnny Haynes, lived until, at the age of thirty-nine, he met my Aunt Ruth at the Hammersmith Palais, got married and moved to Reading. I'm sure that Fulham Football Club must be kept, though, even if the new locals care nothing for the game. Jack still travels in for most matches, and I will not accept that he should be robbed of his culture in the pursuit of developers' profits. Craven Cottage, so full of wonder, cannot be sold so cheaply; it is mine and my history.

I thought all of this, and I thought too that I am going to enjoy being mates with my brother again. Walking to football still makes me think.

Robert Elms, *In Search of the Crack*

❊ ❊ ❊

The history teacher narrating Graham Swift's Waterland *walks his dog in Greenwich Park – the city's open spaces teem with Londoners exercising their dogs – casting an historian's eye over his surroundings while haunted by a catastrophe in his personal history.*

On the top of Greenwich Hill, in Greenwich Park, stands an Observatory, founded by Charles II to search the mysteries of the stars. By the Observatory, set in the asphalt, much bestridden and photographed by visiting sightseers, a metal plate marks the line of longitude 0°. Near longitude 0°, perched on a plinth, becloaked and tricorned, stands General Wolfe, in bronze, staring to the Thames. And beneath General Wolfe, imitating his vigilant pose, stands the history teacher, in coat and scarf, taking in for the umpteenth time the famous view. The Maritime Museum (relics of Cook and Nelson); the Naval College (painted ceiling depicting four English monarchs). History's toy-cupboard. The pastime of past time. The history teacher himself, here in Greenwich at the head of end-of-term outings, his worthy Subject reduced to ice-cream guzzling and clambering over cannons. The river: a steel serpent coiling through clutter – derelict wharves and warehouses, decaying docks ...

From the top of Greenwich Hill it is possible not only to scan the inscrutable heavens but to peel back past panoramas (wind-jammers in the India Dock; royal barges, under Dutch-Master skies, bound for the palace), to imagine these river approaches to London as the wild water-country they once were. Deptford, Millwall, Blackwall, Woolwich ... And, away, out of sight to the east, the former marshes where, in 1980, they are building a flood barrier.

He stands alone and contemplates the view. Every Sunday, weather permitting, by various routes, to the Observatory and back. To longitude 0° and back. Pause on the belvedere; admiration of the view; silent, simultaneous but separate musings; then he to her or she to him (a smile; a shiver at the cold): "Home?" But now he stands alone, beneath the Hero of Quebec.

He stands alone – save for the golden retriever which rubs and nuzzles at his legs and begs to be indulged in more stick-throwing games. [...]

Low winter sun over Flamsteed's Observatory. Fiery high-lights on the roof of the Maritime Museum. The history teacher stands, surveys the outstretched view. Thinks of a student called Price. The only important thing ... If the truth be known he is frightened. If the truth be known, he doesn't know what to think. He is telling himself stories. (How a girl and a boy once ... How ...) He dreads going home. Dreads, now, weekends, Sundays. Dark evenings.

He turns. Stoops suddenly to ruffle vigorously the neck of the impatient Paddy, who, tail-wagging and panting, anticipates the return of his favourite game. He leaves the belvedere and the asphalt, strikes out onto the grass, overtaken by an ecstatic dog. In his gloved right hand he carries an already tooth-marked and saliva-dampened stick.

Graham Swift, *Waterland*

* * *

And to gather together many aspects of this phenomenal city, here's a sweeping view of it by Norman Collins – the 'Preface' to his novel London Belongs To Me. *His love of the city and fascination with every aspect of it fills every sentence. Although originally published immediately after the Second World War, it still rings remarkably true of today's London ... give or take a few small details. And it ends with a look into the future with the birth of a brand new Londoner.*

There may be other cities that are older. But not many. And there may be one across the Atlantic that is larger. But not much.

In fact, no matter how you look at it, London comes pretty high in the respectable upper order of things. It's got a past as well as a present; and it knows it. And this is odd. Because considering its age it's had a remarkably quiet history, London. Nothing very spectacular. Nothing exceptionally heroic. Not until 1940, that is. Except for the Great Fire and the Black Death and the execution of a King, not very much has ever happened there. It has just gone on prosperously and independently through the centuries – wattle one century, timber the next, then brick, then stone, then brick again, then concrete. Building new foundations on old ruins. And sprawling out across the fields when there haven't been enough ruins to go round.

In the result it's been growing up as well as growing. And it must be about mature by now. Even a bit past its prime, perhaps. Beginning to go back on itself, as it were. Maybe. But to see the people, you wouldn't think so.

Every city has its something. Rome has St. Peter's. Pekin has its Summer Palace. Moscow has the Kremlin. In Madrid there's the Prado. In New York there's the Empire State. Constantinople has St. Sophia. Cairo has Shepheard's. Paris has got the Eiffel Tower. Sydney has a bridge. Naples is content with its bay. Cape Town has Table Mountain. Benares is famous for its burning ghats. Pisa has a Leaning Tower. Toledo has a bull-ring. Stockholm has a Town Hall. Vancouver has a view. But London ... London ... What *is* it that London's got?

Well, there's St. Paul's Cathedral. But St. Peter's could put it into its pocket. There's Westminster Abbey. But there are Abbeys everywhere; they're dotted all over Europe. There's the Tower. Admittedly, the dungeons are convincing, but as a castle it's nothing. Not beside Edinburgh or Caernarvon. Even Tower Hill isn't really a hill: it's only an incline. Then there are the Houses of Parliament and the Law Courts. But they're merely so much Victorian Gothic – all turrets and arches and railings and things. There's Buckingham Palace. But that's too new; it hasn't toned in yet. It's just been planted there – a big flat-fronted palace with a made road leading up to it. No, it's the smaller, older palace of St. James's, just round the corner, with its grimy red brick and low windows and little open courtyards, that is nearer the real thing. Is the real thing, in fact. It's a positively shabby little palace, St. James's. And it's got London written all over it. And St. James's Palace – brick and soot and age – is written all over London.

Yes, that's London. Mile upon mile of little houses, most of them as shabby as St. James's. If you start walking westwards in the early morning from somewhere down in Wapping or the Isle of Dogs, by evening you will still be on the march, still in the midst of shabby little houses – only somewhere over by Hammersmith by then.

That's not to say there aren't plenty of fine big houses as well. Take Mayfair. But even Mayfair is distinctly Londonish too, when you come to look at it. The mansions are all squeezed up there side by side, and as a result they are rather poky little mansions, most of them; though the sheer marvel of the address – Mayfair, W.1 – excuses any overcrowding. Not that Mayfair is all mansions or anything like it. It's Shepherd's Market, that hamlet of dark shops and crooked alleyways, rather than Bruton Street or Grosvenor Square, that makes Mayfair.

And what's more it's Covent Garden Market and Smithfield Market and Billingsgate Fish Market and Peckham Market rather than Shepherd's Market – which isn't a real market anyway – that makes London. They are a part of the people, these markets. And London is the people's city. That is why Petticoat Lane is more London than Park Lane. And that is why London is the Mile End Road and the Walworth Road and the Lambeth Road and the Elephant and Castle. Strange, isn't it, how much of the real London still lies south of the river, just as it did in Shakespeare's day, and in Chaucer's day before him? It is as though across the Thames – in London's Deep South – times and manners haven't changed so much as in the Parliamentary North.

But London is more than a collection of streets and markets. It's Wren churches and A.B.C. tea-shops. It's Burlington Arcade and the Temple. It's the Athenæum and the Adelphi Arches. It's Kennington gasometer and the Zoo. It's the iron bridge at Charing Cross and the statue of Eros at Piccadilly Circus. It's the Serpentine and Moss Bros. It's Paddington Recreation Ground and the Nelson Column. It's Big Ben and the Horse Guards. It's the National Gallery and Pimm's. It's the Victoria Palace and Ludgate Hill. It's the second-hand shops and the undertakers and the cinemas and the obscure back-street chapels. It's the Waif-and-Stray Societies and the fortune-tellers and the pub on the corner and the trams. That's London.

And the people. They're London, too. They're the same Londoners that they have always been, except that from time to time the proportion of refugees has altered a little. At one moment the doubtful-looking newcomers are the Huguenots, at another the Jews, and it is the Huguenots who are the Londoners wondering whatever London is coming to. They're all Londoners – the French and the Italians in Soho, the Chinese in Limehouse, the Scotsmen in Muswell Hill and the Irish round the Docks. And the only way in which modern Londoners differ from the Londoners who have lived there before them is that all the Londoners don't live in London any more. They simply work there. By 8 p.m. the City is a desert. Round about six o'clock the trouble starts: the deserters leave. Everyone begins shoving and pushing to get out of the metropolis into the estates and suburbs and garden cities. There they sleep, these demi-Londoners, in their little Tudor dolls' houses, until next morning when they emerge, refreshed, ready to play at being real Londoners again.

Perhaps it is simply the size of London that makes its inhabitants seem somehow smaller. Dolls' houses appear to be the right dwelling-places for these thousands, these tens of thousands, these hundreds of thousands, these half-urban hordes. Stand on the bridge at Liverpool Street Station at a quarter-to-nine in the morning and you see the model trains drawing in beneath you one after another, and swarms of toy-passengers emptying themselves on to the platform to go stumping up to the barrier – toy directors, toy clerks, toy typists, all jerking along to spend the day in toy-town, earning paper money to keep their dolls' houses going.

Of course, there are still plenty of the other kind, too. Real Londoners who sleep the night in London as well as work the day there. Real Londoners – some in love, some in debt, some committing murders, some adultery, some trying to get on in the world, some looking forward to a pension, some getting drunk, some losing their jobs, some dying, and some holding up the new baby.

Norman Collins, *London Belongs To Me*

Selective Index

(* after name indicates writer whose work is featured in the anthology)

242

Acknowledgements

Oxygen Books gratefully acknowledges permission to reprint extracts from:

London: The Biography by Peter Ackroyd. Copyright © Peter Ackroyd 2000. Published by Chatto and Windus. Reprinted by permission of The Random House Group Ltd.

Thames: Sacred River by Peter Ackroyd. Copyright © Peter Ackroyd 2007. Published by Chatto and Windus. Reprinted by permission of The Random House Group Ltd.

Le Silence dans la maison by Renata Ada-Ruata, by kind permission of Éditions Baleine, Paris: Copyright © Éditions de Baleine – Le Seuil, Paris, 2002. Translation copyright © Oxygen Books 2009.

Sorrows of the Moon by Iqbal Ahmed. Copyright © Iqbal Ahmed 2007. Reprinted by permission of Constable and Robinson Ltd.

Brick Lane by Monica Ali. Copyright © Monica Ali 2003. Published by Doubleday. Reprinted by permission of The Random House Group Ltd.

Necropolis: London and its dead by Catherine Arnold. Published by Pocket Books, 2007. Copyright © 2006 by Catherine Arnold. Reprinted by permission of Simon and Schuster UK, Ltd.

Common Pursuits by Margaret Atwood. Published by Virago Press, 2005. Copyright © O.W.Toad Ltd 2005. Reprinted by permission of Little Brown Group Ltd.

According to Queeney by Beryl Bainbridge. First published by Little, Brown and Company, 2001. Copyright © Beryl Bainbridge 2001. Reprinted by permission of Little, Brown and Company.

Metroland by Julian Barnes. Copyright © Julian Barnes 1980. Published by Jonathan Cape. Reprinted by permission of The Random House Group Ltd, and by kind permission of United Agents (www.unitedagents.co.uk) on behalf of the author.

The Uncommon Reader by Alan Bennett. Reprinted by permission of Faber and Faber Ltd.

My First Book by Maeve Binchy. Reprinted by courtesy of The Irish Times and by kind permission of the Christine Green Agency, on behalf of the author.

The Groundwater Diaries by Tim Bradford. Copyright © 2003, Tim Bradford. Reprinted by permission of HarperCollins Publishers Ltd.

We Danced All Night by Barbara Cartland. Copyright © Barbara Cartland 1970. Published by arrangement with Rupert Crew Ltd.

Acknowledgements

Look At It This Way by Justin Cartwright. Copyright © Justin Cartwright 1990. Reproduced by permission of Hodder and Stoughton Limited.

The Great Stink by Clare Clark. Copyright © Clare Clark, 2005. (Viking Books, 2006). By permission of Penguin Books.

London Belongs to Me by Norman Collins, edited with an introduction by Ed Glinert (Penguin Books, 2009). Introduction and Notes copyright Ed Glinert, 2009. Copyright © by Norman Collins, 1945.

The Cricklewood Tapestry by Alan Coren. Copyright © Alan Coren 2001. Reproduced with permission of Curtis Brown Group Ltd. London on behalf of Alan Coren.

'Bus 16: Victoria — Cricklewood' by Diamond Geezer. Copyright © Diamond Geezer. Reprinted by permission of the author.

Winter Notes on Summer Impressions by Fyodor Dostoyevsky. Translation Kyril Fitzlyon. Reprinted by permission of Quartet Books.

The Room of Lost Things by Stella Duffy. Copyright © Stella Duffy 2008. Published by Virago, 2008. Reprinted by permission of the Little, Brown Book Group Ltd.

Home Life by Alice Thomas Ellis. Copyright © Alice Thomas Ellis, 1988. Reprinted by permission of HarperCollins Publishers Ltd.

In Search of the Crack by Robert Elms. Copyright © Robert Elms 1988. Reprinted by permission of the author.

National Service by Richard Eyre. Copyright © 2003 by Richard Eyre. Reprinted by permission of Bloomsbury Publishing.

Limehouse Days by Daniel Farson (Penguin Books, 1991). Copyright © Daniel Farson, 1991. By kind permission of Penguin Books.

Soho in the Fifties by Daniel Farson. Copyright © Daniel Farson 1987. Reprinted by permission of A. M. Heath and Co. Ltd.

Kandahar Cockney by James Fergusson. Copyright © James Fergusson, 2004. Reprinted by permission of HarperCollins Publishers Ltd.

At Freddie's by Penelope Fitzgerald. Copyright © Penelope Fitzgerald, 1982. Reprinted by permission of HarperCollins Publishers Ltd.

East End Chronicles by Ed Glinert. (Penguin Books, 2005.) Copyright © Ed Glinert, 2005. By permission of Penguin Books.

West End Chronicles by Ed Glinert. (Penguin Books, 2007.) Copyright © Ed Glinert, 2007. By permission of Penguin Books.

London Fragments by Rüdiger Görner. Copyright © 2007 Rüdiger Görner. Reprinted by permission of Haus Publishing. Translation © 2007 Debra Marmor and Herbert Danner.

A Concise Chinese-English Dictionary for Lovers by Xiaolu Guo. Copyright © Xiaolu Guo 2007. Published by Chatto and Windus. Reprinted by permission of The Random House Group Ltd.

Acknowledgements

Salaam Brick Lane by Tarquin Hall. Copyright © Tarquin Hall 2005. Reproduced by permission of John Murray (Publishers) Limited.

The Dreadful Judgement by Neil Hanson. Copyright © Neil Hanson 2001. Published by Doubleday. Reprinted by permission of The Random House Group Ltd.

Antic Hay by Aldous Huxley. Copyright © The Estate of Aldous Huxley, 1923. Published by Chatto and Windus. Reprinted by permission of The Random House Group Ltd. and by kind permission of Georges Borchardt, Inc.

'A Hawarden Grove Christmas' by Jemma Leech. Copyright © Jemma Leech. Reprinted by permission of the author.

On Brick Lane by Rachel Lichtenstein (Penguin Books, 2007). Copyright © Rachel Lichtenstein, 2007. By permission of Penguin Books.

A Writer's Notebook by W. Somerset Maugham. Published by William Heinemann, 1951. Reprinted by permission of A. P. Watt Ltd on behalf of the Royal Literary Fund.

Absolute Beginners by Colin MacInnes is published with the kind permission of the Colin MacInnes estate and the publishers, Allison and Busby Ltd. Copyright © 1959 by the Colin MacInnes Estate

'Revisiting Swinging Sixties London', by Rory MacLean. First published in the *Sunday Telegraph*, July 2007. Reprinted by permission of the author.

Saturday by Ian McEwan. Copyright © Ian McEwan 2005. Published by Jonathan Cape. Reprinted by permission of The Random House Group Ltd.

Spider by Patrick McGrath. Copyright © 1990 by Patrick McGrath. Reprinted by permission of Gregory and Company.

A Writer's World: travels 1950–2000 by Jan Morris. Copyright © Jan Morris 2003. Reprinted by permission of Faber and Faber Ltd.

A Word Child by Iris Murdoch. Copyright © Iris Murdoch 1975. Published by Chatto and Windus. Reprinted by permission of The Random House Group Ltd.

The Lodger: Shakespeare on Silver Street by Charles Nicholl (Penguin Books, 2007). Copyright © Charles Nicholl, 2007. By permission of Penguin Books.

Bleeding London by Geoff Nicholson. Copyright © Geoff Nicholson 1997. Reproduced by permission of the Endeavour Agency (U.S.A.) on behalf of the author.

Netherland by Joseph O'Neill. Copyright © Joseph O'Neill, 2008. Reprinted by permission of HarperCollins Publishers Ltd.

Acknowledgements

The Final Passage by Caryl Phillips. Copyright © Caryl Phillips 1985. Published by Faber and Faber, 1985. Reprinted by permission of A. P. Watts Ltd on behalf of Caryl Phillips.

London's Strangest Tales by Tom Quinn. Copyright © Tom Quinn 2008. Reprinted by permission of Robson Books.

Soft City by Jonathan Raban (quoted by Peter Watts in the Introduction), Picador, 2008. (First published, Hamish Hamilton, 1974.) By kind permission of Pan Macmillan.

Portobello by Ruth Rendell. Copyright © Ruth Rendell 2008. Published by Hutchinson. Reprinted by permission of The Random House Group Ltd.

'Voysey and P Diddy: London in Summer' by Eduardo Reyes. Copyright © Eduardo Reyes, 2009. By permission of the author.

The Edwardians by Vita Sackville-West. Copyright © Vita Sackville-West 1930. Reproduced with permission of Curtis Brown Group Ltd, London, on behalf of the Estate of Vita Sackville-West.

Night Haunts by Sukhdev Sandhu. Copyright © Sukhdev Sandhu 2006. Reprinted by permission of Verso.

The Book of Dave by Will Self (Penguin Books, 2006). Copyright © Will Self, 2006. By permission of Penguin Books.

The Lonely Londoners by Sam Selvon (Penguin Books, 2006). Copyright © Sam Selvon, 1956. Reprinted by permission of Penguin Books.

A Start in Life by Alan Sillitoe. Copyright © 1970, 1998. Published by London Books, 2008. Reprinted by permission of London Books.

Constitutional by Helen Simpson. Copyright © Helen Simpson 2005. Published by Jonathan Cape. Reprinted by permission of The Random House Group Ltd.

Lights Out for the Territory by Iain Sinclair. Copyright © 1997 by Iain Sinclair. Reprinted by kind permission of Granta Books.

A Far Cry from Kensington by Muriel Spark. Copyright © Muriel Spark 1988. Reprinted by permission of David Higham Associates Ltd, on behalf of the author.

Waterland, by Graham Swift. Copyright © Graham Swift 1983. Reprinted by permission of A. P. Watt on behalf of the author.

London and the South East by David Szalay. Copyright © David Szalay 2008. Published by Jonathan Cape. Reprinted by permission of The Random House Group Ltd.

'London Lives' by Rebecca Taylor, in *London Calling: High Art and Low Life in the Capital since 1968*. Reprinted by permission of *Time Out*.

In Camden Town by David Thomson. (Hutchinson, 1983.) Reprinted by permission of Martina Thomson.

Acknowledgements

The House by the Thames by Gillian Tindall. Copyright © Gillian Tindall 2006. Published by Chatto and Windus. Reprinted by permission of The Random House Group Ltd.

1700: Scenes from London Life by Maureen Waller. Copyright © 2000 by Maureen Waller. Reproduced by permission of Hodder and Stoughton Limited.

Soho: a novel by Keith Waterhouse. Copyright © 2001 by Keith Waterhouse. Reprinted by permission of David Higham Associates on behalf of the author.

'Rough Magic in the Park' by Peter Watts. Reprinted by permission of The Independent on Sunday.

Kipps by H. G. Wells. Reprinted by permission of A. P. Watts Ltd on behalf of The Literary Executors of the Estate of H. G. Wells.

Karl Marx by Francis Wheen. Copyright © 1999, Francis Wheen. Reprinted by permission of HarperCollins Publishers Ltd.

My Life Closed Twice by Nigel Williams. Copyright © Nigel Williams, 1977. Reproduced by permission of Judy Daish Associates Limited, on behalf of the author.

The Sweets of Pimlico by A. N. Wilson. Copyright © A. N. Wilson, 1987. Reprinted by permission of A. M. Heath & Co Ltd.

Jacob's Room by Virginia Woolf, by permission of The Society of Authors as the Literary Representative of the Estate of Virginia Woolf.

Mrs Dalloway by Virginia Woolf, by permission of The Society of Authors as the Literary Representative of the Estate of Virginia Woolf.

Orlando by Virginia Woolf, by permission of The Society of Authors as the Literary Representative of the Estate of Virginia Woolf.

The London Scene by Virginia Woolf, by permission of The Society of Authors as the Literary Representative of the Estate of Virginia Woolf.

A Journey Through Ruins by Patrick Wright. Copyright © Patrick Wright 1991. From Chapter 10 ('The London Bus Queue Falls Apart') and Chapter 14 ('The Park that Lost its Name'). Reprinted by permission of Oxford University Press.

Every effort has been made to trace and contact copyright holders before publication. If notified, the publisher will rectify any errors or omissions at the earliest opportunity.

city-lit

An exciting and unique city break travel series featuring the best-ever writing on favourite European and World cities

city-lit PARIS

Gertrude Stein: on the origins of the croissant

Julian Barnes: life begins in Paris

Joanne Harris: chocolate in Montmartre

Alex Kapranos: eating out in Paris

Kate Muir: red shoes in the Musée Rodin

Agnès Catherine Poirier: the lure of the Paris café

Marcel Proust: that perfect erotic moment

Victor Hugo: the view from the top of Notre-Dame

Faïza Guène: on not going up the Eiffel Tower

... and over sixty other dazzling writers. The ideal companion for city breaks and for everyone who loves Paris.

'Brilliant ... the best way to get under the skin of a city. The perfect read for travellers and book lovers of all ages' – Kate Mosse, bestselling author of **Sepulchre**

'An essential guidebook ... It maps the Paris of the imagination beautifully' – Kate Muir, bestselling author of **Left Bank**

'A great and eclectic set of writings ... an original book on Paris' – Sylvia Whitman, Shakespeare & Co, Paris

'It's terrific ... all the best writing on this complex city in one place' – Professor Andrew Hussey, author of **Paris: The Secret History**

'An attractive-looking list of destination-based literature anthologies ... The Paris volume contains a great range of writers' – **The Independent**

£8.99 ISBN 978–0–9559700–0–9

Discover **city-lit Berlin, Amsterdam, Dublin, New York, Istanbul, Mumbai** and more – from Oxygen Books, a new publisher of surprising books about all kinds of journeys.
www.oxygenbooks.co.uk http://thecity-litcafe.typepad